# Building Strong Families

## How Your Family Can Withstand the Challenges of Today's Culture

*To: Alma Diaz*
*You're Special!*
*God Bless You —*
*William Mitchell*

# Dr. William Mitchell and Michael A. Mitchell

BROADMAN
& HOLMAN
PUBLISHERS

Nashville, Tennessee

© 1997
by William Mitchell
All rights reserved
Printed in the United States of America
0-8054-6370-4
Published by Broadman & Holman Publishers, Nashville, Tennessee
Acquisitions and Development Editor: Matt Jacobson

Dewey Decimal Classification: 306.85
Subject Heading: FAMILY / FAMILY LIFE EDUCATION
Library of Congress Card Catalog Number: 97-1732

Library of Congress Cataloging-in-Publication Data
Mitchell, William, 1932–
    Building strong families : how your family can withstand
the challenges of today's culture / William Mitchell and Michael Mitchell.
    p.   cm.
    ISBN 0-8054-6370-4 (pbk.)
    1. Family—Religious life. 2. Parenting—Religious aspects—
Christianity. 3. Child rearing—Religious aspects—Christianity.
I. Mitchell, Michael. II. Title.
BV4526.2M49 1997
248.4—dc21
                                                                            97-1732
                                                                            CIP

98 99 00 01 5 4 3 2

To Carolyn

*my wife and partner of forty-three years.*
*She built a strong family at home and was*
*always supportive of my extended families*
*at work, church, and the community.*
*She treated everyone she met with dignity and respect.*
*Now in heaven above, she left a legacy of love.—HWM*

*I can't imagine having a mother finer than*
*the one with which I was blessed.*
*She gave untiringly and unselfishly all her life*
*to those she loved most—her family.*
*Our family will be forever grateful.—MAM*

# CONTENTS

Let's Build Strong Families . . . . . . . . . . . . . . . . . . . . . . . . 1

The Mine Fields of the Home • How Shall We Turn the Tide? • Every Parent Can Do It!

## Part One: The Biblical Foundation for Building Strong Families

1  Characteristics of a Strong Family . . . . . . . . . . . . . . . 9

Meeting the Needs of the Child You Love • A Strong Family Is an Expression of Love • Many Definitions for Good Families • Good Ideas, but Where Is God? • Core Concept #1: Centered on God • Core Concept #2: Caring • Core Concept #3: Connection • Core Concept # 4: Communication • Core Concept # 5: Commitment • Strong Does Not Mean Trouble-Free

2  Every Parent a Leader . . . . . . . . . . . . . . . . . . . . . . . . . 30

Single Parents • Even Communitarians Point to Parents as Key • Home Should Be the Foremost "School" Your Child Attends • Parental Leading Sometimes Means Walking Alongside • Leadership and Authority Don't Require an Adversarial Relationship • Establishing Clear Lines of Authority • Insist that Your Child Respect You • Insist that Your Child Obey You • Set Clear Rules and Boundaries • Justice Is the Basis for Morality • Don't Undermine Your Leadership as Parents • Determine within Yourself the Kind of Leader You Want to Be

3  Identifying Your Parenting Philosophy . . . . . . . . . . . . . . 50

Pouring Yourself into Your Child • Your Vision for Your Child • Your Understanding of Right and Wrong • Your Approach to Discipline • Knowing Who You Are as a Parent

4  Set Your Goals . . . . . . . . . . . . . . . . . . . . . . . . . . . . . 69

Virtues Lists Can Provide Direction • Supreme Trait: Be a Christian • Creating a Climate for Spiritual Growth • Fruit of the Spirit • What If Your Child Rejects Your Faith? • All Virtues Flow from Faith • Framing a Goal Statement • Committing Yourself to the Objectives

5  Managing Your Parenting Resources . . . . . . . . . . . . . . . 92

The Parent's Relationship with the Child's School • Your Relationship with Your Church • Your Relationship with the Business World • Your Broader Community or Extended Family • A Strong Whole

6  What It Means to Train . . . . . . . . . . . . . . . . . . . . . . . 103

Be Dedicated to Training • Training Requires Realism about a Child's Capabilities • Training Requires a Parent to Set and Enforce Limits • Delayed Gratification Is Implied in Training •

## *Part Two:* **Strategies for Practical Application**

7  Tool #1: Team-Building. . . . . . . . . . . . . . . . . . . . . .123
"Togetherness" Routines • Reciprocity: Choosing to Get Along as a Family • A Clear Delineation of Responsibilities and Roles • Developing a Working Plan for Team-Building • Taking Responsibility for Personal Problems • The Waltons: A Family Team

8  Tool #2: Creating a Climate. . . . . . . . . . . . . . . . . . . .143
The Great Blessing of a Happy Home • Positive Presence of Both Parents • Staying Positive about the Future • Positive about Your Potential • A Positive Climate Is Marked by Freedom • Positive All Day! • Positive Results Can Be Expected

9  Tool #3: Conditioning . . . . . . . . . . . . . . . . . . . . . . .161
Good Conditioning • The Power of Role Playing • The Power of Suggestion • The Power of Self-Suggestion • The Power of Habit • Suggestion and Habits Work Together

10  Tool #4: Providing Reinforcement . . . . . . . . . . . . . . .176
Two Types of Reinforcement • Positive Reinforcement • The Goal Is Not Control • Praise as a Reinforcer • Appreciation as a Reinforcer • Rewards as Reinforcer • Recognition as a Reinforcer • Encouragement as a Reinforcer • Success Is Its Own Reinforcer • Overcoming a Negative Disappointment

11  Tool #5: The Parent as Role Model . . . . . . . . . . . . . . .188
Three Types of Modeling • Human Models Are People • The Philosophical Models You Teach • Operational Models Involve Experience • You Are Your Child's "Model Guardian" • Send a Clear Message

12  Running the Drills. . . . . . . . . . . . . . . . . . . . . . . . . .199
The Importance of the "Dailies" • The Best Practice Is Daily Practice • Three Daily Disciplines • Controlling the Media in Your Home • The Daily Discipline of Doing Homework • Fitting It All into a Day

13  Facing the Unexpected . . . . . . . . . . . . . . . . . . . . . . .211
1. Graciously Accept the Great Outpouring of Love, Prayers, and Concern from Others • 2. In Facing an Unexpected Battle, Keep Your Goals and Adjust Them as You Must • 3. Don't Neglect Activities That "Fill Your Cup" Each Day • 4. Live "in the Day" and Savor Each Moment • 5. In a Crisis, Learn a Deeper Meaning of "Commitment" • A Fivefold Approach that Benefits Everyone

14  Legacy of Love . . . . . . . . . . . . . . . . . . . . . . . . . . . .218
Looking to the Long View of Life • The Ripple Effect • Ripples Start with Pebbles • The Legacy of Love • The Legacy of Humility • Leave a Legacy of Obedience to God • A Legacy of Good Memories • Building a Legacy Isn't Always Easy • Start Where You Are Today • Your Family Legacy Is Your Family Treasure

Epilogue. . . . . . . . . . . . . . . . . . . . . . . . . . . . . . . .227

Notes . . . . . . . . . . . . . . . . . . . . . . . . . . . . . . . . . .229

# Let's Build Strong Families

*As are families, so is society.*
—William Thayer
American author (1820–98)

*So encourage each other to build each other up, just
as you are already doing.*
—1 Thessalonians 5:11, TLB

Many parents and grandparents have been heard to say, "My child is special."

How true!

Equally true is the statement: *Your family is special.*

Your family is valuable. It is important. Building up your family in strength is the most important thing you can do—not only as a parent, but as a *person.*

Families are God's design. They are the essential unit of organization in which human life thrives. God placed people in families, tribes, and communities; cities, nations, and empires are all man's ideas. Therefore, recognize that your family, before God, is unique, irreplaceable, and of utmost concern.

The disintegration of the modern family has become a hot topic in today's world. Indeed, the statistics related to the demise of the family are staggering:

- Nearly 18 million American children are living with one parent—double the number in 1970.[1]
- Thirty years of research show that greater family involvement in children's learning is a critical link to achieving a high-quality education and a safe, disciplined learning environment for every student.[2]
- By the time they [children] reach driving age, American children have seen close to 100,000 beer commercials.[3]

- An estimated 10 to 20 million Americans suffer from alcoholism or alcohol-related problems. For every one person who suffers from alcoholism, another four persons (usually family) are directly affected in adverse ways.[4]
- A recent U.S. Department of Education handbook on drug education states flatly: "In American today, the most serious threat to the health and well-being of our children is drug use." The United States has the highest rate of teenage drug use of any industrialized nation (ten times greater than that of Japan).[5]
- By the year 2000, one in four children will live in poverty.[6]
- One of two U. S. marriages now ends in divorce. Our divorce rate, which has more than doubled since 1960, is the highest in the world.[7]
- The suicide rate of children in the U.S. has risen 300 percent during the past three decades.[8]
- Over a twenty-year period (1968-88), there was a 53 percent increase in all violent crime—murder, rape, robbery, and assault—for males and females seventeen or under.[9]

Compared to a child growing up in 1960, the child of today is more likely to

- commit a violent crime
- assault a parent or teacher
- abuse drugs or alcohol
- become sexually active before age eighteen
- have a child out of wedlock
- become depressed
- become an underachiever
- create discipline problems in group settings
- have reading problems

In addition to what seem to be modern-day problems, every generation also seems to suffer from "age-old" problems that have never been remedied.

It has been written: "Our youths love luxury. They have bad manners, contempt for authority—they show disrespect for their elders, and love to chatter in place of exercise. Children are now tyrants, not the servants of their households. They no longer rise when their elders enter the room. They contradict their parents, chatter before company, gobble up food, and tyrannize teachers." Do you suppose this was written by a parent today? Far from it! This statement was made by Socrates in 400 B.C.

We inevitably ask ourselves: Who is to blame? Who is at fault? Where did we go wrong?

Fifty studies conducted by the National School Board Association have concluded that parents are the most important influence in a child's academic success. The curriculum of the home is *twice* as predictive of academic learning as family socioeconomic status.

A sad example of parental malpractice is evident in the statistics related to the physical abuse of children. We hear and read so much about abuse in media reports today that we seem to be desensitizing ourselves to this problem. The shocking fact remains that tens of thousands of children each year are maimed or killed because of abuse by parents and caretakers. In 1995, the number of children killed was estimated by the U.S. Advisory Board on Child Abuse and Neglect to be at least 2,000 (the vast majority age four and under), with 18,000 children permanently disabled and 142,000 seriously injured. The number of children who die at the hands of abusers total more than those who die in car accidents, house fires, falls, or drownings. *The majority of the abuse cases involve fathers, stepfathers, boyfriends, or other male caretakers, while neglect cases are more commonly caused by mothers.*

Such abuse seems to occur regardless of the socioeconomic or educational status of parents. There seems to be a hidden rage in our nation that infects virtually every segment of our society.

# The Mine Fields of the Home

Several years ago I saw a television documentary about an effort to clear mine fields in Cambodia. People there frequently were being blown apart or maimed as a residual effect of a war fought in that area decades ago.

I couldn't help but liken this problem to our families today. Our families are being blown apart by:

- financial pressures, often the result of an over-emphasis on material possessions
- a lack of values and virtues instilled in the family
- sexual laxness of parents, which is imitated by teens when they enter puberty
- a high divorce rate, exemplifying to children a transient quality to relationships
- verbal, physical, and sexual abuse
- children being used as pawns in divorce battles
- alcohol abuse

- mothers glued to daytime television shows or romance novels, rather than spending time with their children
- heavy-handed dictatorial roles played by fathers who regard tenderness and expressions of love as signs of personal weakness
- selfishness on the part of parents who place their own desires above the emotional needs of their children
- chemical abuse, including illegal drugs and over-use of prescription medications
- excessive fault-finding and criticism

The mine fields in Cambodia may eventually be cleared. As in the case of many areas that have been torn apart by war or armed conflict—such as Western Europe during World War II—once a political settlement is reached, a child has a reasonable hope for healing and peace.

The internal mine fields of a war-torn family, however, are far less easily resolved, and, in some cases, children may never recover from the loss of innocence, peace, and inner confidence that should have been part of their childhoods.

In many cases, it is not what we *do* to our children that is the most damaging, but what we *don't do*. Equally potent mine fields occur when we don't do what we know to do: teach our children the values and train our children in the attitudes and behaviors that will lead to their living successful, fulfilling, meaningful lives.

## How Shall We Turn the Tide?

What can be done? How can we turn the tide and begin to build strong families?

Perhaps first and foremost, we must recognize that the home is the *primary training school for building character*. This is not the primary job of the school or even the church. Character formation begins at home. We must shoulder the responsibility that is ours as parents and grandparents.

And secondly, we truly must begin to *train* our children. There is a great difference between caring for, raising, providing for, and *training*. The Scriptures instruct us to train children in the way they should go. It is a concept that many parents don't seem to be implementing.

Proverbs 22:6 says, "Train up a child in the way he should go: and when he is old, he will not depart from it." I believe this statement from Scripture represents an absolute truth which parents can rely upon. *If we train up a child according to biblical principles, when he is old, he will not depart from it.* But my experience indicates that living out the practice of "training up a child in the way he should go" produces an emotionally and spiritually healthy adult.

For more than fifteen years, I have researched and written books on the importance of the home and the parents' role in a child's education. As a former teacher, principal, and superintendent of schools, and now as the chairman of the POPS (Power of Positive Students) International Foundation, I believe strongly that kids can and do turn out OK. The key word to this success is *training*.

I have concluded that many children do not turn out with bright futures because they have lacked genuine *training*. They may have been "raised" in homes with adequate income and good parents, but they were never really *trained* in the habits necessary for reaching their dreams and goals.

Training has to do with the formation of habits—behavior that is repeated and reinforced to the point where it truly has become ingrained as an automatic response in a person's life. At the root of training are attitudes and values.

It is parents who are responsible for training their children. That is the primary responsibility of neither the school nor church. Schools and churches reinforce the training that parents do at home, but the home is the primary place where training occurs. Therefore, while training is an activity we generally associate with "teachers," the key to training up children lies with the parents. Parents must be educated in *how* to train children. Parents must remain dedicated to God and hold fast to their own godly values and positive attitude, continue to receive instruction and learn all they can about good parenting, and remain intrinsically motivated to build strong families—if children are to be "trained up" successfully.

Educating parents in the training process is the purpose for this book.

## Every Parent Can Do It!

The good news about values education is that you can train your child in morals and sound spiritual principles, regardless of

- your educational background. Uneducated parents can train children in virtues and values as well as educated parents.
- your socioeconomic status. Parents who make a great deal of money and provide material luxuries for their children sometimes do a poor job of teaching morals and ethics to their children. By the same reasoning, parents who are poor and capable of providing

only the bare necessities for their children still can teach ethical and moral behavior.

• your physical home environment. Children learn values just as well in huts of grass and straw as they do in mansions of brick and wood.

It doesn't matter what type of neighborhood you live in or what type of climate or terrain you call home. Children learn values from parents who care and provide for them. They learn virtues from living human beings, not from things that are given to them (or not given to them).

You can build a strong family.

It's important that you do so!

# The Biblical Foundation for Building Strong Families

A commitment to building strong families requires first and foremost a commitment to personal development. Each member of a family must always be encouraged to develop his or her personal identity and to grow strong spiritually, mentally, physically, emotionally, and socially. No family can be stronger than the "sum" of its individual members.

Over the years, I have referred frequently to the Four I's that I believe are at the core of personal development:

1. **Improved daily.** Each person in a family must be encouraged to be better by sunset than he was at dawn. We must challenge ourselves to grow toward greater excellence on a daily basis.

2. **Inspired daily.** We each must seek out our own sources of daily inspiration. For my family this involves a mixture of reading God's Word, reading inspirational books, listening to motivational and inspirational tapes and fine music, taking time to enjoy nature, and engaging in positive conversations. Our source of inspiration should never be limited to a periodic seminar or lecture, or to a fifteen-minute sermon on Sunday morning. We must actively seek out *positive* inspiration on a daily basis because our world feeds us so much negative input *on a daily basis!* Every morning, we each wake up with an "empty cup" and have a need to fill it with good ideas, good values, good feelings about ourselves and others, and the goodness of God.

3. **Involved with others.** We each must seek out a daily means of being involved with others. Most people encounter other people on a daily basis, but being *involved* with people means that you know something about them and care about what happens to them. In return, you make yourself vulnerable and available

to them so that they can know something about you and show their care for you. In sum, you develop a relationship with the people with whom you work, enjoy recreational activities, and worship. You connect at deep levels with those in your own family. Unless you are involved with other people, you cannot fully express or receive love. And love is our basic emotional need. Without it, we are not whole people and we cannot build strong families.

4. *Interested in others.* We each must choose to stay interested in the world around us—to seek out new people and enjoy positive, new experiences. When a person loses interest in life, he loses a great deal of hope. Without hope, there is very little will to live. And when that happens, there is nearly always a rapid decline in a person's quality of life, including the person's overall family life.

It is only as we are committed to strong personal development that we can begin to develop the family—to create a team and a sense of oneness in which each member of the family helps the others to grow spiritually, physically, mentally, emotionally, and socially.

The tools you will find in the second section of this book are ones that can help parents stay focused on building strong families and develop habits that in turn build character. In this first section, you will find information about what it means to be a leader, train a child, develop a parenting philosophy, and set parenting goals. Each of these chapters is aimed at helping you "step up to the plate" and assume your full responsibility for being the best person you can be, and in that context, being the best parent you can be.

As a part of preflight information given to airline passengers, instruction is given regarding the use of oxygen masks. We all no doubt have heard a flight attendant advise, "Be sure to put on your own mask before attempting to help a child put on his mask." The same holds true for parenting! As you seek to be the best person you can be, you will desire to be the best parent you can be. In the process, you will become a better role model for your child. More than from any other source, your child will learn how to *be* an adult from you, his or her parent. To a very great extent, the person you are is the person your child will become!

## Chapter One

# Characteristics of a Strong Family

*There is no doubt that it is around the family*
*and the home that all the greatest virtues, the*
*most dominating virtues of human society, are*
*created, strengthened, and maintained.*
—Winston Churchill

*Build your lives on a strong foundation.*
—Jude 1:20, TLB

Do you truly treasure your child?

One of the most endearing statements about children that I have ever read was one made by President Herbert Hoover:

*Children are the most wholesome part of the race, the sweetest,*
*for they are freshest from the Hand of God. Whimsical, ingenious,*
*mischievous, they fill the earth with joy and good humor. We*
*adults live a life of apprehension as to what they will think of us, a*
*life of defense against their terrifying energy, a life of hard work to*
*live up to their great expectations. We put them to bed with a sense*
*of relief—and greet them in the morning with delight and antici-*
*pation. We envy them the freshness of adventure and the discovery*
*of life. In all these ways, children add to the wonder of being alive.*
*In all these ways, they help to keep us young.*

Is that the way you feel about your child? That certainly is the way I feel about my children and grandchildren. I can't think of anything that I wouldn't do for them.

## Meeting the Needs of the Child You Love

Every individual, which means every member of your family—no matter how old or young—has a need for these ten things:

- to belong
- to feel secure and safe
- to have status
- to feel free
- to have loyalties

- to contribute
- to grow
- to be independent
- to experience love
- to have self-esteem

Meeting these needs can mean a balancing act at times. For example, a person may need to balance the need for independence and freedom with responsibilities related to belonging and contributing. To the greatest extent possible, however, it is a parent's responsibility not only to have these needs met in his or her own life, but to help meet these needs in the life of each child. The desire to meet a child's needs flows from the heart. It comes from a parent's love.

How is your home? How is your family? To answer those questions, you need to first ask yourself, "How is my heart? What are my *true* desires for my family? What do my actions say about my attitudes?"

In asking these questions and answering them honestly, you may discover that your home does not match your heart's desire for a strong, healthy family. Don't be dismayed! It *is* within your power to create the kind of family atmosphere you desire. The changes begin with the one thing you have complete control over—you.

# A Strong Family Is an Expression of Love

One of the greatest expressions of love you can make to your child is to build for him or her a strong family. The building blocks are simple and can be found in the phrase *building strong families*.

### STRONG

*Strong* implies both endurance and permanence. We seek to build families that have a "lasting quality" for both values and relationships. Strong families have what it takes to stick together through all kinds of circumstances and crises.

Not everyone in our culture is pro-family, although you might conclude that from some news reports. One Cornell University professor has said, "The family is not currently a social unit we value or support."[1] Examples of this are evident in virtually every corner. If all Americans gave more than lip-service to the importance of the family, abuse and divorce would be practically nonexistent. That simply isn't the case.

Some sociologists see the family as being of great harm to the child. They rarely offer suitable alternatives, but these sociologists can make a strong case in arguing that families *hurt* children as often as they help them. F. M. Estiandiary was quoted in the *Los Angeles Times* as saying, "To free the child, we must do away with parenthood . . . marriage must go. We must settle for nothing less than the total elimination of the family."

That certainly is not the perspective of this book.

I am a strong believer in the family unit and, even more importantly, an advocate for *strong* family units. It isn't enough just to *be* a family. We must build strong families to withstand the cultural bombardment parents and their children face.

## FAMILY

Families have many definitions in our world today, but, ultimately, the godly family is a three-part pillar: God at the top, the parent(s) in the middle, and the child at the base. Ideally, a parent is a child's natural birth mother or father. However, we are remiss if we think that only these two people are capable of parenting a child. A "parent" may also be a grandparent, foster parent, or another adult or relative who is fulfilling the parental role in a child's life. More important than genetic or blood relationship is the two-sided element of authority and responsibility. A family is a unit of organization in which a definite pattern of authority and responsibility exists.

In today's world, the family itself has been redefined. In virtually any neighborhood, church, or school setting, you will find:

- widows and widowers who have remarried and blended their families
- traditional homes with a husband and wife raising children together
- divorced men and women who have remarried and created new family units
- separated mothers and fathers who try to spend equal amounts of time with their children as they sort out their marriages
- divorced single parents who are struggling to raise their children without the ongoing presence of a second parent in the home
- unwed or divorced women and men who have returned home to live with their parents, who assist in raising their children

Each of the above situations can and should be defined as a family. Each has a potential for being a strong family. We cannot dismiss a single-parent home or a grandparent-involved home as being a home in which a family cannot thrive. Those who are experiencing these circumstances *can* build strong families, although they often must exert greater effort and energy to do so.

# Many Definitions for Good Families

A number of organizations, educators, child psychologists, and child-development researchers have created definitions and criteria for good families and healthy, strong homes. I want to present four of them to you so you can get a sense of the common threads that seem to run through studies which were not aimed precisely at the Christian family.

## HEALTHY FAMILIES

Parent-educator Dolores Curran of Denver polled five hundred social workers, counselors, and other experts to determine what makes for a happy home. She reported these thirteen traits in her book, *Traits of a Healthy Family*:

1. A willingness to speak and listen thoughtfully to each other. (Close attention also paid to body language, sighs, touches, and periods of silence.)
2. The ability to bring quarrels to a quick and satisfying conclusion— without bearing grudges.
3. Cooperation among family members in helping each other maintain a secure and positive self-image.
4. An atmosphere of playfulness and humor without sarcasm or put-downs.
5. Clear parental guidelines on right and wrong.
6. A system for sharing responsibility, particularly important in single-parent homes.
7. Creation of a strong sense of unity and a respect for family traditions.
8. Easy interaction among all family members. Everyone is encouraged to participate in activities, and creation of factions is discouraged.
9. The sharing of some common religious or ethical core.
10. Respect of each other's privacy.
11. Development of a spirit of volunteerism and community service beyond the family's immediate needs.
12. A desire to share some leisure time, but not all.
13. A willingness, when serious problems can't be solved, to go outside the family for help.

Note how many of these relate directly or indirectly to communication! The flow of communication within a family is vitally important to each member of the family feeling personally happy.

## SUCCESSFUL FAMILIES

A study among Mormon families, who place high importance on the family unit, focused on families who had been through the strains of teenage years with at least one child. Some two hundred families were selected to complete a lengthy questionnaire that had more than five hundred variables, and then many of the families were interviewed by phone.

The researchers concluded that there was no precise profile for a successful family. Some of the families showed a great deal of physical affection; others didn't. Some parents spanked their children; others didn't. Some controlled the amount of television viewed in the home; others didn't.

What the researchers found was a few common threads that emerged among the successful families:

- A strong commitment to their faith. Almost 100 percent of the families paid tithes, attended church meetings as a family, and accepted "callings" in the church.
- A strong commitment to building a good family and spending the time necessary to do so. Nearly all of the parents defined their parenting goals and communicated these expectations to their children. In some cases, the parents didn't really believe they could determine their "successfulness" in raising a family until they saw how their grandchildren turned out. These parents had goals that extended beyond their immediate families to the next generation.

  The parents spent both quality and quantity time in working with their children, talking with their children, being with their children, and teaching their children. Older brothers and sisters supported one another. The parents encouraged their children to be involved in music, sports, drama, school elections, scouting, and other activities—and the parents were willing to get involved with them as chaperones, leaders, and mentors.
- The establishment of general rules about lifestyle—doing what is right because it's right—rather than specific lists of do's and don'ts.
- A great deal of communication. Almost all the parents in the study placed a high importance on talking to their children, reading to them, and communicating with them about their faith and their studies.
- Visible affection. Hugs, kisses, and saying "I love you" were common in these homes, with some 81 percent of the parents stating

that they showed some kind of physical affection to their children on a daily basis.

The successful families in this study were by no means problem-free. One farmer put his family problems into perspective with this statement: "They last from one to the next." But the successful families had learned to be flexible, to ride out the storms, and to bend with adversity rather than break under it. They chose to endure through tough times.

## STRONG FAMILIES

In the mid 1970s, Nick Stinnett became interested in learning more about what makes for strong families. A professor of family studies at Oklahoma State University at the time, he was disturbed about much of what research and popular literature was saying about families. Much of the material seemed to be pointing out what was wrong about to-day's families, and while Stinnett recognized the validity of such an emphasis, he saw a crying need for balance. He set out to see what a *strong* family looked like, and his quest led to a nationwide study. For families to qualify for his study, they had to demonstrate a high degree of marital happiness, a high degree of parent-child satisfaction, and the family needed to appear to meet individual family member needs in a way that was mutually satisfactory. Through questionnaires and interviews, Stinnett concluded that these six qualities appeared in a remarkably high percentage of the families he studied:

1. appreciation expressed
2. good communication patterns
3. time spent together
4. commitment to family
5. high degree of religious orientation
6. ability to deal with crises in a positive manner

## EFFECTIVE FAMILIES

The National Institute of Mental Health asked fifty parents who had "successfully" raised their children to become productive, well-adjusted adults for tips on raising children. Their responses were grouped into these ten basic principles:

1. Love abundantly. Love gives a child a sense of security, belonging, and support.
2. Discipline constructively. Give clear directions and enforce limits on a child's behavior. Emphasize "do this" instead of "don't do that."

3.  Spend time together. Play with your children, talk with them, teach them.
4.  Give priority to personal and marital needs. Child-centered households produce neither happy marriages nor happy children. Don't neglect your spouse or your own personal needs. Your poor health—physical, emotional, or financial—and an unhappy marriage (especially if it ends in separation or divorce) have much greater potential for harming your child than if you occasionally place your own needs before those of your child.
5.  Teach right from wrong. Help children learn basic values and manners. Set before them personal examples of moral courage and integrity.
6.  Develop mutual respect. Treat your children with respect. Say "please" and "thank you" to your child even as you teach him to say "please" and "thank you." Treat your child as you desire to be treated.
7.  Listen actively. Give your child undivided attention. See life through your child's eyes.
8.  Offer guidance. Be brief; don't nag.
9.  Foster independence. Gradually allow children more and more freedom to make their own choices and decisions; give them more and more responsibility for possessions and the management of their own lives. Let them earn freedom and responsibility privileges by showing you their trustworthiness.
10. Be realistic. Expect mistakes and allow for failures.[2]

## Good Ideas, but Where Is God?

All of the above studies list good ideas, and many of the concepts overlap from list to list. While each of the four mentions religious faith or a strong moral and ethical component, none of the authors or organizations attempts to rank or sequence the traits that contribute to wholeness and strength in a family.

We each know from practical experience that some principles in life are more important than others. Some concepts are foundational, while others are good but not necessarily vital. Are there some concepts that are more critical than others? Do they have a direct relationship to a strong family?

*Building* is a process. It is incremental, in stages, and by design. In building a strong family, we need to have a foundation and then build upward upon it.

I believe there are five vital concepts at the core of a strong family. These concepts are each powerful but they are not equal. They build upon each other like blocks. They are the five C's of building strong families:

1. Centered on God
2. Caring
3. Connection
4. Communication
5. Commitment

Let's take a look at each in turn, keeping in mind that each concept builds upon the one preceding it and sets the foundation for the concept that follows.

# Core Concept # 1: Centered on God

God must be kept at the center of the family at all times and in all circumstances. This is the foremost and most foundational of all principles for you as a Christian parent as you build a strong family.

If every person in the family is trusting God, keeping God's commandments, and relying upon God for his or her identity, the family will thrive and every member of the family will regard the home as a safe haven. Placing God at the center includes placing a high priority on association with other godly people—for example, church attendance and involvement and participation in family-related activities with other families who share the same commitment to the Lord Jesus and to the development of personal faith.

Those things which tear families apart or weaken them are invariably things that are in opposition to God's plan for humankind and, very specifically, in rebellion to God's commandments. A child who does not have a physical father present in the home can be taught to rely upon his or her heavenly Father. A child who does not have a physical mother present in the home can draw great strength from the nurturing and love expressed through the church.

When God is at the center of a family—with parents taking the lead—values, and the teaching of values, become an automatic priority. Teaching a child about God's love includes teaching a child about God's mercy and judgment. God not only woos us to Himself continuously, but He chastises us when we stray from Him. God's commandments are a framework for teaching a child right from wrong. Our values flow from our faith.

A family's faith in God forms the rock-solid foundation from which all attitudes, values, virtues, and habits are built.

# Core Concept # 2: Caring

Another way of saying *caring* is to say love and appreciation. Genuine caring compels a parent to meet the needs of a child—physical, emotional, and spiritual. Loving care results in sacrificial giving, the expression of affection, and continual attendance to a child's nurturing and growth. Love within the family must be rooted in forgiveness and coupled with understanding and compassion.

This kind of caring love does not exist in a vacuum. It doesn't spring spontaneously into a parent's heart upon the birth of a child. A parent, whether Christian or non-Christian, loves his child with an earthly, natural, parental love—"storga" love, as it is referred to in the New Testament. But the Christian parent who has God at the center of his or her life, and who chooses to keep God at the center of all family life, is a person who is also endowed with a divine quality of love—"agape" love—that is unconditional, sacrificial, and unshakable. Agape love is love in its purest form and represents the kind of love God the Father had for us in giving His Son, Jesus, to die on a cross on our behalf.

Before any of us can wholly care for another, we must first believe that someone cares for us—loves us, believes in us, respects us, and wishes the best for us. Let me assure you today that God feels this way about you as an individual and a parent, and He will help you become the best parent possible.

All human beings have a great need to be appreciated. Those who matter to us most in life are the members of our own family; therefore, it is most important to us that we appreciate, and are appreciated by, our family members. When total strangers compliment us or express thanks for things we have done, we grow in esteem. But when our own parents, grandparents, siblings, and other family members we trust show their appreciation to us, we grow *greatly* in esteem and in confidence that we are able to face the outside world with strength and ability.

Appreciation needs to be expressed often for a relationship to grow. It is easy to express appreciation for services or favors that are performed. We are a performance-driven society. But of even greater value are expressions of appreciation simply for *who* a person is and the character traits he is displaying. Let your child know you appreciate the qualities of character you see growing in him, the faith that he is exhibiting, and the good habits he is developing.

Ephesians 4:29 says, "Do not let any unwholesome talk come out of your mouths, but only what is helpful for building others up according to their needs." In 1 Thessalonians 5:11 Paul also said, "Therefore encourage one another and build each other up, just as in fact you are doing" (NIV).

These admonitions of Paul were not for the church only. They apply to the home as well.

Compliment your child at least once a day. Make your compliment genuine and specific. Ask your child to share with you ways in which you can show appreciation to him or her.

Occasionally gather your family together and have each member tell what he or she appreciates about other family members. Ask your children to keep a running "I appreciate . . ." list (and you do the same). Thanksgiving, Christmas, and Easter are excellent times for this discussion, as well as any other occasion when the extended family is together.

## Core Concept #3: Connection

Caring that is based upon one's faith compels us to reach out to our children and forge a "connection" with them. You cannot believe in and embrace God's love—and love your child—without wanting to form a bond with him or her.

Connections are forged in several dimensions:

- *Time.* You must spend time with your child for him to feel connected to you. This means not only quality time, but a quantity of time and a consistency of time. You can't be accessible one day and inaccessible the next. Your child must know that he can get in touch with you twenty-four hours a day, seven days a week. If your job requires travel, you need to make an extra effort to stay in touch with your child and teach him how to contact you if a need arises.

  In one study, some fifteen hundred school children were asked, "What do you think makes for a happy family?" It is good to note what the children did *not* list. They did not list money, fine homes, big-screen television sets, or dozens of Christmas presents. The answer they gave most frequently was "doing things together."

  Children spell love *t-i-m-e.* You can't buy your child's affection with any currency other than time.

- *Space:* You need to be in physical proximity with your child. Make the effort to get down on the floor and play with your young child. Let your child sit close to you on the sofa as you watch a video together. Invite your child to ride with you as you go on an errand. If you travel in your business, you need to spend as much of your "home time" as possible with your child.

- *Touch.* Be affectionate with your child. A pat on the shoulder, a quick hug, a kiss goodnight, a hand held. Your affection shouldn't smother a child, but your child should feel that you approve of him or her. Approval is conveyed most powerfully through the sense of touch.

  Your touching, of course, must always be within the bounds of affection and never cross over into inappropriate behavior. One of the great tragedies of our time is the amount of sexual abuse that occurs within families. Touching among family members must always be pure and innocent, never sexual in its context. If you have questions or concerns about what is appropriate for children at various ages, talk to a professional counselor. If you see within yourself tendencies to hurt or inflict pain upon your children, even under the guise of "discipline," or if you were the victim of abuse yourself as a child, I encourage you to seek counseling. Abuse is preventable.

- *Frequency and Consistency.* Connections remain solid only if a parent and child are spending time together, sharing space, and showing affection to one another frequently and consistently. It isn't enough to hug your child once every six months or to spend time with your child once or twice per month (if you and your spouse are not living together). You need to have regular contact with your child for him or her to feel "connected" to you.

## PRESENCE VS. PRESENTS

So many parents are concerned about the material substance and the luxury items—the "presents"—they give their children. The best gift you will ever give your child is the gift of yourself.

Once a mother was celebrating a birthday, and the other family members treated her to a party. They instructed her to sit in her favorite living-room chair. Then the father and older children came in from the kitchen bearing their gifts on a tray. One by one, they solemnly presented their gifts to her, as if to royalty.

The youngest child, too young to have had much of a role in selecting presents, felt left out of this joyous gift-giving ceremony. But after watching the procession for a few minutes, she went into the kitchen and came out bearing an empty tray. Approaching her mother, she placed the tray on the floor and then stepped onto it. With a childish wiggle of exuberance, she exclaimed, "Mommy, I give you *me!*"

There could have been no greater gift to that mother. Conversely, there is no greater gift a child can receive than a parent's time, attention, and affection. Many families today are attempting to move from having two incomes to only one, so that one parent can stay home with the children. In the majority of cases, children are more than willing to exchange the luxury of "things" for their parent's presence.

You may think that your child doesn't want you around or that you are unimportant to your child. That simply isn't the case. Make yourself available. Eventually, even the most reluctant, reticent child will open up to a parent who is available, not only in physical presence but in eagerness to listen and communicate.

A boy was asked by his father what he wanted as a present for his sixth birthday. The boy was usually very specific about the gifts he liked his father to buy him, often giving his father great details about the names of certain toys and their color, size, and location in the toy store. The boy's response surprised the father. He simply said, "I'd like a ball."

"Great," the dad said, "what kind of ball?"

"A football or a soccer ball."

"Which do you want more?" Dad asked.

"Well," the boy said after a few moments of thought, "if you have time to play catch with me, then I'd like a football so we could throw it back and forth in the back yard. But if you're too busy, then I'd like a soccer ball because I can play soccer with the kids in the neighborhood."

The father quickly realized that what the boy *really* wanted was more time with Dad. The ball was just a means to an end.

**CARVING OUT FAMILY TIME**

A "lack of time" is something virtually every family in our busy society experiences. We sometimes think it was far easier for families in the past to spend time together. That wasn't necessarily so. In the past, men often worked much longer hours at harder labor than they do today. A work schedule of dawn to dusk was the norm even as recent as the last century. Many times the men in a family—not only fathers but older male children—were away at war or had to travel a great distance to find work.

In many cultures, both ancient and modern, children are required to work, often away from the home. Other children have a legacy of boarding schools or long school days, with a necessity of traveling many miles on foot or by horseback to get to school.

In sum, don't assume that people in the past weren't as busy as we are today or that time was any easier to carve out for family togetherness. What people in past decades did have to their advantage, perhaps, was a different set of priorities. Once the family was together for the evening, the family tended to stay at home. Meals were more likely to be eaten together as a family; evening hours were more likely to be spent together, with a greater likelihood for conversation or activities within a shared space. Family occasions—whether Sunday dinners with the extended family or chats on a front porch with nearby neighbors and friends—were more likely because society was less mobile.

Spending time together has always been, and is today, a matter of *priority*. The family that *wants* to spend time together does.

Here are some practical suggestions for carving out valuable family time:

1. Limit the number of activities to which you or your children are committed. This means putting a cap on the number of sports your children play, the number of clubs to which you or your children belong, and the number of organizations you serve as a volunteer.

2. As much as possible, control your work schedule (as opposed to it controlling you). Many young men and women today believe they are *expected* to work ten- to fourteen-hour days to appear "committed" to their employers or practices. There may come a point where you have to choose between a job that requires that degree of time and energy and settling for a less demanding position (and perhaps less money) to have more time with your family. Frequently, couples who try this are pleasantly surprised to discover how easily they adjust to a smaller salary, especially if they are spending more time with their children and hiring fewer baby-sitters, spending less money on expensive entertainment, and eating fewer dinners away from home.

3. Plan for family time. Set aside one night a week as family night. You may need to have a periodic family conference to schedule events during the upcoming month. Certainly you should not strive to do everything together as a family; such a family is likely to be as unhealthy as a family that spends no time together. The

key is to schedule enough events or activities together, while allowing time for individuals' events or activities.

Keep in mind that outside activities are always going to be vying for "family time." Bolster yourself for this and make a firm decision that when family events are scheduled, they take precedence over any other event that may come along.

### TANGIBLE CONNECTION

When you can't be with your child, give him or her something—whether tangible or intangible—to hold on to.

I recently heard of a mother who developed a wonderful daily ritual with her child. Each morning when she took her daughter to school, she'd kiss the palm of her daughter's hand and her daughter would kiss the palm of her hand. Then they'd each close their hands up tightly and put their hands (and the kisses) into their pockets.

The idea was this: if either the mother or daughter felt lonely during the day, all she needed to do was reach into her pocket, take out her kiss, and place it on her cheek.

What a nice way to help your child through a day, a performance, or a scary moment.

# Core Concept # 4: Communication

When we choose to build connections with our children by spending time with them and being available to them, we pave the way for communication. You can't communicate with someone who isn't (physically and emotionally) "there" for you.

In her book, *Traits of a Healthy Family,* Dolores Curran concluded that the stronger a family was, the less TV it watched. This may be the result of the fact that when the TV set is turned off, there's a greater likelihood for family members to talk to one another!

Communication within a family needs to have certain qualities for a family to become strong. One can't simply "convey information" or toss off trite and eventually meaningless phrases and consider the communication to have been genuine.

It is from you, the parent, that the child learns most of his vocabulary and facility with language. In one study, researchers concluded that by the age of three, children have acquired more than half the language they will use throughout their lives.[3] You may never have thought of yourself as a vocabulary or grammar teacher, but you are!

Don't talk "baby talk" to your child. Don't talk "down" to your child. But do talk to your child. Talk, and talk, and talk. Offer explanations. Give opinions. Share ideas. All the while, you are presenting concepts that are received and internalized by your child, becoming the foundational concepts and structures for your child's ability to think, reason, and communicate.

### SPONTANEITY

Royce Money, author of *Building Stronger Families*, has noted that most of the strong families he has observed have had a high level of "spontaneity" in their communication. Conversations are spirited, with natural interruptions. They are marked by a sense of humor, although never humor that ridicules. The pattern of communication is described as "free" and "free-wheeling."

While this type of communication pattern may be difficult to define formally, we all know how it feels to be engaged in such communication. There is an easiness, a relaxed flow that is comfortable.

Adults in the family set the tone for this type of communication. This means, of course, that the quality of your marriage directly influences the family communication pattern. If you and your spouse are at odds or have unresolved difficulties, the communication between you—and therefore the communication between your children and between adults and children—is likely to be stifled or stiff.

### ANSWERING QUESTIONS

Communication is not simply a matter of talking and listening. It's very possible for two people to take turns talking and listening and not have any real communication occur. Listening isn't merely being quiet until it's your turn to speak again. It requires that you listen to what is being asked or said and then respond to *that*, not to your preplanned agenda.

In one of her columns, Erma Bombeck addressed this problem, noting that many times people respond to questions with questions. One of her readers wrote her about an incident that occurred in their home. Their sixteen-year-old daughter had called from upstairs, "Has anyone seen my new sweater?"

Her father called back, "You mean the one that cost $20?" Her sister said, "You mean the one you won't let me wear?" Her brother replied, "You mean the stupid one that makes you look fat?" Grandma chimed in, "You mean the one with the low neckline?" And Mom asked, "You mean the one that has to be washed by hand in cold water?"[4]

Everyone in the family was talking about the same sweater, but no one had answered the teenager's question. No real communication had taken place; rather, each person had made a "statement" in the form of a question.

## CAREFUL LISTENING

A story is told of children in a family who begged for a hamster until they were given one. They named the hamster Danny and fawned over it for a couple of weeks. Two months later, however, when Mom found herself solely responsible for feeding the hamster and cleaning its cage, she found a new home for Danny and informed the children the time had come to take Danny to his new home.

One of the children said, "He's been around here a long time. We'll really miss him!"

Mom agreed, saying, "Yes, but he's too much work for one person, and since I'm that one person, I say he goes."

Another child offered, "Well, maybe if he wouldn't eat so much and wouldn't be so messy, we could keep him."

Mom stood firm. "No, it's time to take him to his new home. Go and get Danny's cage."

With one voice the children shouted, "Danny? We thought you said, 'Daddy'!"

Listen *closely* to what your children say. Never assume you know fully what they are thinking or are going to say. What you hear and what they say may be two different things.

Good listening involves far more than merely being silent while someone is talking.

Listening also entails paying close attention to the nonverbal language of your child—her facial expressions, the way the child walks, the lack of a smile or a laugh.

Listen without getting caught up in teaching, explaining, or solving all your child's problems. You don't need to give your child your opinion about *everything*. Sometimes a child benefits simply from having an opportunity to express his feelings and state his problems. He may not be looking for an answer or solace—rather, for an opportunity to get something off his mind.

Listen actively. Don't just insert an occasional "uh-huh" or "mmmm" as a response. You should be able to repeat back to your child what he is saying to you.

Sometimes listening requires clarification. If you have questions about what your child has said or is feeling, ask. Be sure to ask in a nonaccusatory, noninterrogating manner. An example might be, "Let me be sure I understood you correctly. Did you say . . . ?"

Accept your child's early-language imperfections. The English language is one of the most difficult to learn since it doesn't always have consistent rules. Your child is going to make mistakes. If you note a pattern of error that your child is making over a period of weeks or months, you should point that out to your child and let your child know why you want to help him correct his grammar or make better vocabulary choices. Don't, however, interrupt your child frequently to correct language use. You'll only stifle your child's eagerness to communicate.

Start listening early. The parent who fails to listen with interest to the ramblings of a three-year-old will probably find that his thirteen-year-old doesn't care to tell him a thing!

### KEEP YOUR COMMUNICATION POSITIVE

Your words carry tremendous weight with your child. Take inventory of your own vocabulary. What words do you hear yourself using most frequently? Words like *ugly, stupid,* and *jerk* are generally understood among adults as being figures of speech. But they have no place in conversations with children, who take their meaning far more literally.

Words can create a mind-set of achievement or failure within a child. What attitude do your words portray? You can't tell a child on one occasion that you believe in him, pray for his highest and best, and that you desire for him to put his faith and trust in God . . . and then bombard that child day in and day out with messages that say "You can't," "You aren't," and "You won't."

Of course, communication within a family can't be all positive. That's an unrealistic goal. There is a time and place for negative statements to be expressed, and withholding them can create quite an unhealthy climate in a home. Over time, bottled-up emotions can become volatile and erupt in ways that are even more negative than the initial feelings!

Saying no, pointing out areas in the lives of our children that need to be corrected, and giving voice to things that frustrate us are all part of parenting. Sometimes parents and children are going to have a clash of opinions since we each see the world from a unique viewpoint. Hopefully, however, positive comments outweigh negative ones. A healthy ratio to strive for is 80/20: 80 percent positive and only 20 percent negative. In most homes, that ratio would reflect a vast improvement toward the positive!

## RESOLVE ARGUMENTS FOR GROWTH

Since arguments and disagreements are unavoidable, finding ways to resolve conflicts so that growth or improvement result is crucial. Those who have studied communication tell us that less than 7 percent of total communication is in the message itself.[5] The remaining communication lies in voice tone and nonverbal expressions and gestures. It is important not only to take a look at *what* is said in your family, but also *how* it is said.

Most parents would benefit greatly in the communication department simply by lowering their volume and speaking in a kinder tone of voice.

Paul told the Ephesians that one of the marks of Christian maturity is to "speak the truth in love" (Eph. 4:15). We have all heard the old saying, "The truth hurts." At the same time, we all want to be told the truth and want others to hear the truth from us. The key lies in speaking truth with an attitude that conveys these messages:

- I want the very best for you.
- I'm sure this negative can be turned into a positive.
- I believe in you and your ability to grow and change.
- I love you regardless of your behavior.

We need to make certain that when we speak the truth to other family members, we do so without bitterness, anger, slander, or any form of malice. "Be kind and compassionate to one another, forgiving each other, just as in Christ God forgave you" (Eph. 4:32, NIV).

Several things can be done to keep your family communication positive, to build consensus, and to resolve differences in a constructive way:

- Don't allow blanket statements of criticism, i.e., statements such as "you always" or "you never." Keep criticisms and negative comments specific to current issues.
- Keep disagreements in the present tense. Don't allow past failures or errors to be woven into the argument.
- Defuse the anger. If tempers are raging, have a cooling off period before you discuss the matter.
- Tone down the rhetoric. Some words are obvious "triggers" to an argument. These words vary from person to person, family to family. Don't allow those words to be used.
- Don't end a discussion of the negative too soon. It's easy for some people to stomp out of the room, leave the discussion in a pout, or clam up and refuse to discuss the matter further. However, it's

more productive to work your way *all the way through* the matter at hand.

- Try to sift the minor and irrelevant from the truly important. Most arguments are loaded with trivia that really is of no major consequence.
- Insist that those in an argument repeat back to the person speaking what it is that they "heard." What a person says is sometimes not what others hear, and vice versa.
- Voice your empathy. "I see what you mean" or "I'm trying to understand better" are important phrases in conflict resolution. Be sure you mean these phrases, however, and aren't only using them as a ploy.

Families tend to develop patterns of communication that are predictable over time, including the way they argue. The point may come when you need an outside counselor or mediator to help you find new ways of communicating with one another. If you suspect that's the case, get help. It takes two to agree. It also takes two to agree to agree!

## Core Concept # 5: Commitment

Commitment is like icing on a cake or the roof on a house—it covers everything else. When we build on a strong foundation of faith in God, love takes on a Christlike quality. Our deep caring for our child leads us to build connections with him, and those connections pave the way for open, free-flowing, and honest communication. Commitment is our resolve *always* to keep our families centered on God, *always* love, *always* build bridges to our children, and *always* communicate to the best of our ability. It also includes our commitment to *be* a family, no matter what circumstances or situations arise.

Strong families don't happen by accident. They involve willful choices, often made daily. We as parents must choose to maintain our motivation and be consistent, steadfast, and focused on our goal to train children who will be productive and happy adults in our society-at-large. Parenting is a twenty-four-and-seven job: twenty-four hours a day, seven days a week. Always remember:

There is no vacation from parenting if a parent is to be successful.

## Strong Does Not Mean Trouble-Free

We each would like to conclude that if we build strong families, we will never have any family problems. That simply isn't the case. No family is problem-free. You only need to read a few chapters into the Bible to discover this ancient truth. David, Solomon, Jacob, Esther, Samson, Joseph, Job, Ruth, and Hosea (among others) all faced major family problems of different types. Each family has to learn to deal with pain, frustration, disappointment, and conflict—as well as with the joys that can come from being part of a loyal, loving group.

The difference tends to be this: when trouble strikes a weak family, the family scatters, becomes frayed, and individual members become isolated, experiencing even more pain. When trouble strikes a strong family, the family bonds tighter, presents a unified front, and individual members are strengthened and helped through tight bonds of love and loyalty.

Consider the way that geese fly when they migrate. As each bird in the group flaps its wings, it creates an uplift for the bird following it. By flying in a "V" formation, the entire flock adds 71 percent greater flying range than if each bird flew alone. Whenever a goose falls out of formation, it suddenly feels the drag and resistance of trying to fly alone. It quickly gets back into formation to take advantage of the lifting power of the bird immediately in front of it. When the lead goose gets tired, it rotates back into the formation and another goose flies up to the point position.

Have you ever wondered why geese honk as they fly? Those who have studied these birds believe it may be a form of encouragement to those in front to keep up their speed.

If a goose gets sick or wounded, two geese drop out of formation and follow it down to the ground to help and protect it. They stay with the injured bird until it is able to fly again or dies. Then they launch out on their own or join another formation.

What wonderful lessons these are for our families. The family that is closely knit creates a "lifting power" for each individual member. Children in such a family have a much greater desire to stay true to family ideals and to do nothing that would destroy family ties. Encouragement in a family needs to be free flowing, and when one person is down—physically or emotionally—the others need to rally around and support that person until they are "flying" again.

Dr. Jerry Lewis made an interesting observation in his book, *How's Your Family?* He believes that strong families are ones that don't develop chronic, internal stress. Poor family relationships tend to create a stressful climate, with each member taking on a certain amount of discomfort, stress, and feelings of frustration or pressure.

In times of crisis, the dysfunctional family tends to come apart at the seams because it has no energy left to deal with the problem. It has drained itself along the way on chronic, everyday problems. In contrast, the strong, healthy family has lots of stored-up energy—created by expressions of love and values—to tackle the problem. The strong family isn't destroyed by the emergency; rather, individual members tend to turn inward to support one another and upward for guidance from God.

Choose today to become a strong family, and remain one, regardless. Your faith in God and your love for your children compel you to do so. Make the effort to continue to connect and to communicate. Seal your family with a strong commitment to *be* a family, no matter what may come your way.

# Chapter 2

# *Every Parent a Leader*

*I did not have my mother long, but she cast over me
an influence that lasted all my life. The good effects of
her early training I can never lose. If it had not been
for her appreciation and her faith in me at a critical
time in my experience, I would never likely have become an inventor. I was always a careless boy, and
with a mother of different mental caliber, I would
have turned out badly. But her firmness, her sweet-
ness, her goodness, were potent powers to help me on
the right path. My mother was the making of me.
The memory of her will always be a blessing to me.*
—Thomas Edison

*Let them follow the way you teach and live; be a
pattern for them in your love, your faith, and your
clean thoughts.*
—1 Timothy 4:12, TLB

Every eight and a half seconds a miracle happens in the United
States—a baby is born.

That birth rate translates into 420 babies born each hour, or 10,080 a
day. By the end of a year, almost four million babies are born in our
nation.

Training this army of potential citizens is a formidable task that is
shared by the home, school, and community. It involves a shared commitment to help a child acquire the skills, knowledge, and attitudes required for a rich, fruitful life.

The parents of the newborn may not think of themselves as teachers,
but they are a child's first and foremost teachers nonetheless. As soon
as they take their tiny infant from the hospital, they embark on a training program that will continue until the child is an adult. The question

is not, "Will you be a leader and a teacher as a parent?" Rather, the question is, "What *kind* of leader and teacher will you be?"

Children are essentially raw material to be converted into finished products. Like unimproved property, their full value cannot be realized until their traits and capacities are developed. Education, both at home and at school, is the primary process that transforms the illiterate, untrained child into the capable adult.

Contrary to popular thought, parental influence is critical *throughout* a child's growing-up years, not only in the first few "formative" years. Though high-schoolers' needs are vastly different from a small child's, their need for parental involvement is just as great. They need to be told "I love you" when their peers tag them as unlovable. They need to hear that beauty comes from within when popular culture says they're too heavy or too thin. Perhaps most importantly, they need to see their parents modeling Christ in a time when they are most vulnerable to the spiritual chaos surrounding them.

## Single Parents

What about the single parent? In 1994, a U.S. Census Bureau report showed that more than one-fourth of American children are now living with one parent. That translates to some 17.9 million children. Another study reported that 23.3 percent of children are living with "mother only."

It is especially critical that a single parent step up to the plate and *choose* to be a parent. Without the daily assistance of a spouse, she bears a much greater responsibility of being her child's role model, disciplinarian, and ballast during the storms of childhood and adolescence on a constant, ongoing basis.

## Even Communitarians Point to Parents as Key

At a seminar in 1991, a group of thirty social theorists from diverse political backgrounds forged a document titled, "The Responsive Communitarian Platform: Rights and Responsibilities." The "communitarian" vision for society that they proposed is one in which parents put children first, schools teach values, politicians don't cave in to special interests, citizens honor civic duties, and communities take steps to curb disease and crime. The "best place to start" in building such a community, the group argued, is the family, "where each new generation acquires its moral anchoring."

"Moral education is not a task that can be relegated to babysitters, or even professional child-care centers. It requires close bonding of the kind that typically is formed only with parents, if it is formed at all," the document stated. While the group did not agree unanimously on the root causes or cures of the problems plaguing our society, the scholars did agree on this: parents—whether by economic necessity or to sustain their standard of consumerism or personal advancement—too often "come home too late and too tired to attend to the needs of their children."

This group attempted to avoid religious overtones to their platform statement, stressing that a communitarian philosophy could stress "values Americans share" such as human dignity, tolerance, peaceful resolution of conflicts, and the merits of democratic government, truth, work, and self-reliance.

## Home Should Be the Foremost "School" Your Child Attends

Parents have far more time than a school in which to train and influence a child. Consider the example of an eighteen-year-old who has just graduated from high school. We often envision this young person having spent most of his life in school, and yet, if you do the math, you'll discover this young person spent only a small portion of his time in school.

If our graduate attended school 180 days a year for twelve years, he spent 2,160 days in school. Average in his extracurricular activities and say he spent eight hours a day in school, and you have 17,280 hours. But in eighteen years (allowing eight hours a day for sleep), he has lived a total of 105,120 waking hours. School only accounted for about 16 percent of those hours!

Many parents have the mistaken idea that children *only* learn when they go to school and that the remainder of the time they are in a static state—watching TV, eating dinner, or visiting with friends. Nothing could be further from the truth. Children are learning every waking moment, in a constant state of taking in and processing information. That's why it's so important for parents to exercise control over where, how, and with whom their children are spending their time.

Too frequently, parents not only rely upon the school system to teach their children, but on the Sunday school teachers in their church to pass along biblical principles of Christian living. I can't begin to count the number of children I have met who attended Sunday school and church regularly, and yet had never had anyone tell them about Christ. Do you really know what goes on in your child's Sunday school class or children's church program? For years, many of these programs focused on "activities" far more than on true training in Christian living. Children were supposed to learn about Jesus from coloring pictures of Him!

It is not the Sunday school's responsibility to make sure your child knows who Jesus was and is, and how He desires to impact your child's life. That is your responsibility as a parent. The home is the place God intended to be the center of your child's spiritual formation and growth.

Remember these words in Deuteronomy 6:4–9 (KJV):

> *Hear, O Israel: The LORD our God is one LORD: And thou shalt love the LORD thy God with all thine heart, and with all thy soul, and with all thy might. And these words, which I command thee this day, shall be in thine heart: And thou shalt teach them diligently unto thy children, and shalt talk of them when thou sittest in thine house, and when thou walkest by the way, and when thou liest down, and when thou risest up. And thou shalt bind them for a sign upon thine hand, and they shall be as frontlets between thine eyes. And thou shalt write them upon the posts of thy house, and on thy gates.*

Moses went on to tell the people that when their children asked questions about why they kept certain customs and adhered to certain laws and rules, they should tell their children, "And the LORD commanded us to do all these statutes, to fear the LORD our God, for our good always, that he might preserve us alive, as it is at this day. And it shall be our righteousness, if we observe to do all these commandments before the LORD our God" (Deut. 6:24–25).

In other words, we are not only to teach our children right and wrong, but to tell our children *why* we do certain things and don't do other things. God's laws are a means of our serving God. His laws are always for our good—our preservation and joy. Obedience is our way of staying in a right relationship with God.

It is never enough to tell your child *what* to do. You must also tell him *why* to do it.

Furthermore, training, teaching, and leading are all considered to be part of the natural flow of life within a family. There's no "break between classes" or "grade" system in the home. Training is seamless and ongoing.

# Parental Leading Sometimes Means Walking Alongside

Most of us think of leadership as being "out front" with a parade of people behind us, being "up front" with a group of people before us, or being "up the ladder" with a group of people on an organizational chart below us.

Leadership within a family structure is very likely a matter of steering a child's negative impulses into a positive expression.

A story has been told through the years about one of Poland's most famous concert pianists, who later became a prime minister—Ignace Paderewski. Once Paderewski was scheduled to give a performance, and a mother, desiring to encourage her son's progress at the piano, bought tickets. When the night arrived, she found their seats near the front of the concert hall and then turned her attention to talk to her friends and neighbors who were seated around her. Her son, however, had his eyes glued on the grand piano that sat center stage.

Promptly at eight o'clock, the house lights dimmed and the audience quieted. Only as the spotlight came up on stage did the mother realize that her son was no longer by her side. She looked up as the audience gasped to see her son, perched proudly on the bench of the grand piano on stage, begin to innocently pick out "Twinkle, Twinkle, Little Star." Before she could make it to the stage to retrieve her son, the master himself walked onto the stage and quickly moved to the keyboard. He whispered to the boy, "Don't quit; keep playing," as he leaned over him. With his left hand, Paderewski began to fill in the bass part. His right hand moved to the other end of the keyboard and began to add running obbligatos. Together, the old master and the young novice held the crowd mesmerized.

Your child's life is unpolished and unformed. Mistakes and errors that are made are generally made in innocence. Leadership requires that a child's errors be redeemed, and the child be trained, without destroying the child's spirit—which can readily happen if a child is embarrassed in front of others, reprimanded with a severity that is beyond the "crime" of the child's error, or if the child is given a punishment that is punitive but not corrective (in other words, a punishment that hurts but isn't coupled with positive alternatives so that a child truly learns what to *do* as well as what *not* to do).

Parental leadership requires a balance between insisting that your child exhibit right behaviors and, thus, learn right values, and reassuring your child continually that you are at the keyboard with him and that you love him unconditionally.

# Leadership and Authority Don't Require an Adversarial Relationship

We often hear of parents who say, "I'm great friends with my child." In fact, many parents desire to be "pals" with their children along with the role of authoritative figure.

Communication and affection are hallmarks of both friendship and parenthood, but a parent must never lose sight of the fact that the parent is filling a leadership role. The parent is the authority within the home because the parent bears the responsibility for the child's actions.

The concepts of authority and responsibility go hand in hand. The more your child assumes responsibility for his own life, the more authority he should have over his life. But until your child bears the *full* responsibility for his behavior before God and society, the parent is in authority over that child.

Perhaps because so many people work in environments in which supervisors or other figures of authority have an adversarial relationship with them, many parents come to assume that leaders and followers are necessarily "enemies." Nothing could be further from the truth from God's standpoint, especially as far as leadership is to be exerted in the home. Consider again the verse in Deuteronomy, which indicates a pattern of teaching children while sitting, walking, lying down, and rising up. This infers ongoing, active communication encompassing a broad range of activities, including work, play, and relaxation.

Leadership does not mean that you must be aloof or that you must set aside all of your own childlike curiosity and delight in the world. Having authority doesn't mean that you must become a curmudgeon.

Keep in mind always that as a parent:

*You are the most interesting thing in the world to your young child.* No other sight, sound, smell, or experience can rival what Mom and Dad do. The same holds true for others in your child's life who are beloved—grandmothers and grandfathers, aunts and uncles, older siblings and other relatives. *People* count to children far more than things.

A woman once wrote about a trip she took to Kenya to visit her parents. She took her children along on what she considered to be the adventure of a lifetime. The children experienced many new things— flying in a jumbo jet, seeing elephants and prides of lions in their natural habitats, trying new foods, and seeing new sights. After the family had cleared customs at the airport on the return trip, the children rushed into the arms of their waiting father. "Daddy, Daddy, guess what?" one of the younger children exclaimed. "Granddad can take his teeth out!"

What you consider to be noteworthy may not be at all what catches the eye or incites the imagination of your child. Be sensitive always to the fact that your child's foremost fascination is with you and others in his family.

*Your child benefits when you see the world through his eyes.* Get down on your child's level occasionally. Sit on the floor and play with him. Imagine what the world must look like from his vantage point. Being a leader with authority and responsibility doesn't mean that you cease to relate to your child or to care about his perspective and desires.

A father once became quite upset over the length of time it was taking his son to walk home from school. He made the journey himself to see how long it took to cover the several blocks from school to home, and calculated that twenty minutes was plenty of time, even allowing for his son's shorter legs and slower pace. His son, however, was taking well over an hour to get home.

Finally the father decided to make the walk with his son. Upon arriving home he said to his wife, "I thought twenty minutes was sufficient time, but I had failed to consider important things—such as side trips to track down a trail of ants, watch a man fix a flat tire, or gaze up at birds in a nest. I'd forgotten that it takes time to swing around at least a half-dozen telephone poles and to play hopscotch in the chalk diagram made by a neighborhood child. I'd forgotten how long it takes for a boy to get acquainted with two stray dogs. In short, I had forgotten what it means to be eight years old."

*Your child benefits when you continue to take delight in your own world.* Being a parent does not mean that you can no longer express childlike delight in the world. Being child*like* is a Christian virtue. Being child*ish* is something quite different. To be childlike means to adore God, place utter dependence upon God, obey God without question, and to come to God with your petitions as you would to a heavenly Father who loves you and desires only your best. To be childish means to act in a self-centered, the-world-must-revolve-around-me manner.

The story is told of a distinguished elderly gentleman who walked through a toy department and stopped to admire a train. It whistled, belched smoke, deposited milk cans—in fact, it did virtually everything a real freight train does. After looking at it for some time, he finally said, "I'll take it. Please have it wrapped."

The clerk commented, "Excellent! I'm sure your grandson will love it."

The elderly gentleman said thoughtfully, "I suppose you're right. Maybe you'd better give me two of them."

There's nothing in the definition of being a parent that says you must lose your sense of humor or ability to have fun, that you no longer can delight in games and hobbies, or that you must never play with toys and gadgets. The Lord meant for you to enjoy life, which includes enjoying all of creation, the work of your hands (and that of others), and the wonders of things that reflect His natural laws at work.

# Establishing Clear Lines of Authority

There should be no questions about the chain of command or the line of authority within your home. If you have questions about that line, I suggest you turn to the Scriptures for advice. The Books of Proverbs, Ephesians, and 1 Peter give very specific instructions to both fathers and mothers. We are wise to heed its advice.

A husband and father is to

- love his wife
- regard children as a blessing
- derive happiness from the family
- trust in God, keep His commandments, and teach His commandments in the home
- be a willing wage earner
- be dedicated and motivated in both marriage and parenting
- be a model of virtues and values
- encourage children even in times of discipline
- promote loyalty and fidelity within the family and the spiritual community-at-large

A wife and mother is to

- submit her life to God and submit decision-making authority in the family to her husband
- show respect for her husband
- be committed to her family
- exemplify self-control, kindness, purity of mind, confidence, and wisdom
- do her work eagerly and vigorously, both within the home and in ways that are beneficial to the family outside the home
- teach and love her children

Children, too, have a specific role. They are to
- honor and obey their parents
- obey God's Word
- give God praise
- think about and talk about God daily
- do God's will and flee from sin
- work hard and avoid procrastinating
- desire instruction

These are lofty ideals, and yet they are do-able. We simply must make a commitment to keep God's ideals as our priority.

I certainly am aware that many women today have questions about what it means to "submit" to a husband. From my perspective, submission relates to ultimate decision-making about the direction that a family is going to take and the tone that a family is going to adopt. Most women I know have no difficulty in submitting this final decision-making to the husband if the husband is fulfilling his role in loving her, trusting God, working diligently to provide for the family, modeling virtues and values, and is dedicated and devoted to the marriage and to the family. For their part, most men I know don't have difficulty in loving their wives and leading their families if they have full confidence in their wives' respect, virtue, love, and commitment.

Together, parents have authority over their children, and that is the critical point to be made. Children are to honor and obey their mothers and fathers. Exodus 20:12 clearly states, "Honor your father and your mother" (NIV). From a child's point of view, both Mom and Dad are to be honored. Both are in authority over his life.

Be very clear about teaching your child his proper role in your family. Encourage your child to memorize Ephesians 6:1–3: "Children, obey your parents in the Lord, for this is right. 'Honor your father and mother'—which is the first commandment with a promise—'that it may go well with you and that you may enjoy long life on the earth'" (NIV).

Talk to your child about what you expect in terms of obedience and "honor," or respect.

# Insist that Your Child Respect You

Insist that your child show respect for you and for your spouse as parents, regardless of their age. Teens often reach a rebellious stage in which they delight in "putting down" Mom and Dad in hopes of elevating themselves. The way to rise in life and in the esteem of others is never by putting others down. Teach this to your children early.

The story is told of a visit Pope John XXIII received from his mother, a simple woman who had lived all her life within the shadow of poverty. Like others who were expecting an audience with the Pope shortly after being elected to the papacy, she stood in a line of people to greet him. As each person approached the Pope, he or she offered their congratulations and then bowed and kissed his papal ring. When it was the mother's turn, she also knelt before her son in good Roman Catholic fashion and acknowledged his authority by kissing his ring. But then she did an unusual thing. She held out her hand to him, pointing to her wedding band, and said, "Now, Son, you kiss this ring. Because if it were not for *this* ring, you wouldn't have *that* ring." He did as she requested. They both laughed, and Pope John rose to take his mother in his arms.

### PRACTICAL EXPRESSIONS OF RESPECT

Insist that your child speak to you with courtesy and politeness. Don't allow your child to speak to you with rudeness, cynicism, sarcasm, or disregard in his tone of voice. Don't allow your child to use crude or vulgar language in speaking to you. If your child is allowed to show disrespect to you, he will most likely show disrespect to all adults and others who may have authority over his life. This lack of respect will surely result in disdain and, ultimately, disobedience. By encouraging disrespect, you are helping to create a child who is unduly proud and arrogant when you let him get away with speaking to you in an unkind, disrespectful way.

Help your child to understand that to honor a parent does not necessarily mean that he agrees with everything the parent does and says. It does not mean that you lie about, cover for, or deny the bad behavior of an abusive parent. It does mean that you do not actively seek to undermine the well-being of a parent or to dismiss with disregard the good things that a parent has done or is doing.

What about a parent who is abusive or engaged in self-abusive behavior, such as alcoholism? A child is perfectly within his rights to seek his own safety from danger and to report an abusive parent to authorities. A child is also doing an honorable thing in participating in an intervention to get an addictive parent into a program where the parent can be treated medically and assisted psychologically and spiritually to make new choices and develop new habits. In reporting abuse or intervening in cases of addiction, a child is not being disrespectful to the parent primarily because the child is not seeking to undermine the well-being of the parent. Rather, it is the child's attempt to get *help* for the parent. Indeed, the dishonorable thing to do would be to walk away from such a parent and never seek to require the parent to face his own destructive or self-destructive behavior.

In the Jewish tradition, honoring parents included taking responsibility for elderly parents and providing for them. Jesus spoke well of those who fulfilled this responsibility. One of the best things you can do as a parent is to show respect for your child's *grandparents* and do your best to help them as they advance in years. Your example of honor and respect will likely reap dividends in your relationships with your own children!

### NO "CON" OR "SNOW" JOBS

Children are always testing the limits of good behavior, and they can readily become skilled "con artists" if you aren't aware of their schemes.

Beverly Sills admits to having been good at this craft. As a child, she sang on the "Capitol Family Hour," and part of the program was devoted to her conversations with Major Bowes, host of the Sunday night broadcast. On one occasion, Bowes asked Beverly what she wanted for Christmas. When she replied that she would like a sled, listeners sent sixty-five sleds to her. A few weeks later when she mentioned how much she wanted a Mickey Mouse watch, listeners sent in dozens of them.

She admits to being shameless. On one program Major Bowes described the little ruffled dress her mother had made for her, and Beverly cut in, saying, "Yes, but my mommy won't make me a long dress and I want one." Her mother was so annoyed at the long dresses that came pouring in that she confiscated them all and then sat down to sew Beverly a long dress of her own creation.

The game was up for Beverly the day she told her listeners about her father's hernia operation. She said she hoped her Papa would be all right so he could go back to work soon because her family needed the money he earned. Her father was listening from his hospital bed and was not amused. He certainly wasn't a charity case, and he did not want his "Bubbly" to extort money from people listening to the "Capitol Family Hour." Beverly's days as a panhandler were over.

Also be on the alert for your child's attempts to compliment you or shower you with affection in an effort to get you to comply with his wishes against your better judgment. This is simply your child's attempt to manipulate you with praise. If you give in to these attempts, you are only encouraging your child to continue a pattern of manipulation—a pattern that becomes very hard to break over time.

# Insist that Your Child Obey You

There are many parallels in the Bible between God and His people (Israel) and parents and their children, but none so vivid as the concept of obedience. God commanded strict obedience of His people, and the consequences of disobedience were severe. But God also explained the reasoning behind His "discipline policies," which always came around to it being for their own good.

So, too, with the parent-child relationship. Rules should reflect what is fair, just, and reasonable, for the good of the child and the family community. Children should be taught early in life that obedience is to be immediate, exact, and unquestioning.

*Immediate.* Such obedience could mean the difference between life and death. Require your child to obey you the *first* time you tell her to do something. Don't wait to threaten punishment on the fourth request and then exact punishment on the seventh request. Insist that your child take seriously your commands.

Your child should obey you *exactly.* Not half-heartedly or with a motive of seeing how much he can get away with. Insist that your commands be followed precisely and entirely. You are not being over-dictatorial in this; rather, you are helping your child learn the important lesson of following instructions—a lesson that will reap benefits in school, in jobs, and in all of life.

Finally, insist that your child obey you *without question.* This does not mean that your child cannot ask you why *after* he or she has heeded your command. Questions are important for a child to gain understanding of the reasoning for certain behaviors. Good answers to such questions can help a child become self-motivated toward right behavior, but your child should obey you without question and *then* ask questions. A child who balks at obeying until an explanation is given is a child who is going to have great difficulty later in life in yielding to authority figures. We all are under the authority of *somebody* in some area of our lives, for all our lives. Ultimately, we are under God's authority. Learning to operate under authority and to be submissive to that authority is part of learning how to yield our lives in humility to the Lord.

# Set Clear Rules and Boundaries

In his book, *The Christian Family,* Larry Christensen gives this description of a good mother:

*"I had the meanest mother in the world," a housewife wrote. "While other kids ate candy for breakfast, I had to have cereal, eggs, or toast. When others had Cokes and candy for lunch, I had to eat a sandwich. As you can guess, my supper was different than the other kids' also. But at least I wasn't alone in my sufferings. My sister and two brothers had the same mean mother.*

*"My mother insisted upon knowing where we were at all times. You'd think we were on a chain gang. She had to know who our friends were and what we were doing. She insisted if we said we'd be gone an hour, that we be gone one hour or less—not one hour and one minute.*

*"We had to wear clean clothes and take a bath. The other kids always wore their clothes for days. We reached the heights of insults because she made our clothes herself, just to save money.*

*"The worst is yet to come. We had to be in bed by nine each night and up at eight the next morning. We couldn't sleep till noon like our friends. So while they slept—my mother actually had the nerve to break the child-labor law. She made us work. We had to wash dishes, make beds, learn to cook, and all sorts of cruel things. I believe she lay awake at night thinking up mean things to do to us.*

*"She always insisted upon our telling the truth, the whole truth and nothing but the truth, even if it killed us—and it nearly did.*

*"By the time we were teenagers, she was much wiser, and our life became even more unbearable. None of this tooting the horn of a car for us to come running. She embarrassed us to no end by making our dates and friends come to the door to get us. If I spent the night with a girl friend, can you imagine, she checked on me to see if I was really there? I never had the chance to elope to Mexico. That is, if I'd had a boy friend to elope with.*

*"Through the years, things didn't improve a bit. We could not lie in bed 'sick,' like our friends did, and miss school. If our friends had a toe-ache, a hang-nail, or another serious ailment, they could stay home from school.*

*"My mother was a complete failure as a mother. Out of four children a couple of us attained some higher education. None of us has ever been arrested, divorced, or beaten his mate. Each of my brothers served his time in the service of this country. And whom do we blame for the terrible way we turned out? You're*

*right—our mean mother. But look at all the things we missed. We never got to march in a protest parade, nor to take part in a riot, burn draft cards, and a million and one other things that our friends did. She forced us to grow up into God-fearing, educated, honest adults.*

*"Using this as a background, I am trying to raise my three children. I stand a little taller, and I am filled with pride when my children call me mean. Because, you see, I thank God He gave me the meanest mother in the world."*

It is the parent's responsibility to set rules and boundaries that define and regulate virtually every aspect of a child's life. Your child should have:

- an established bedtime
- a set of chores that are to be done daily or weekly
- rules regarding manners, including table manners
- rules regarding how your child addresses you ("Ma'am" and "sir" are not only for southern children!)

Very specifically, your child should have set rules regarding school, where your child can go, and what your child is allowed to take into his life.

### RULES ABOUT SCHOOL

In *Strong Families, Strong Schools*, Secretary of Education Richard Riley cited a study done by Barton and Coley in 1992. The study revealed that most of the differences in achievement observed across the states could be attributed to *home* practices more than school practices. Three factors mentioned in the study—student absenteeism, the variety of reading materials available in the home, and excessive television watching—accounted for nearly 90 percent of the differences in the average state-by-state performance of eighth grade mathematics test scores.

Certainly every parent can insist that his or her child attend school; drop-out students are as much a result of parental irresponsibility as student or school irresponsibility. It is the parent who can turn off the television set, or insist that homework be completed before television is watched. It is the parent who sets the tone about how many and what types of books are available for a child to read. It costs nothing but a little time and interest for a parent to go with a child to the library on a weekly basis! In addition to books, the public library is a great source for magazines, videos, and a wide variety of audio tapes. What a difference a parent can make in the school success of a child by doing these three simple things: go to the library, turn off the TV, and make sure a child goes to school.

Do children welcome this involvement? Absolutely. In one study, almost three-quarters of the students between the ages of ten and thirteen said they would like to talk to their parents more about schoolwork.[1]

### RULES ABOUT "INPUT"

*Input* pertains to everything that goes into your child's life—physically, mentally, and spiritually. Input includes defining who may be a friend and how much time can be spent with that friend. It includes how much time and what programs might be allowed on television, stereo, or computer. It includes participation in activities and events that have "input" into your child's moral and spiritual development, and emotional well-being.

One day a mother was scraping and peeling vegetables for a salad when her daughter came to her and asked permission to go to a movie that had a number of offensive scenes and was filled with bad language. When the mother refused to give permission, the girl cried, "But all the other girls are going. *Their* parents think it's OK."

While she continued to plead for permission to go to the movie, she noticed that her mother was picking up various bits of the discarded vegetable peelings and putting them into the salad bowl. "M-o-t-h-e-r, what are you doing?" she cried. "You're putting garbage into the salad."

"Oh," the mother said calmly. "I thought that since you didn't seem to mind garbage going into your mind and heart, you wouldn't mind a little garbage going into your stomach."

The girl picked out the offensive material from the salad and then quietly went to tell her friends that she would not be able to go with them.

Your child may not come to you until he or she is much older to tell you how much he appreciates the fact that you told him no when he asked to participate in certain events or parties at which immoral or illegal behavior was allowed. But deep inside, your child does and will appreciate that you have done your best to safeguard him from evil.

# Justice Is the Basis for Morality

Justice is not usually a concept we associate with family life, but it is a very important one. Justice is the quality of being true or correct, and is the basis for morality. Morality is conformity to a code of behavior based on what is just. As a Christian, justice is based unequivocally on the Bible and its principles. An excellent place to begin teaching justice to a young child is the Ten Commandments. This discussion, followed to its natural conclusion, will lead to an understanding of consequences and, of course, forgiveness.

Carrying out justice is a matter of establishing rules and boundaries that you insist be kept. These rules and boundaries must be firmly fixed. They must last from day to day and, as much as possible, from year to year.

As your child grows, some rules or boundaries should expand. For example, a parent might limit a child's play to a backyard area when the child is small, then extend that limit to include the front yard, and then extend it further to include the entire neighborhood block. You must be certain your child knows when the rules or boundaries change.

Rules related to virtues and values—such as telling the truth, showing respect, or doing work honestly and diligently—should never be relaxed or compromised.

Children who keep the rules and stay within the designated boundaries should enjoy great freedom of expression, creativity, and decision-making. Those who break the rules should expect, and receive, negative consequences.

For justice to prevail, you as the parent must make sure that your children understand the rules, as well as the consequences for breaking the rules and the rewards for keeping them. These rewards and consequences must apply to all children involved, not only one or a select few. And the rewards and consequences should be reasonably linked to the behaviors required or the rules that are established.

Be fair in your establishment of punishments and rewards. Even as Paul admonished children to obey and honor their parents, he admonished parents, "Do not provoke your children to wrath, but bring them up in the training and admonition of the Lord" (Eph. 6:4). Unfair, unnecessary, or overly harsh punishments can create a seething anger in a child. Punishment must never include deprivation of your child's basic needs (such as food, water, shelter). A most effective punishment for children seems to be isolation from the rest of the family for a period of time or denial of something that the child wants (as opposed to needs). As one parent phrased it, "Time outs and no desserts."

Make sure that you punish your child when you yourself are calm and in control of your own emotions. If you spank your child, spank her privately and make certain that she knows why she is being spanked and what you expect in terms of behavior in the future.

Finally, for justice to prevail, punishments and rewards must not be delayed. When good behavior is observed, reward that behavior quickly with a word of praise, recognition, or appreciation. When bad behavior is observed, punish the child as soon as possible so there will be no doubt in the child's mind that the punishment is linked to the breaking of a specific rule or the overstepping of a designated boundary.

To maintain the self-worth and self-esteem of your child, I recommend that you punish your child in one-to-one conversation, in private. Nobody else in the family, neighborhood, or a radius of ten feet in a public setting need know that your child is being corrected for wrong behavior. In private, you can get directly into your child's face and speak in a low tone of voice—which lets your child know that you mean business (and aren't just grandstanding for others) and, at the same time, that you respect him as a person (by not embarrassing him publicly).

On the other hand, much benefit can be derived from rewarding your child in the presence of others. Let your child know that you appreciate his keeping the rules and staying within boundaries. Part of the reward may be the setting of new, expanded boundaries. This shouldn't be simply because your child has reached a "magic age" or because you are becoming more relaxed as a parent. The new boundaries should be stated clearly as a reward for exemplary behavior and trustworthiness.

Boundaries can also be tightened and rules made more strict if you discover that you have been too lax or that your child is not yet ready for expanded freedoms and responsibilities. Again, make sure your child knows why you are tightening the reigns and what the new boundaries are, with what related consequences and rewards.

In summary, to have a moral home, you must have a "just" home. This means that as a parent you must:

- clearly state your expectations to your child; identify rules and boundaries and stick by them
- clearly identify fair and reasonable rewards and punishments associated with good and bad behavior
- act quickly, decisively, and privately in punishing your child
- act quickly in rewarding your child (which may include public recognition or praise)

How is justice linked to morality? Morality is a framework of right and wrong that you establish in training your child. Ultimately, right and wrong are absolutes. It is from such a framework of right and wrong that all behaviors flow. If you are lax in creating rules and boundaries that reflect right and wrong to your child, or if you are lax in enforcing those rules and boundaries, you send your child a message that there are no absolutes. That message is contrary to God's Word, which says there are.

A child who is taught that all behavior is relative, and that all bad behavior will ultimately be overlooked or have no consequences, is a child who grows up having no regard for God's absolutes. Such a child is in grave danger of experiencing God's justice, which is always inevitable, always exact, and frequently swift.

# Don't Undermine Your Leadership as Parents

Sometimes parents "shoot themselves in the foot," so to speak, by undermining their own leadership. Children are to respect and obey their parents, and the best way to ensure that they do so is for parents to present a united front to their children (regardless of the warmth or solidarity of their relationship with each other).

In my experience, there are eight events that have a highly negative impact on children. These negatives are exacerbated in broken homes:

1. One parent puts down the other parent. Don't criticize your spouse, or former spouse. You not only are establishing a critical spirit in your home—which can translate easily into cynicism, sarcasm, and negative speech in your child—but you are tearing away at the self-esteem foundation of your child. After all, this other parent *is* your child's father or mother, and regardless of how you feel about your spouse or former spouse, your child is related to that person for life and a certain amount of his or her identity is derived from that parent.

2. One parent thinks the children are spending too much time with the other parent. At different stages in life, children need one or the other parent more. It's not uncommon for this emphasis to shift back and forth several times as a child grows up. Share your child willingly and generously with your spouse or ex-spouse.

3. Relatives speak negatively about the parents. Your child's grandparents, aunts, uncles, or other relatives should not be allowed to speak negatively about you to your child. If you suspect this is happening, confront the person who is criticizing you. Let him know he is undermining your authority, creating a negative spirit in your child, and impacting your child's self-esteem. If he doesn't

change his ways, don't allow your child to be with him. Such a person is a source of negative input to your child.

4. One parent instructs a child not to tell the other parent something. A family is a place to share intimate feelings, not create secrets. The parent that engages in this activity is building a wall in the communication pattern of the home. He or she is disrupting an atmosphere of freedom and security; after all, if a child is asked to keep a secret about a parent, what secrets must others be keeping about the child? Your child needs to live in an atmosphere of trust and openness.

5. Parents talk to their children about their marital problems. Keep your problems to yourselves. Your marital problems become a burden to your child and make your child feel less secure. Eventually, your child will have less respect for you if you continually load him with an emotional burden he shouldn't have to bear.

6. Parents make a child feel he has to choose between Mom and Dad. This often happens in broken homes when it comes to custody battles, deciding where a child will live or determining how time is to be spent with a parent on weekends. In homes that are intact, this conflict can arise when both parents "vie" for a child's attention, each parent holding out fun activities or rewards in a type of marital competition.

7. Parents communicate through their children. Some parents send "hate" messages through their children to their former spouses. Others involve their children in their disagreements and ask children to be message carriers. The parent who does this is not only making a child feel less secure, but is firing a torpedo at family communication. Never ask your child to be a "go-between."

8. One parent overrides the decision of another parent. Talk to your spouse or former spouse directly about rules and privileges, reach some kind of common ground, and then stick to your decisions. A child who can get something from Mom that he can't get from Dad, or vice versa, is a child who loses respect for both parents and, ultimately, is a child who has problems with authority.

To put this into the positive, parents are wise when they:
- speak well of each other to their children
- are generous in spending time with their children
- seek out the positive support of other relatives
- keep their marital problems to themselves
- communicate openly, without creating family secrets

- freely share their children, without jealousy
- communicate directly with each other
- present a common front to a child when it comes to rules, privileges, and responsibilities

Don't allow your child to drive a wedge between you and your spouse, or to play one parent against another. Even if your spouse or former spouse engages in "warfare" tactics against you, be the parent who does the right thing.

## Determine within Yourself the Kind of Leader You Want to Be

Ultimately it's up to you to determine what kind of leader you want to be as a parent. Part of your decision will include coming to grips with what kind of *person* you want to be.

Various groups have attempted to identify the characteristics of good Christian leaders. Below are ten qualities which seem to be listed almost universally, adapted to reflect parenting.

1. Be a parent who is growing in Christian faith and spiritual understanding.
2. Be a parent who is working to improve his or her parenting skills.
3. Be an active member of a Christian church.
4. Have a teachable spirit.
5. Have a healthy attitude toward children.
6. Possess good interpersonal relationship skills.
7. Be open in attitude.
8. Be a self-starter.
9. Be available to spend time with your children.
10. Have the ability to facilitate.

If you aren't the leader that you desire to be today, make a start toward becoming that type of leader. Turn to God's Word to help you discover who you are in Christ Jesus and what He calls you to be and do. I can assure you of this: the kind of person you are is the kind of person your child will be. Who you are as an adult will determine greatly who your children will grow up to become.

# Chapter 3

# *Identifying Your Parenting Philosophy*

*Character is not cut in marble;*
*it is not something solid and unalterable.*
*It is something living and changing.*
—George Eliot
English novelist (1819–80)

*We . . . do not cease to pray for you, and to ask*
*that you may be filled with the knowledge of His*
*will in all wisdom and spiritual understanding;*
*that you may walk worthy of the Lord, fully*
*pleasing Him, being fruitful in every good work*
*and increasing in the knowledge of God;*
*strengthened with all might, according to His*
*glorious power, for all patience and*
*longsuffering with joy.*
—Colossians 1:9–11, NKJV

Most parents have a clear understanding that they bear responsibility for providing their children with food, shelter, clothing, an education, and medical care. Parents are equally responsible for giving their children discipline, mental stimulation, and moral and spiritual training.

When most parents think of the kind of parent they want to be, however, few come up with the word *self-sacrificing*. Being a good parent inevitably involves putting a child's needs above one's own, and giving up a tremendous amount of time, material resources, and devotion that a self-serving person would just as soon hang on to.

Several years ago, Erma Bombeck wrote the following column about mothers. Many mothers no doubt saw in her column the type of mother they desired to be, while others likely read a description of the type of mother they had as a child.

*When the good Lord was creating mothers, He was into His sixth day of "overtime" when the angel appeared and said, "You're doing a lot of fiddling around on this one."*

*And the Lord said, "Have you read the specs on this order? She has to be completely washable, but not plastic. Have 180 movable parts . . . all replaceable. Run on black coffee and leftovers. Have a lap that disappears when she stands up. And have a kiss that can cure anything from a broken leg to a disappointed love affair. And six pairs of hands."*

*The angel shook her head slowly and said, "Six pairs of hands . . . no way."*

*"It's not the hands that are causing me problems," said the Lord. "It's the three pairs of eyes that mothers have to have."*

*"That's on the standard model?" asked the angel.*

*The Lord nodded. "One pair that sees through closed doors when she asks, 'What are you kids doing in there?' when she already knows. Another here in the back of her head that sees what she shouldn't but what she has to know, and of course, the ones here in front so that she can look at a child when he goofs, and say, 'I understand and I love you' without so much as uttering a word."*

*"Lord," said the angel touching His sleeve gently, "Come to bed. Tomorrow . . . ."*

*"I can't," said the Lord. "I'm so close to creating something so close to myself. Already I have one who heals herself when she is sick . . . can feed a family of six on one pound of hamburger . . . and can get a 9-year-old to stand under a shower."*

*The angel circled the model of a mother very slowly. "It's too soft," she sighed.*

*"But tough!" said the Lord excitedly. "You cannot imagine what this mother can do or endure."*

*"Can it think?"*

*"Not only think, but it can reason and compromise," said the Creator.*

*Finally, the angel bent over and ran her finger across the cheek. "There's a leak," she pronounced. "I told you that you were trying to put too much into this model."*

*"It's not a leak," said the Lord. "It's a tear."*

*"What's it for?"*

*"It's for joy, sadness, disappointment, pain, loneliness, and pride."*

*"You are a genius," said the angel.*

*The Lord looked somber. "I didn't put it there."*

A parent of compassion, uncompromising virtue, and unending energy and enthusiasm—that's a parent description almost too good to be true. Yet the Lord calls parents—both moms and dads—to just this challenge: to be the lover, keeper, and foremost mentor of their child's life. Such a challenge requires that we give up a big part of what we want, desire, and hope for in order to give ourselves to our children's needs and dreams. Good parenting is selfless giving.

The story is told of a newly married woman who was calling on a friend. When she saw the sick woman's two children in quiet play at her friend's feet, she said, "Oh, I'd give my life to have two such children."

The friend replied, quietly but in earnest, "That's exactly what it costs."

It may not sound like much of a goal to say that your ambition as a parent is to pour your life into your children, but that is what it takes to raise children with positive attitudes, high values, lofty aspirations, good habits, and noble behavior.

"It's too high a price," you might say.

No, it's the price for having something of eternal value and something that is infinitely rewarding on this earth.

As you begin to develop your parenting philosophy, keep in mind always that if you choose to be a self-centered, selfish person, you can never be a truly good parent.

## Pouring Yourself into Your Child

In pouring yourself into your child, you are primarily pouring into your child your vision for him, your understanding of right and wrong, and your approach to discipline.

The vision you have for your child will create your child's self-esteem. Your understanding of right and wrong will create your child's value structure. Your approach to discipline will mold your child's behavior. His habitual attitudes and behavior, in turn, will form his character. Finally, his character will form his reputation.

A simple triangular model may help you envision this:

Your Vision for Your Child

Your Child's Self-Esteem

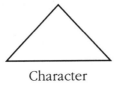

Your Understanding
of Right and Wrong

Your Approach
to Discipline

Your Child's Values

Your Child's Behavior

Character

Reputation

# Your Vision for Your Child

Most parents have expectations for and about their children. You may have heard the story of a mother who was walking with her two young children in the park. She met a friend, who asked, "How old are your children?" The mother replied, "Oh, the lawyer is two and the doctor is four."

While we might find such a story humorous, how many parents do we know who define the future of their children almost solely in terms of the career and social standing that they desire for their children to have?

Paul Noxon has written a wonderful essay titled "What Is a Child?" As you read through it, ask yourself, "What is the vision that I have for my child? How do I regard my child and his or her potential?"

*What are you my child? A match that needs to be struck, potential to light up our world and make it a cheerier place.*

*What are you my child? Dynamite awaiting the plunger to be set, potential to destroy the earth, or rightly directed to move a mountain of an obstacle to a better life.*

*What are you my child? Ground awaiting the plow, potential to bring forth a garden of weeds or a crop to feed the starving of the world.*

*What are you my child? A lump of clay ready to be formed, potential to be a vessel unto honor and serve kings and queens, or a vessel for dishonor and shame fit only for the trash heap.*

*What are you my child? A book ready to be written, potential to be a trashy novel, or a biography to sit on library shelves for all time to encourage and exhort future generations.*

*What are you my child? A foundation awaiting construction above, potential to be a palace beautiful or the greatest eyesore in the community.*

*What are you my child? A piece of wood in the hands of crafts-men, potential to be a rod of destruction or a bridge of peace.*

*What are you my child? A soul desperately needing a work of grace, potential to enter the broad gate to destruction, or walk the streets of gold in eternity.*

Your child is a slate that has yet to be written upon. The foremost writer on that slate will be you, your child's parent.

In one report, young children were asked to give their foremost complaints about the way their parents related to them or communicated with them. The children gave these top ten responses:

1. They have little or no interest in things that really matter to me.
2. They break promises they make.
3. They make me feel unnoticed or unappreciated by ignoring me.
4. They don't consider me as a thinking, feeling person.
5. They appear too busy to care about me and listen to me.
6. They don't take the time necessary to understand what I'm trying to say.
7. They speak before thinking through how what they say will affect me.
8. They don't explain the reasons behind their decisions involving me.
9. They build me up and then let me down by not following through.
10. They make me feel as if they wish they had never had me in the first place.[1]

The children in this study were not teenagers, but children in elementary school! Can you imagine how strongly these children will feel by the time they reach adolescence if a change hasn't been made in their homes?

## YOU ARE THE AUTHOR OF YOUR CHILD'S SELF-ESTEEM

In the Power of Positive Students program founded a number of years ago, we have developed a list of things that we encourage teachers to do to build up a child's sense of self-esteem and to create a positive climate in the classroom. I believe all of these techniques can be applied to the home. They are adapted here to refer to parents rather than classroom teachers.

1.  Use your child's name often in conversations.
2.  Be generous in your use of "we" and "our" to promote feelings of belonging.
3.  Give your child as much honest and specific feedback as possible.
4.  Admit to your child when you don't know the answer to a question or the solution to a problem. Ask your child for suggestions if that is appropriate. A parent who adopts the posture of having an answer for everything is setting himself up for failure because eventually his child will realize he has been lying.
5.  Let your child participate in decisions. You can do this easily by giving your child two or three choices from which to decide. Screen the choices in advance and then let your child experience the esteem-building action of making the final choice. For example, suggest two or three things that you might fix for dinner and let your child make the decision. Or, give your child two or three options of after-school treats.
6.  Greet your children individually and warmly when you come together at the end of the day.
7.  Smile at your child. It takes fewer muscles to smile than to frown. So many children rarely see their parents smile *at them!*
8.  Be a good listener. Concentrate on what your child is saying and give your child as much undivided attention as possible.
9.  Tell your child that you missed him while he was away from you and that you appreciate the time you can be together.
10. Take time for personal contact with *each* child.
11. Use positive statements in evaluating your child's work. Here are some examples:
    *   "Keep trying. Come to see me if you need help."
    *   "Keep working. It appears to me as if you almost have it."
    *   "Apparently I did not explain this very well. Let me try again."
    *   "Don't be discouraged. There will be better days."
    *   "You usually do this very well. What happened today?"
12. Touch your child. A pat on the back, a quick hug, or a kiss on the forehead—all show affection that helps a child feel secure.

Most of your child's self-esteem will be established during the first six years of her life. Those are critical years for doing the following:
*   Showing your child he is loved unconditionally. Tell your child that you love him. Touch and hold your child.
*   Communicating with your child frequently.
*   Disciplining your child within established rules and boundaries.

- Praising your child often and encouraging your child to try new things that are within your child's ability.
- Looking for things to reinforce positively.
- Encouraging your child to make choices for himself and to do things for himself.

In sum, set up successes for your child and applaud him when success comes. At all times, assure your child that you love her whether she succeeds or fails.

If your child is between the ages of six and twelve, emphasize the following:

- Encourage your child to become involved in group activities that are positive (such as a church youth group, a scout group, or a group activity sponsored by the YMCA).
- Take your child to plays, concerts, and games. Give your child experience with the world outside your home.
- Provide an opportunity for your child to develop special talents. This may involve giving your child lessons (such as art, music, or ballet) or special coaching. You may be able to find a mentor for your child in an area of her interest—such as a person employed in that career area or a person who has the same interests. Sometimes specialty clubs are available to help your child, such as a chess club.
- Support your child in developing friends. Invite other children to spend the night at your house. Host parties. Invite your child's friends to go along to cultural or athletic events.
- Look for the good in your child and praise it.
- Encourage your child to make good choices. Guide your child's choices, but let your child experience the full consequences of the choices he makes as much as possible.

During the teen years, you can do these things to help your child continue to grow in self-esteem:

- Respect your child's individuality. Invite his expression of opinions. Don't invade his privacy or insist that you be in his presence at all times. Give your child a sense of "space" in which to develop his own ideas and identity.
- Expand your child's opportunity to make choices and, again, to live with their consequences.
- Do things together that your child might consider to be "adult" activities—such as volunteering together in the community or participating in church outreaches, going out to dinner together, or

going to concerts or other cultural events together. Take your child with you to the golf course or the spa.

- Communicate with your child, remembering that communication works both ways. Give your own opinions and ideas, but not in a dogmatic you-must-do-it-my-way tone. Invite your child to share her ideas by asking genuine questions and showing interest in what interests her.
- As your child shows herself to be trustworthy, trust her with greater responsibilities and freedoms.
- Encourage your child to bring his friends home. Take time to talk to his friends and get to know them.

## KNOW YOUR CHILD'S LIMITATIONS

A woman noticed a father and son in the grocery store. The boy was carrying a rather large basket, one the woman thought might be too big a load for the boy. She said to him, "That's a pretty heavy basket for a boy your age, isn't it?" The boy replied, "Oh, don't worry. My dad knows how much I can carry."

Know your child's limitations. Believe in your child. Balance the two. Encourage your child to believe he can do more than he thinks, but never expect him to do more than he can.

Building your child's self-esteem includes helping your child to know his own aptitudes and to develop a realistic understanding of what he *wants* to do vis-a-vis what he is *capable* of doing. Young children often have highly unrealistic dreams about having five careers simultaneously or about attaining goals that may be mutually incompatible. A five-year-old once told me that he wanted to be a fireman and a star in the NBA and a teacher. That was fine for age five. But if a fifteen-year-old holds the same vision for his life, it's time for his parents to take notice. Limiting your child's focus is not damaging to self-esteem as long as you let your child aim high within that focus. We've all heard the phrase, "Shoot for the moon, and if you miss, you'll still land among the stars."

The primary focus of self-esteem always is this: I love you because of who you are—my child. I believe in you, and I want the best for you. You have great potential—use it and be all you can be!

A poem by Douglas Malloch captures that ideal of doing one's best:

*If you can't be a pine on the top of the hill*
*Be a shrub in the valley but be*
*The best little shrub by the side of the hill;*
*Be a bush if you can't be a tree.*

*If you can't be a bush be a bit of grass*
*And some highway happier make;*
*If you can't be a muskie then just be a bass,*
*But be the liveliest bass in the lake.*
*We can't all be captains, we've got to be crew,*
*There is something for all of us. There*
*Is big work to do and there's lesser to do*
*And the task we must do is the near.*
*If you can't be a highway then just be a trail;*
*If you can't be the sun be a star;*
*It isn't by size that you win or you fail.*
*Be the best of whatever you are.*[2]

## RESPECT YOUR CHILD IN YOUR COMMUNICATION

We've all heard the phrase, "Sticks and stones can hurt my bones, but words can never hurt me." It isn't true. Words produce feelings, including pain. And feelings determine actions, sometimes negative ones. In fact, emotional pain results in some highly negative behaviors in some people.

Watch what you say to your child.

*A careless word may kindle strife;*
*A cruel word may wreck a life;*
*A bitter word may hate instill;*
*A brutal word may smite and kill;*
*A gracious word may smooth the way;*
*A joyous word may light the day;*
*A timely word may lessen stress;*
*A loving word may heal and bless.*

—Anonymous

# Your Understanding of Right and Wrong

We've all heard the phrase, "Do the right thing." A child isn't born knowing right from wrong. He doesn't know what the "right thing" is!

Your parenting philosophy will be the foundation that shapes the values and behaviors your child exhibits not only while growing up, but when he is grown to adulthood.

## RIGHT BEHAVIORS

Ask yourself the basic question, "What is right behavior?" Make a list of these behaviors, and you will also come up with a list of values. Consider the following list, and feel free to add to it:

| RIGHT BEHAVIORS | VALUES |
|---|---|
| *To tell the truth* | *Truthfulness* |
| *To deal with others honestly* | *Honesty* |
| *To "play fair"* | *Fairness* |
| *To give to others with a generosity of spirit* | *Love* |
| *To have a bright, optimistic attitude toward life* | *Joy* |
| *To have an inner contentment that God is in control* | *Peace* |
| *To be patient with people and irksome situations* | *Patience* |
| *To confront evil in appropriate ways* | *Courage* |
| *To refuse to provoke others to mean or evil behavior* | *Gentleness* |
| *To have the inner fortitude to say yes to good and no to evil* | *Self-control* |
|  |  |
|  |  |
|  |  |

## RIGHT FAMILY VALUES

You may want to try summarizing your understanding of values in a way that educators would describe as "operational"—identifying values along with a description of each value as it might be expressed in your home. In effect, this becomes something of a parent's manifesto.

Here are a dozen such values to consider as a start:

1. Love. We choose to make our home a place where each family member gives freely and shares generously with others—not only material possessions, but compliments and praise.

2. Faith in God. We choose to incorporate what we believe into our daily conversations and habits. We will make family prayer a norm. We will attend church together and get involved in church activities as a family.

3. Hope. We will expect good things from one another and work to help one another succeed. We will look to the future with a positive attitude and an expectation that God has something wonderful ahead for us individually and as a family.

4. Happiness. Happiness flows from having a positive attitude toward life. We will *choose* to be happy—to look for and emphasize the good in every situation.

5. Enthusiasm. We will choose to be passionate in our loyalty and support of one another. If we undertake a task together as a family, we will pursue it with our whole heart. We will be enthusiastic toward our jobs, school, daily tasks, and the family. We will let our children know that we are excited about their progress in school and in the other activities in which they are involved.

6. Integrity. We will be honest with ourselves and with others in the family. Because home is a place where children readily see if words match deeds, we will practice what we preach. We will follow through on the commitments we make.

7. Courage. We will stand up for what we believe. We will support those causes that are in line with our values.

8. Perseverance. We will complete the tasks we start. We will stick with friends through thick and thin. We will maintain our personal and family loyalties through good times and bad.

9. Reciprocity. We will choose to practice the Golden Rule, "Do unto others as we would have them do unto us." We will use good manners, complete our chores, and be willing to compromise when it comes to family schedules and choices that must be made.

10. Responsibility. We will become a family in which each person has responsibilities and learns self-discipline in the process of fulfilling those responsibilities.

11. Patience. We will have a relaxed atmosphere in our home that allows for family members to make mistakes. We recognize that learning is a *process* that isn't accomplished in a day. We will give our child the opportunity to learn delayed gratification and self-control.

12. Excellence. We will not settle for a mediocre family. We will choose to build a strong family and to leave an excellent legacy of love, values, and faith to our children and grandchildren.

You may want to add more. . . .

## IDENTIFY THE BENEFITS

You must also identify for yourself—and then for your child—what you believe to be the benefits of doing the right thing, or holding the right values. It is important to do this so that when you are feeling tired, discouraged, and unsure of yourself as a parent, you can remind yourself that what you are seeking to instill in your child *is* worth the effort!

Below is a partial list of such benefits. Again, add to it insights and ideas you may have.

As you talk to your children about values, always remind them that all behavior has consequences. Good behavior yields positive consequences; bad behavior yields negative consequences. These consequences may not occur immediately—some may not be experienced for months, years, or perhaps not until eternity—but they will occur eventually.

Also, some of the consequences are internal, not external. Doing the right thing doesn't always translate into material or physical reward, but it does always translate into a spiritual, mental, or emotional reward.

### BENEFITS OF GOOD BEHAVIOR AND RIGHT VALUES

1. Inner peace. A life of good behavior and right values is a life that brings greater contentment.
2. Self-confidence and self-esteem. Be content that you have acted in a way that is right before God and mankind.
3. Being in a position to receive God's many rewards to the "righteous." You may want to look up some of these verses and read them with your child from time to time as your child matures. You may even want to memorize them together as a family so you can readily call them to mind.

   | Psalm 146:8    | Proverbs 10:30 |
   | Proverbs 10:21 | Proverbs 11:21 |
   | Proverbs 10:24 | Proverbs 16:13 |
   | Proverbs 10:25 | Matthew 25:46  |

   Use a concordance to find many other verses that speak of the rewards to the righteous! God's Word is filled with them.
4. More loving family ties. When family members display good behavior and have the right values, the entire family is marked by an increase in love and care.
5. Closer relationships with friends. When your child acts in right ways and has the right values, he attracts better and closer friends—one of the greatest assets in life.

6. A greater willingness to give. Right behaviors and values always express themselves eventually in the act of giving to others, which may be displayed as simply as yielding the right of way to another person on a freeway, or as profoundly as sacrificing one's position or possessions to help a person in need.

   Giving always results in receiving in God's economy—and receiving in greater abundance than the gift given. Luke 6:38 tells us, "Give, and it shall be given unto you; good measure, pressed down, and shaken together, and running over, shall men give into your bosom. For with the same measure that ye mete withal it shall be measured to you again" (KJV). God always has a special reward for those who give.

7. Feelings of satisfaction and fulfillment. When one has peace of mind, loving relationships, a habit of giving and receiving, and a relationship with God (the source of all right values and the author of all good behaviors), that person can truly experience a *meaningful* life.

_____

_____

_____

### A BIBLICAL APPROACH

Any time you have questions about what your parenting philosophy should be—what behaviors to emphasize with your child or what values to hold out as good and right before God—go back to your Bible. See what God's Word has to say about the matter.

I especially recommend the Book of Proverbs to you as a parent. One of the best things you can ever do for your child is to acquaint him or her with the guidelines within this book.

Read the Proverbs aloud with your child. Some families do this by having a "box" of proverbs available, from which a child can draw one a day and commit it to memory. Some families read through a chapter of Proverbs together every day. (Some balance this by reading a parable of Jesus or a psalm every day, or having a reading sequence of a passage from Proverbs three mornings a week, a passage from Psalms three mornings a week, and a passage from the Gospels every evening.) Find the method that works best for you and your family, but read from the Bible regularly. Over time, your child will commit the truths he learns to memory, and they will become his "mind set" for behaving in right ways.

Be sure you have a working definition for righteousness. The simplest definition I know is this: doing the right thing in God's eyes. The number one "right thing" to do in God's eyes, of course, is to accept Jesus Christ as Savior and then to follow Him in a daily way as Lord. There is nothing greater that you can teach your child.

Present Jesus to your child as the Son of a loving heavenly Father. Tell your child how Jesus died for your child's sinful nature so that your child might enjoy all the benefits of personal salvation and live with God forever in heaven after he dies. Children *can* receive this message and their lives *can* be changed forever. Don't fall into the trap of thinking that your child must wait until adulthood to accept Christ. The message of God's love and Christ's sacrifice is not a complicated one, nor is it too difficult for children to understand. More than understanding with the mind, faith is *believing with the heart*, and children are quite adept at believing with their hearts.

Once a child has accepted Jesus as his Savior, he must be encouraged daily to trust God and to follow the leading of the Holy Spirit (and yes, the Holy Spirit does prompt children to do good and convict them of unrighteous behavior). Train your child to:

• talk to God often, asking for His protection, provision, and guidance. Encourage your child to tell God freely, immediately, and openly about all the events and activities in his life—including faults and errors, victories and triumphs.

• look for the good things in life. All of the good things your child experiences are "gifts" from God to your child. Encourage your child to recognize them as such and to thank God for all His many blessings. Even very young children are capable of praising God, and they delight in doing so. Some children are quite creative in their expressions of thanksgiving and praise!

• find creative ways of giving to others. This can be in the form of giving compliments, giving service, writing notes of encouragement and thanks, and making little gifts (of artwork or flowers from the garden). Giving is an expression of love, and all gifts from the heart of a Christian are an expression of God's love in the world.

How can parents *train* a young child to do this?

Pray daily with your child, and she will imitate the way you pray. Talk to God in conversational, easy-to-understand terms. Talk to God about lots of things, but as a parent, always ask God to protect and bless your child. Let your child hear you pray for him, and express your trust in God to love and care for him always.

As you ride in the car with your child, invite her to play this game: look out the car window and then take turns thanking God for all the pretty, nice, and good things you see. As you take a hike with your child—or even walk together in your neighborhood—turn your conversation to praise for the people who live near you, the blessings God has given you, and the very nature of God as our loving heavenly Father.

The way to train your child to talk to God, praise Him, and have an optimistic, positive outlook is by getting your child to *voice* his petitions and praise with you as coach. The child who grows up talking to a loving God is a child who is trained to have an ongoing relationship with a loving God.

Encourage your child to give gifts to others. This turns your child from self-centeredness to generosity. Suggest gifts and expressions of love. Invite your child's own creative input. You'll probably be amazed at the good ideas your child has for showing love to others!

God freely gives us His commandments about good behavior and right values. He tells us quite plainly in His Word what He considers to be good and evil. We simply need to read what the Bible says and then do it.

### YOUR CHILD'S VALUE STRUCTURE

As you identify your own beliefs—the biblical values that you feel are important and the benefits related to good values—and then attempt to instill these truths into your child, you will have a solid framework for identifying what it is that you want your children to believe and how you want your children to act. The parent who hasn't thought through his own understanding of right and wrong is a parent who is truly operating on "instinct" and the past performances of his own parents. Don't simply mirror your own past upbringing, however good it may have been. Identify for yourself what it is that you hope to instill in your child. Be intentional about what you hope to accomplish as a parent.

The stronger the value structure you give to your child, the more meaningful and fulfilling your child's life is likely to become.

# Your Approach to Discipline

Whether or not you discipline your child is going to determine what actually becomes a habit in your child's way of thinking and acting. You can value your child's life highly and have high standards of right and wrong, but unless you choose to guide your child's behavior through discipline, your child will not become all that you want him to be.

Discipline is not an option for the parent who wants to instill Christian values into his children. But beware! Discipline can easily overshadow other forms of communication. A study by the National Family Institute found that the average parent spends 14.5 minutes a day communicating with each child. Of that time, 12.5 minutes are devoted to parental criticism or correction.[3]

Discipline without a moral dimension to it is not discipline at all, but "control." It is setting up boundaries and lists of infractions and correlating punishments.

Discipline with a moral dimension is just as easy to establish, although it takes greater intention. In establishing a moral dimension, you must first state *why* certain behaviors are valued, which gives meaning to why certain rules are in effect and why certain consequences result when those rules are broken.

Establishing a moral dimension means seeking to manage a child's values and attitudes, not only his behavior. What children believe will give rise to how they behave.

Discipline with a moral dimension inevitably requires conversation and discussion. It involves making statements about what you believe, inviting questions, and taking the time to answer those questions.

Conversations about moral and ethical issues rarely take place only once in the course of a child's life. They are ongoing—sometimes day to day, sometimes month to month, sometimes year to year. As a child grows in his understanding of the world around him, he is capable of understanding more complex reasons as to why certain attitudes, virtues, values, and behaviors are being emphasized and required. He is able to make stronger correlations between values and what he sees in the world around him, and to discern more clearly the results of moral breakdown.

Discipline is *not:*
- screaming and yelling
- making autocratic demands
- nagging
- venting anger physically or verbally
- belittling, or using sarcastic "put downs"
- entrapping your child in misbehavior
- imposing guilt or shame

- physical punishment
- coercion
- denial of basic needs

Discipline is a training process. It involves setting goals, rules, and standards for your child—ones that your child knows, understands, and is capable of achieving. In other words, your child must be able to do—fairly easily—the things that you require her to do.

Certainly you can establish challenges for your child, but with challenges, you must be willing to accept mistakes and failures. You can challenge your child to learn something new or to achieve a higher level of performance, and the acquisition of that new level or skill is going to take trial, error, and practice. Areas of "challenge" are not areas that should be subject to discipline. Your child should be able to do, with a high degree of reliability and success, anything that you consider subject to discipline.

When your child fails to adhere to the rules or standards of behavior that you have set, you must correct your child and reinstill in him the importance of keeping the rules, staying within the boundaries, or keeping the standards of behavior that you have established.

## CORRECTION

Correction involves:

- getting your child's attention. You must have your child's undivided attention. This likely means getting alone with your child or speaking directly to your child in a way that your child has eye contact with you and you alone.
- stating what it is that you want changed. Your admonition to your child should be simple and direct, such as, "Stop what you are doing." In doing this, you are sending a clear message to your child that you do not approve of his current behavior.
- telling your child what you want him to do instead. Politely command your child to begin showing the positive behavior that you want him to display. Parents tend to fall short in this area of discipline—they tell their children what not to do but then neglect to tell them what to do. I once heard about a young boy who asked his mother, "How do I be good?" This boy's mother obviously had told him to "be good" but hadn't told him precisely what that involved!

    If your son is punching his sister, you might say, "Stop hitting your sister. Keep your hands to yourself and look out the car window to see how many red cars you can spot."

- if your child refuses to obey you, follow through on consequences that you have previously established with your child. Let your child know what the consequences are for bad behavior. The consequences should be ones that are meaningful to your child, i.e., the deprivation of something your child "wants" but does not need.

Explain to your child in clear terms, and in private, that he has disobeyed you and, therefore, he must experience the consequences for disobedience.

Discipline involves the establishment of authority and the correction of bad behavior. You undermine the effectiveness of your own disciplinary actions if you mete out discipline in frustration or anger. Say what you mean to your child with a tone of voice that conveys, "I mean what I'm saying."

Don't make idle threats.

Don't barter or bargain with your child for obedience or good behavior.

Don't negotiate away the rules you have established.

Insist that your child obey you and keep the rules and boundaries that you have established in your family.

### RESTRAINT

A twelve-year-old boy decided that while his parents were out of town, he'd take the key to his father's old pick-up and start it up. The only problem was, he didn't know the difference between a standard and an automatic transmission. As soon as he turned the key, without putting in the clutch, the truck lurched forward violently, pushing a deep freeze through the wall behind it. The family dining room was suddenly visible from the garage!

The boy panicked. Certain that he would be spanked, he went to a friend's house to avoid the inevitable. But eventually his parents came home, and he had to face the inevitable. His mother greeted him at the door and immediately sent him to his room to wait for his father. As the young man sat on the edge of his bed, he truly thought his life might be over.

Then his father came into the room. He walked over to his son, put his arms around him, and hugged him. He said, "Son, I want you to know that I love you. I'm disappointed in what you did, but nothing that you do can ever make me stop loving you." The boy never forgot that moment. In fact, when he told the story twenty years later he couldn't recall fully what his punishment had been for his misbehavior.

The punishment had come and gone—but the expression of love from his father had lasted through the years.

Never fail to couple your discipline with love. It's the part of the learning process that lasts!

## Knowing Who You Are as a Parent

The processes of identifying your own willingness to sacrifice yourself for your child, of describing the value you place on your child, of identifying your own belief structure, and of better understanding your own approach to discipline all flow together to create your unique parenting philosophy.

Not all parents approach parenting precisely the same way, and of course not all children are alike. While many values, virtues, and behaviors flow directly from God's Word, others do not. They are a reflection of your personality and desires. Furthermore, you as a parent are likely compromising some of your personal parenting philosophy with that of your spouse.

Identify with your spouse what you hope to be and to accomplish—as a married couple and also as parents. Coming to grips with your parenting philosophy is a precursor to setting the specific goals and putting into place the plans that will enable you to build a strong family!

# Chapter 4

# *Set Your Goals*

*The secret of success is constancy to purpose.*
—Benjamin Disraeli
English statesman (1804–81)

*Set your mind on the things above.*
—Colossians 3:2, NASB

The goals and plans you set for your child should be at the forefront of your own thinking, day in and day out. This requires a constancy on your part, a deep commitment to parenting.

In educational and business terms, the word *objectives* has become more popular than the word *goals*. Goals tend to be more vague than objectives. Goals are the broad, general ideas that form your parenting philosophy. Objectives are specific. They involve behavior that can be observed, measured, and set into time.

As you begin to envision the specific objectives that you desire to accomplish as a parent, I encourage you to spend time in these three activities:

*First, meditate upon God's Word and what it says about family.* To meditate means "to repeat and rehearse" what God's Word says. Commit to memory verses of Scripture about family life. Think about those verses often. The Bible presents quite a clear picture of our mission in life and the role of the family. Discover it for yourself and make it your own mission.

*Second, visualize your family in action together.* How do you imagine your family would respond if faced with a major storm, such as a hurricane or tornado? What if you lost most of your worldly possessions? Can you imagine your family on a trip together, laughing and having a good time? What are you doing? How about envisioning your family on a short-term missions trip, perhaps helping with a Vacation Bible School program at an impoverished church in the United States or overseas?

I once heard of a woman and her husband who had spent considerable time thinking about the goals for their family and their overriding vision was this: their family standing together before God's throne and hearing Him say to them, individually and as a family, "Well done, good and faithful servants." Nothing else mattered to her except that her children stand with her and that as a family they be rewarded for their faithfulness to the Lord.

*Third, pray for your family.* Pray for your spouse and for each of your children by name every morning. Pray for specific needs that they have during the day ahead. Pray for the qualities that you desire to see develop in your children. And pray for their future—that they will become strong Christian witnesses in whatever profession they enter, that they will be surrounded by Christian friends and be active members of a church body, and that they will marry Christians and raise children who will serve Christ all their lives. Take seriously your privilege and responsibility to pray for your children.

# Virtues Lists Can Provide Direction

A number of lists of significant character traits have been compiled by various organizations and researchers. I am going to present six of these to help boost your own creativity as you prepare to set objectives for your child's training.

### PARENTS' CHOICE

In a survey of 2,300 parents, these were the top ten characteristics identified as the traits they would most like for their children to exhibit:

1. self-confidence
2. responsibility
3. eagerness to learn
4. self-directive
5. able to work well with others (cooperative)
6. sensitive to others
7. kind
8. hard worker
9. getting good grades
10. amiable[1]

## PUBLIC SCHOOL CHOICE

A study conducted by the Public Agenda Foundation in 1994 noted that these were among the values that those surveyed desired to see emphasized in public schools:

- good work habits, including being on time and doing homework
- being dependable and disciplined
- honesty and the importance of telling the truth

## LAWMAKERS' CHOICE

Lawmakers in the United States Senate formed a "Character Counts Coalition" early in 1995. The "Character Counts" program that they advocated, and which is now being implemented in some schools, cites these six traits as being the "core elements" of good character:

1. trustworthiness
2. respect
3. responsibility
4. justice and fairness
5. caring
6. civic virtue and citizenship

## TEEN TRAITS

I recently read a report that cited these five characteristics of adolescents in our nation today: apathetic, distrustful, dishonest, uncaring, irresponsible. If you turn these into positives, you would have a fine profile of what a teenager *should* reflect as character qualities:

- involved and productive
- trustworthy and trustful
- honest
- caring
- responsible

## BLOOM'S "ACHIEVERS" QUALITIES

Noted educator Benjamin Bloom has observed these five qualities of "high achievers" in our society:

1. drive
2. determination
3. hard work
4. encouragement from home
5. encouragement from school[2]

In looking at Bloom's list, I couldn't help but note that there is substantial research to support the fact that students who receive encouragement from home tend to do better in school, and thus are likely to receive more encouragement from school than they might otherwise. Also, parents are key role models in teaching their children the qualities of drive, determination, and hard work. Requiring that a child set goals, work to meet them, persevere to the completion of tasks, and have chores and responsibilities are also ways that a parent can become involved in training a child to develop drive, determination, and a good work ethic.

### CITIZENSHIP VIRTUES

There are virtues that have been associated with good citizenship. They include:

- loyalty
- labor
- courage
- thrift
- honor
- honesty
- unselfishness
- cooperation

We sometimes think of good citizenship as voting, serving in the military when called to, paying taxes, and knowing the words to the Pledge of Allegiance and "The Star-Spangled Banner." Good citizenship really means to live in a "good relationship" with others whom we would call our neighbors—whether they be neighbors in our area of town, neighbors in a city, neighbors within our state, or neighbors in our nation as a whole. To be a productive, effective, law-abiding, positive influence in the secular community at large is to be a good citizen.

### THE CHRISTIAN HOME LIST YOU MAKE!

Each of the six lists above can provide you with insight, direction, and ideas for framing your own list of specific objectives about who you want your child to be. As a Christian parent, however, your goals should be rooted in your faith, in keeping God at the center of your home and at the foundation of your training efforts with your child.

In 1979, the Pittsburgh Pirates won the World Series. They had as their theme, "We Are Family." From their perspective, family meant togetherness. They had a unified goal to which every member of the team made a commitment: win the championship. In our Christian families, our supreme goal, of course, must be this: serve God.

The objective or goal to "serve God" is not primarily a goal about what your child will do or accomplish in life, but a set of character traits that your child will manifest in behavior. As Christian parents, we should be concerned primarily with what our children will "be" in life. Our primary concern should be about the attitudes they express, the habits they adopt, and the behaviors they exhibit. Too many parents have a goal for their children to be "well off" financially, to have successful careers, or to live in specific neighborhoods with a certain degree of status. While they also say they want their children to have good spouses and fine children, note the emphasis on "have," even in these noble areas of acquisition.

Be more concerned as a parent about who your child *is* and the way in which people see your child, not your child's position, status, or possessions.

Most Christian parents I know desire their children to exhibit the following "be" traits and characteristics. As you read through these next several pages, make notes as to what it is that *you* desire the "Character Profile" of your child to be. What specifically do you desire to see your child reflect in his or her behavior?

# Supreme Trait: Be a Christian

Being a Christian is primarily something a child *is*. Simply doing Christian activities does not make a child a Christian. Accepting God's forgiveness, offered on the basis of what Jesus Christ did in giving His life as the definitive, complete, and perfect sacrifice on the cross, is what makes a child a Christian. Lead your child to Christ. Accompany him to the cross. Don't push your child to Jesus. Don't guilt-trip your child to acceptance of Christ. Lead your child to Christ by your own example, by your prayers, and by speaking often to your child about Christ's love for him or her.

### ESTABLISHING AN ENVIRONMENT

It is God who creates a relationship between your child and Christ; it is a sovereign work on His part. He works through the Holy Spirit to woo your child to Himself and then assures your child of His love and forgiveness and fills your child with His own presence. God saves your child. You cannot.

What you can do is create a climate in which accepting Jesus' love is as natural as breathing for your child, as normal as growing up and going to school, or as easy as receiving a present from a loved one. As your child sees you pray to God and praise God, as your child sees you faithful in your commitment to other Christians and to your church, as your child sees you witnessing to unbelievers about your faith, and as your child watches how you display the fruit of the Holy Spirit in your life, your child will want to follow in your footsteps and become a Christian, like you. Keep your child by your side in every Christ-honoring habit and activity in which you participate.

In an earlier chapter we referred to the mine fields of the home, which included the things we ought *not* to do. Yet the things we should do but fail—through negligence, oversight, and carelessness—are equally destructive to the home, although the results may not be as explosive, visible, or apparent. Breakdown in many families is due to slow leaks, not major blow-outs. Either way, the family falls flat.

Some of the slow leaks might be

- parents who never talk about God, praise God, or thank God
- a total lack of prayer in the home
- a lack of emphasis on the Bible and what it has to say
- a failure to attend church regularly
- a parent who never compliments a child
- a parent who does not require a child to perform certain chores or tasks that benefit the family

### YOUR CHILD'S ACCEPTANCE OF CHRIST

I am amazed at the number of parents who believe that a child develops spiritual capacity after puberty! A child is born with spiritual capacity, just as a child is born with intellectual capacity and certain physical capabilities. A child's spiritual capacity is apparent in very young children, who often instinctively shy away from evil environments and respond openly to those who reflect the love of God. Very young children are capable of prayer and praise.

As a child continues in his or her walk with God, he reaches a point where he makes a decision with the *will* that he is going to seek the forgiveness made available through Christ Jesus and to live in close fellowship with God. Once that decision is made, the child is as much a Christian as any adult who makes a willful decision to renounce sin and turn to God through Christ Jesus. He has a relationship with the Holy Spirit, who manifests "fruit" in the child's life. The development of the qualities we call fruits of the Spirit is not something that a parent alone can develop in a child. Rather, they are qualities that a parent can nurture as part of a child's relationship with God by encouraging the child to trust the Holy Spirit to be at work in his life.

The story has been told of a family who came forward in their church to have their infant baptized. The baby lay cute and content in her mother's arms as the pastor began to ask a series of questions to the congregation and family. Among the questions were these: "Do you believe in Jesus? Do you confess Him as your Savior? Will you teach this child the Scriptures and give careful, reverent attention to your child's attendance at church?"

As the pastor moved away from the questioning segment of the ritual to prepare for the infant's baptism, he was surprised to hear a tiny voice say loudly, "I do! I do! Oh yes, I do!" He turned to see little Katie, the baby's five-year-old sister, standing next to her parents. She had been listening intently to all that had been said and asked, and with all of her being, she was responding.

No one had been paying much attention to Katie, other than including her in the ceremony. She took it all in and made perhaps one of the purest confessions of Christ that has ever been made.

That story embodies what it means to lead a child to Christ. We include our children in all aspects of our own belief and worship. We invite them to answer the questions for themselves as we each answer them for ourselves, "Do you believe in Jesus? Will you follow Him?"

### FOLLOWING CHRIST

Your child's relationship with Christ is sealed by the Holy Spirit, but you can reinforce your child's relationship with Christ by encouraging him or her to pray in times of crisis and need, to praise God always, to give to God in a wide variety of ways (including money and service), to be active in church activities, and to talk about Jesus to his or her friends.

# Creating a Climate for Spiritual Growth

Much of what a parent does is simply create a climate in which God is allowed to work.

A woman was working once with her young son in the family garden. Mom was pulling up weeds and not paying much attention to her son. She eventually looked over at him and noticed that he had taken a daffodil bud and was trying to force it open into full bloom. Frustrated, he said, "Mommy, why is it when I try to open the bud, it just falls to pieces? How come it doesn't turn into a flower?"

Before his mother could give an answer, he drew his own conclusion and said, "Oh, I know! God works from the inside."

That's the perspective we need to keep as parents.

God is always at work inside your child. You may plant good seeds—good attitudes, good ideas, good information—and water and fertilize those seeds with good experiences and the training of a child to have good habits, and then weed out bad behavior through appropriate disciplinary measures; but God does the growing and the maturing. Trust God to do His work in your child.

### PRAYER

Memorized prayers are fine, but don't limit your child to them. Teach your child to pray on his own. Russell Baker was a Pulitzer Prize-winning columnist for *The New York Times*. In his biography, *Growing Up*, he told how his mother had often helped him with his homework and prayed diligently for him as he faced important exams. When Baker applied to Johns Hopkins, he was required to take an entrance examination. Baker knew it was critical that he do well, not only for entrance to the university but also so he might receive a much needed scholarship. Unlike his mother, however, he had little faith in prayer.

Even so, as the examination papers were distributed, Baker said, "I sat at my desk silently repeating, 'Now I lay me down to sleep, I pray the Lord my soul to keep. . . .' At the end I improvised a single line of my own and prayed, 'Dear God, help me with this test.'" The exam took four hours, but in the end, Baker won a scholarship.

While I rejoice at Baker's success and his moment of reliance on prayer, I also recognize in his telling of this story that as much as Baker's mother must have believed in prayer and prayed for her son, she had not taught him to pray for himself or to trust God to meet his needs. Baker's trust was in his mother's prayers, it seems, more than in the Lord's power and desire to answer Baker's own prayers.

Assure your child that the Lord will hear and answer your *child's* prayers and that there is nothing too big or too small to talk over with God.

When my wife was ill, our grandson Matthew came to her bedside and announced to her, "Mamoo, I don't want you to be worrying. I'm praying for you every day." He then proceeded to pray for her right there by her bed. Tears came to all our eyes as Matthew prayed from his heart. We had a new understanding of what a clear line of communication he has with God—not one that has been performed and prepackaged, but one that reflects his own creativity and will. He has total freedom to express himself to his heavenly Father.

Encourage that in your child too. The child who knows he or she can communicate openly with God at any time and in any place, about any situation or circumstance, is a child who is confident in faith and in God's abiding love.

## THE SCRIPTURES

Reading, memorizing, and meditating upon the Word of God are critical to building a strong spiritual foundation in your home. Your children not only need to know what the Bible says, but should be required to obey its commandments.

Some parents attempt to require their children to obey the commandments they "believe" to be found in the Bible, and yet they have never read these commandments for themselves. They never tell their children precisely what the Bible says or read it to them, and they never encourage their children to read the Bible for themselves.

We should never assume that we know what the Bible says on a particular matter unless we have read it for ourselves. I once heard of a woman who thought that "an apple a day keeps the doctor away" was a verse from the Bible!

The story is told of a young man who robbed a bank while his brother, who had devised the plan but hadn't participated in the caper, demanded half of the money as his fair share of the heist. The two brothers argued for a while about the "fairness" of this. The nonparticipating brother insisted that the Bible required an equal division of goods. The bank robber laughed at the mention of the Bible and said, "All right, if you want to bring the Bible into this, I'll agree but on one condition. Before I give you any of this loot, you have to quote something from the Bible to me." He felt certain his brother would not be able to comply with this request.

The brother immediately said, "Now I lay me down to sleep. I pray the Lord my soul to keep."

The bank robber replied, "Oh, all right, you win. I'll split the money with you. I didn't think you could do it!"

Know what the Bible says. If you are going to make the Bible the basis for your understanding of right and wrong, you had best know what the Bible teaches!

## OBEDIENCE

It isn't enough, of course, only to know what the Bible says. We must be "doers of the word, and not hearers only" (James 1:22).

Obedience to God's Word has many benefits associated with it. The Bible itself promises that those who are obedient in following God's commandments and principles:

- are treasured by God
- have happiness in life
- are not ashamed
- have understanding
- know how to avoid evil and are empowered to do so
- have guidance for life
- are freed from anxiety
- enjoy God's blessing
- have a love for God
- have the promise of God's presence always
- have the assurance of salvation and a heavenly home.

When Joshua was called upon to succeed Moses, God gave him the key to his eventual success: meditate upon God's Word. He was to meditate upon it day and night, which means "at all times." He was promised both prosperity and success in the task that lay before him and the children of Israel as they left the wilderness and entered the land God had promised to them.

To meditate upon God's Word means that you rehearse its teachings over and over to understand the many implications to life's various situations. When we meditate upon a passage of God's Word, we inevitably memorize it because we are repeating it to ourselves so many times in the course of a day, week, or month.

Meditating on God's Word—passage by passage, day in and day out—creates in our minds a "way of thinking." Some call this a mind-set, a perspective, a cognitive framework, a predisposition, an attitude. Whatever terminology you use, it is a systematic way of thinking that results in behavior. If you are thinking in ways that line up with God's Word, your behavior will line up in ways that conform to God's commandments and statutes. The process is virtually automatic. As we think, we act.

# Fruit of the Spirit

It is good for us to be reminded periodically of the qualities known as the "fruit of the Spirit" (Gal. 5:23):

- love
- joy
- peace

- long-suffering
- kindness
- faithfulness
- gentleness
- goodness
- self-control

Just as we hope to reflect these qualities in our own adult lives, so we can help develop the manifestation of these qualities in our children. Make these character traits your prayer for your child. You can be certain that such a prayer is totally in keeping with the will of heaven!

While the character of a Christian is considered to be a bundle of virtues, note that the fruit of the Spirit is "singular" in nature. Paul doesn't write of the *fruits* of the Spirit, but of *fruit*. As the Holy Spirit dwells within us, He manifests His character through us, which results in the manifestation of these noble qualities.

A parent can expend a great deal of energy attempting to instill each of these virtues into a child's life, but the supreme focus should be on your child's acceptance of Christ and his sensitivity to the leading of the Holy Spirit as he follows Christ. The Holy Spirit bears *His* fruit in your child. Anything else that you do simply supports the work of God that is already under way.

Note, too, that values tend to have a cumulative effect in your child's life. They build upon one another. Consider these words from 2 Peter 1:5–8 (KJV): "Add to your faith virtue; and to virtue knowledge; and to knowledge temperance; and to temperance patience; and to patience godliness; and to godliness brotherly kindness; and to brotherly kindness charity. For if these things be in you, and abound, they make you that ye shall neither be barren nor unfruitful in the knowledge of our Lord Jesus Christ."

Faith is at the root of all other virtues in your child. In keeping the focus on your child's relationship with God, you are setting the stage for all other values to have a rightful place and a solid foundation.

# What If Your Child Rejects Your Faith?

Don't overreact if your child rejects, tests, or expresses doubt about the faith that you have championed in the home. There is always a transition time in which the "inherited" faith of the family must be internalized and accepted on an individual, personal basis by each child. This transition time is often marked by periods of rejection, testing, or doubting. Continue to pray for and love your child. Your love and affirmation during this time—without criticism—is likely to be the most powerful of all statements to your child.

# All Virtues Flow from Faith

All character traits that you may desire to see in your child flow from the fountain of faith. At first, this faith may be mostly resident in you and manifested by you. As your child grows and matures, however, he will manifest his faith in various ways. You can do much to encourage your child's faith to grow and bear fruit. Perhaps the foremost thing you can do is to speak openly to your child about the virtues and values that you desire your child to learn and reflect. Talk about the importance of having values and living them out. Let your child know *why* virtues are important to you. Repeat the benefits of cleaving to right values daily.

The traits that follow are only a handful of the many that flow naturally from a relationship with God that is vital, vibrant, and practical.

### TRAIT #1: LOVING

Every parent I know desires that their child establish loving relationships with others—that their child be able to give and receive love openly, yet within a moral framework; that their child be generous in giving to others of their time, talents, and resources; and that their child place a high value upon love.

Love is not merely an emotion. Let your child know that love is a commitment of the will to seek out and then do the best for another person and to receive the best from that person. Love involves a willful choice to have:

- a good relationship with God
- a good relationship with other people
- a good relationship with one's own self

Never let your child dismiss another person as being unworthy of love. Separate clearly a person's behavior from a person's spiritual identity before God. Every person is worth loving. The child who comes to believe otherwise is a child who will discount what Christ did on the cross for him, and who may at times discount himself as being unworthy of love from others.

### TRAITS #2 AND 3: CONTENTMENT AND JOY

Most parents I know would probably say that they desire for their children to have a twofold attitude in life: peace and joyful enthusiasm.

Such a child is a pleasure to be around and is usually eager to embrace life fully.

On the surface, these two traits seem contradictory. One appears placid and calm; the other, energized with exuberance. At a deeper level, they are like two sides of a coin. The contented child is capable of experiencing joy. The joyful child exudes an aura of confidence that is rooted in contentment.

**Contentment.** To be content, or to have an inner peace, results in part from recognizing openly the talents one has been given and being willing to use them for good. Talents are a blessing, not a burden, but they do carry responsibility. To whom much is given, much is required (see Luke 12:48).

At the same time, contentment has a dimension of accepting one's own limitations and believing in God's ultimate sovereignty and control. In Milan, Italy, a mechanics union once took a group of children to the circus. The children were either deaf or blind, yet all seemed thrilled at the experience of attending the circus. One little girl who was blind said she hoped the deaf children had enjoyed the show as much as she had, but then added, "But they probably didn't. They couldn't hear the marching band or the noise of the crowd. Or even worse, they couldn't hear the lions roar!" This little girl expressed no self-pity. She had accepted fully her own limitations and actually saw in them opportunity for thanksgiving.

**Joy.** Joy and happiness are not the same. Happiness is an emotion that is felt in those moments when things are pleasing, amusing, or satisfying. Happiness is dependent upon outward circumstances, events, and other people. Happiness comes and goes.

In contrast, joy is an inner quality that lasts. It is not dependent upon outward circumstances or other people, but on having an inward sense of relationship with God, a purpose in life, and a destiny that is being fulfilled.

Too often I hear parents say, "I just want my child to be happy." No, what you really want is for your child to have inner joy. Joy is acquired in part by having a sense of growing, of accomplishing, of facing up to a challenge and coming away a winner (not necessarily literally, but on the inside, in values and integrity).

Contentment is balanced with joy. Joy is not related to a person's given talents, strengths, weaknesses, or circumstances—but to who God is and what He has done. We have a duty to joy, whether we are adults or children. Joy is a response to what God has created, given, and planned.

How can we train our children for these traits of contentment and joy? In part, by refusing to let our children complain and whine. We can say no to their expressions of self-pity. We can refuse to allow our children to compare themselves to others in a negative, I'm-not-as-good, I-don't-have-as-much, or I'll-never-be-as-much manner.

We can train our children—by example and discipline—to look for the good in themselves and others, to find their talents, acknowledge them and then use them, and to be grateful for what they have rather than focus on what they don't have.

## TRAIT #4: INTEGRITY

Every parent I know wants his child to be honest, moral, and trustworthy. Among the fruit of the Spirit, this kind of integrity is called "goodness." One of the finest examples of personal integrity I have ever read about is an example set by a child.

In the fourth round of a national spelling contest in Washington, eleven-year-old Rosalie Elliot from South Carolina drew the word *avowal*. She spelled it in her soft Southern accent. Judges questioned whether the seventh grader used an "a" or an "e" as the next to last letter in the word. For several minutes they listened to tape recording playbacks, but the critical letter was accent-blurred. The chief judge, John Lloyd, finally put the question to the only person in the room who knew the answer with certainty. He asked Rosalie, "Was the next to last letter an 'a' or an 'e'?" Surrounded by whispering young spellers, Rosalie knew by now the correct spelling of the word, but without hesitating, she replied that she had misspelled the word and walked from the stage.

The audience stood and applauded, including fifty or more newspaper reporters, one of whom later remarked that this was the most inspiring moment he had experienced in several years. While Rosalie didn't win the contest, she was nevertheless a winner. Her parents must have been proud of her in that heartwarming and inspiring moment. And most of all, Rosalie should have been proud of herself. She displayed great personal integrity that day.

Insist that your child tell the truth.

Insist that your child follow through on verbal promises he makes.

Insist that your child do his own work—not plagiarizing the work of others or copying the homework of friends. Never do your child's homework for him.

### TRAIT #5: KINDNESS

You may be tempted to think, *Children are incapable of kindness. They are too self-centered to be kind to others.*

All children are capable of kindness. But not every child has been trained to be kind and consistently mentored in kindness.

Jim Schibsted of the First Congregational Church of Anaheim, California, once told this story:

> While Penny and I were walking the park the other day, a ten-year-old boy came racing around a tree, almost running into us, and said, "Dad, where's Amy?" Instantly he realized his mistake and said, "Sir, I'm sorry. I thought you were my Dad. I made a mistake."
>
> I replied, "That's OK. Everybody makes mistakes."
>
> As he began to walk away, I noticed he had a limp as well as the features of a child with Down's syndrome. After having walked about ten yards, as an afterthought, he turned around and started retracing his steps toward us.
>
> "My name is Billy," he said. "You both were very nice to me. Can I give you a hug?"
>
> After giving each of us a tight hug, he said, "I just wanted you to know that you're my friends and I'm going to be praying for you. I have to go now and find my sister, Amy. Good-bye and God bless you."
>
> Tears came to both [our] eyes as we watched Billy, that child with Down's syndrome, limp to the playground to play with his little sister. After Billy went down the slide, his mother came over to him and gave him a big hug. It was obvious that he was a special child to her.

If a child like Billy can show such spontaneous kindness, certainly any child can be trained to be kind to others. An unkind child is a child untrained in kindness.

Don't let your child get away with pushing, shoving, or bullying other children. Don't allow your child to go unchastised for speaking unkindly to another child. Don't let your child criticize other children as being unworthy of their friendship.

### TRAIT #6: SELF-DISCIPLINE

I have never met a parent who did not desire for his or her children to become self-disciplined or manifest self-control. We all want our children to make right choices regarding their own behavior.

There are six keys to acquiring this important attribute:

*1. Control your emotions.* Proverbs 25:28 (TLB) tells us, "A person without self-control is as defenseless as a city with broken-down walls." When your child becomes angry or sullen, invite him to take a few moments by himself to bring his emotions under control. Encourage him to face the fact that his emotions are running rampant, and then verbalize to himself what it is that he is feeling and why. Then ask him to identify a response that will yield a positive result. You may need to work with your child on this until he learns the new pattern and it becomes an almost automatic response.

It's not a sin to feel angry, frustrated, or hurt. But your child needs to own up to his feelings and be able to express precisely what he is feeling and why. This is important for good mental and emotional health! Perhaps a friend insulted him on the playground or walked away with his toy or other possession. Sometimes simply stating the problem alleviates a good deal of the hurt or tension because your child realizes that he may have overreacted.

In identifying a positive response you are encouraging your child to act upon his feelings, but to use the energy of his emotions to bring about a positive result. Ask your child, "What can you do to change this situation?" Yelling, crying, and slamming fists into walls rarely bring about positive results. Confronting the offending party, perhaps with a mediator present, is likely to be the more positive approach—although it is often a difficult route to take.

The best advice you can offer if your child is struggling with self-control is prayer. Only God can change the heart, where anger and hostility are born. Pray with and for your child, and suggest that he continue in prayer on his own.

*2. Guard your words.* Proverbs 13:3 (NASB) says, "The one who guards his mouth preserves his life." Positive words build; negative ones tear down. Much is said that is better left unsaid. A child who learns to think before he speaks is going to find himself in far fewer arguments and confrontations.

At times, you may need to encourage your child, "Think about what you just said. Could you have said something more positive?"

Old speech habits are hard to change. Give your child opportunities to practice positive speech.

*3. Refrain from acting.* "Just say no" is not only a useful phrase to use when you are tempted to try drugs or other harmful substances. All of us need to learn to say no to negative impulses which could lead to wrong actions.

Teach your child early that:

- not all suggestions are worth taking
- not all invitations need to be accepted
- not all people are good to have as friends
- not all activities are healthful or helpful
- not all associations or relationships are beneficial

Proverbs 19:11 (TLB) tells us, "When someone wrongs you, it is a great virtue to ignore it." You can spend a great deal of time and energy plotting revenge or retaliation for wrongs you believe have been committed against you. Sometimes it's best to say no to those impulses and continue to live your life, ignoring the barbs, slander, or attacks from others.

*4. Stick to plans.* Help your child learn to set goals, make plans for reaching them, and then stick to the plans. Proverbs 16:9 (TLB) advises, "We should make plans—counting on God to direct us." Encourage your child to pray first, asking for God's wisdom and guidance as he makes plans and sets goals.

Self-discipline also includes keeping commitments to people. When your child makes a promise to someone or agrees to a "date" or an "appointment"—even just to a friend to go to an event together—insist that your child keep his promise. Children sometimes are quick to say yes to one invitation and then to accept what appears to be a better offer later on. Don't let your child walk away from commitments he makes. Teach your child that his word is something you and others need to be able to count on.

*5. Manage money and material resources wisely.* The self-disciplined person not only controls his emotions, his behavior, and his commitments, but also his money. Proverbs 21:20 (TLB) says, "The wise man saves for the future, but the foolish man spends whatever he gets." Budgeting and saving are important habits to instill in your child.

There's an old saying, "If you exchange all your bricks for mortar, you still have nothing with which to build." Make your money count. Use it wisely to help you reach your goals. And teach your children to do the same.

*6. Strive to maintain good health.* When a person has health, he has hope. With hope, the doors to life swing open wide.

Name anything that you desire in life—family, friends, a savings account, a good job, a car. Without health, you will not be able to enjoy any of the other things in life that you desire to have. In 1 Thessalonians 4:4 (NIV) we read, "Each of you should learn to control his own body in a way that is holy and honorable."

If you are not self-disciplined as an adult, you will find it difficult to instill self-discipline in your child. Your own behavior will speak louder to your child than your words. The good news is that God will help us acquire self-control. Paul told Timothy, "God did not give us a spirit of timidity, but a spirit of power, of love and of self-discipline" (2 Tim. 1:7). Ask God to help you become more self-disciplined and to show you ways in which you can help your child acquire this important trait.

## TRAIT #7: GOOD DECISION-MAKER

Help your child learn to make good decisions. You can do this by giving your child a limited number of options from which to choose. Don't ask your child, "What do you want to eat?" Rather, say to your child, "Would you rather have a hamburger or fried chicken?" Don't ask your child what he wants to wear. Rather, ask your child if he wants to wear the blue outfit or the red one.

Teach your child that a deferred decision is also a decision—it's a decision to let someone else decide! Former President Ronald Reagan learned this as a young man.

An aunt took him to a cobbler to have a pair of shoes custom made. The shoemaker asked, "Do you want a round toe or a square toe?"

Young Ronald hemmed and hawed, so the cobbler said, "Come back in a day or two and tell me what you want."

A few days later the cobbler saw Reagan on the street and asked what he had decided. "I haven't made up my mind yet," Reagan answered.

"Very well," the cobbler said. "Your shoes will be ready tomorrow."

When Reagan picked up the shoes, he discovered that the cobbler had given him one shoe with a round toe and one with a square toe. He said, "Looking at those shoes taught me a lesson. If you don't make your own decisions, somebody else makes them for you."[3]

A part of decision-making is goal-setting and plan-making. Encourage your child to set goals for himself—ones that are a challenge, but which are attainable through effort and perhaps learning a new skill. Show your child how to make a plan for achieving his goals.

In making decisions, setting goals, and making plans, your child develops two great qualities that are part of the fruit of the Spirit: faithfulness and patience. Faithfulness is steadfastness—sticking to a course, standing by a person, remaining true to a relationship. Patience is having the ability to wait until the thing you are aiming at, hoping for, or desiring comes to pass.

### TRAIT #8: GOAL SETTER

Inspire creativity and help your child set new challenges for himself in every area of his life. We each need to have hopes for the future and an eye toward what we want to accomplish in order to give our lives meaning and motivation.

A young boy once complained to his father that the hymns sung in church were boring and old-fashioned, with tiresome tunes and words that were out of date. His father challenged him, "If you think you can write better hymns, why don't you?"

The boy did! He immediately went to his room and wrote his first hymn. The year was 1690. The young man's name was Isaac Watts. Among the 350 hymns he produced in his lifetime are "Joy to the World" and "When I Survey the Wondrous Cross."[4]

There may be traits other than these eight that you see as vitally important to your definition of being a Christ-follower. Identify them as part of your specific objectives for your child's character profile. You may want to write your objectives here:

CHARACTER PROFILE OF MY CHILD

_____

_____

_____

It is very popular in business circles these days for a business to have a "mission statement." The mission statement drives the corporate activities and sets a direction for the future. In many ways a "character profile" is a mission statement for your child. It will help you set priorities and make decisions related to parenting.

Such a character profile places emphasis on the type of behavior you desire to see your child manifest as an adult, what qualities you want your child to display in the future, and what you hope others will say objectively about your child. What do you believe the Lord longs to say to your child one day within the gates of heaven? Honest answers to questions such as these frame your goals for each child and give rise to a mission statement for your family.

Note that your child's character profile is not stating what it is that you believe your child should do with his life. You are not making career or "interest" choices for him. You are not stating that you are preparing your child for a position as a pastor or missionary, or that you are training your child to become a teacher, nurse, engineer, or corporate president. These are goals for your child to set for himself as he matures.

You also are not identifying what it is that you desire for your child to have or possess in the way of material goods. Again, those goals are up to your child to establish as he or she begins to understand God's unique plan and purpose for his life.

Finally, a character profile does *not* define your child's future relationships. A child who bears the traits identified in this chapter *will* be a person who has the potential for deep and abiding friendships and lasting relationships, including a successful marriage. But we need to keep in mind that Christians also have spiritual enemies who do not want to see the cause of Christ extended on the earth. Furthermore, not every child will marry or have children. We err greatly if we attempt to engineer our child's future relationships. That, too, is an area subject to your child's desires and to the leading of the Lord in his or her life.

## Framing a Goal Statement

Once you have identified a specific character profile for your child, you should be able to come up with a single summary statement that reflects in only a few words what you want your child to *be*.

Your goal statement should be succinct, each word filled with meaning.

I recently read, and was very impressed by, the goal statement for a company called Chick-Fil-A: "To glorify God by being a faithful steward of all that is entrusted to us; and to have a positive influence on all who come in contact with Chick-Fil-A."

Chick-Fil-A has quite a low turnover rate among its employees. Its growth has been steady. From the first restaurant in 1964, the company now has 365 restaurants and ranks third in the nation in chicken fast-food sales. Furthermore, the company has rewarded more than seventy-six hundred students with one-thousand-dollar scholarships. The students have all worked for the company more than twenty hours a week for two years.

The goal statement for this company not only reflects the company policy, but also the heart of its founder. The same will be true for your goal statement related to your child. It will not only establish your "parenting policy" toward your child, but will also reflect your heart. To illustrate what I mean, let me tell you a little about Chick-Fil-A's leader, Truett Cathy.

Truett Cathy, the CEO and founder of Chick-Fil-A, doesn't fit the stereotypical profile of a high-powered corporate executive. He has a gentle smile and relaxed southern accent. But behind his easy manner is a strong determination. What motivates him? A belief that succeeding in the fast-food chicken business is God's mission for his life.

The thing that Cathy likes best is giving. He has said, "Jesus said something that everyone knows but few believe—it is more blessed to give than to receive, especially to those from whom you don't expect anything in return. The greatest gift of all is the promise of eternal life. If we are going to be the recipients of eternal life and God's blessings upon us, we have a duty to give."

Cathy sponsors four foster homes in the United States and one in Brazil. He also established the WinShape Centre Foundation, which supports summer camps for children and teens from seven to sixteen years of age. He gives scholarships worth up to ten thousand dollars to more than one hundred students at Berry College in Rome, Georgia.

He also teaches a Sunday school class of thirteen-year-old boys at First Baptist Church in Jonesboro, Georgia. He teaches his students that if they fail in any one of the areas below—which he calls the three M's—they are going to have trouble:

1. Who will be your Master?
2. What will be your Mission?
3. Who will be your Mate?

Cathy's restaurants are closed on Sunday. He has heard all the arguments for staying open seven days a week, but he can't be convinced. His restaurants usually generate more sales in six days than others do in seven.

When he was a child, an elementary school teacher required Cathy and the other students to submit a favorite Bible verse. He chose Proverbs 22:1, "A good name is rather to be chosen than great riches."[5]

How does Cathy's story relate to you and the goal statement you generate for your child? The statement you have for your child cannot exist apart from the broader goal statement (or parenting philosophy) that you have for your overall family. The two must be virtually one and the same.

Cathy's personal Christianity is reflected in his company, in his philanthropic endeavors, and in his church.

Your goals as a parent—for yourself and your family—inevitably become your goals for your child.

Check the goal statement you have written for your child against what you identified as your parenting philosophy. The two should be in agreement if there is to be consistency and harmony in your efforts to train your child.

## Committing Yourself to the Objectives

You can establish all the objectives in the world for yourself and your child, but unless you actually commit yourself to the *doing* of them, you will have wasted your time. Establishing goals is a meaningless gesture unless you are willing to put out the effort to pursue those goals and achieve them.

The name Julius Caesar commands respect. It is a name linked with victory and leadership. What gives Caesar this reputation in history?

Julius Caesar was a field general under Pompey the Great, the ruler of the Roman Empire. He had a difference of opinion with Pompey, however, and found himself wondering if he should march on the capitol and attempt to wrest the empire from Pompey's control.

In 49 B.C.E., Caesar led his soldiers to the Rubicon, a river in northern Italy that served as a boundary of Caesar's territorial command. The Rubicon was considered something of a sacred landmark, one which required special permission from the Roman Senate to cross. If Caesar crossed the Rubicon without permission, he clearly would be expressing his intent to make the entire Roman Empire subject to his command. Caesar knew that in crossing the Rubicon, he would likely cause a civil war between his followers and loyalists to Pompey. Many lives would be lost, possibly his own, and the entire Roman Empire would be engaged in struggle.

Caesar carefully considered all his options and then made up his mind. He would march on Rome. Caesar declared, "The die is cast," and thrust himself into the waters of the Rubicon, followed closely by the soldiers under his command. The rest is history.

Caesar's dramatic decision is one from which every parent can learn, regardless of whether you agree with Caesar's reasoning or attempt to overthrow Rome. The lesson is this: know what you want and be willing to sacrifice in order to attain it. Once a decision is made, don't engage in second-guessing or doubting. Stick to your commitment to attain or accomplish the objective you have established.

Caesar knew the importance of total commitment. He had no alternative or escape-route plans. When he led his troops to capture Britain, he made sure his soldiers understood his total commitment to victory. After the men and supplies had been unloaded from the ships, he ordered that the ships be sailed out into the harbor and, in the still of night, be burned. There would be no turning back. Caesar knew that human beings have a great ability to exert an above-average effort when they are faced with a tremendous adversity or challenge. He was counting on this intensity of effort to result in victory, and he was right.

Decide today what it is that you want to accomplish as a parent. Then set your face toward the work that is necessary to fulfill your goals.

# Chapter 5

# Managing Your Parenting Resources

*The qualities that we admire in people—*
*honesty, cheerfulness, thoughtfulness,*
*cooperation—must be learned in the*
*home and developed by society.*
—Lou Holtz
Former head football coach,
Notre Dame University

*For the man who uses well what he is given*
*shall be given more, and he shall have abundance.*
—Matthew 25:29, TLB

The stress many parents feel from the pressures of work and home can be intense. However, the communities they live in can provide resources which help parents and children grow and thrive. A study by Massachusetts Mutual in 1989 revealed that 48 percent of Americans believe people need support from their local communities, beyond their immediate families, to help raise their children. This figure rose to 60 percent when those asked were single parents or lower-income parents.

While most parents would agree wholeheartedly with this need for community involvement, many parents don't know *where* to turn for help.

For most of us, a community has four components: church, school, business, and the extended family of friends and other community relationships. The model on the next page can help you visualize the relationships your family has naturally.

The important thing to note about the relationship that your family has with these various entities is that the relationship is a two-way street. If the flow were only one way, either you would be a drain on

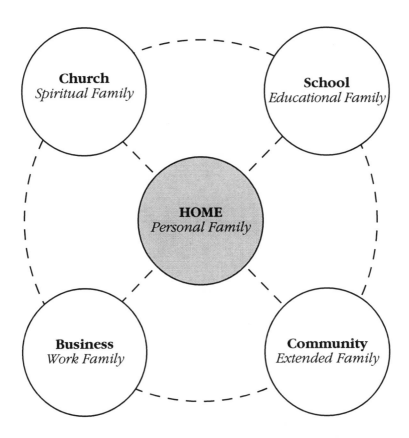

society, or you would be drained by society. Just as give-and-take is an important concept in personal relationships, so it is a vital concept in your family's relationships with the broader community.

## The Parent's Relationship with the Child's School

One of the foremost resources that many parents overlook is the school, specifically, their child's teachers and coaches. Some parents had a bad school experience themselves and are reluctant to return to school for conferences with teachers; others feel intimidated and are unsure about the value of their contributions compared to those of a teacher. Yet one of the most valuable things a parent can do is to *ask* his or her child's teacher for assistance. Very specifically, ask your child's teacher—as well as your child's coach, band leader, or other teachers involved on a regular basis with your child—to give you guidance or suggestions on how you might improve your child's level of achievement and socialization in school.

Be sure to attend all parent-teacher conferences that are scheduled by the school. If at all possible, both parents should attend these conferences. Ask questions. Get details about your child's performance and behavior at school. It isn't enough to know that your child is getting a *C* in math and an *A* in reading. Ask how your child interacts with other children and what values your child is displaying in the school setting. Assume going into such a conference that the teacher is on your side. Your child's teacher is your ally in desiring to see your child maximize his potential and become a solid citizen. Some parents are too sensitive to a teacher's criticisms of a child's behavior; assume that *together* you and the teacher can help resolve the difficulties your child may be having. All children have adjustment problems from time to time; as they grow and their bodies mature, their environments shift around them, and their peers change.

Attend open house nights or school fairs that give parents an opportunity to visit the classrooms, see the students' work on display, and talk to teachers and school specialists. These events at school are far more important to your child than your child is likely to admit.

If your child's teacher recommends tutoring or a special program to help your child in a particular learning skill or subject matter, the teacher may have information about tutoring programs—perhaps ones offered through the school district or available through a nearby college or university where education students are required to provide tutoring services as part of their coursework.

As much as possible, be present to applaud your child's performances. As a coach, I knew how valuable it was to have parents in the stands when my players took the field. The same is true for school concerts and plays, art shows, and other programs such as speech contests or chess tournaments.

The schools with high parental involvement are the best schools in our nation. Three decades of research have shown that parental participation improves students' learning.[1] We are tempted to think that better schools simply have finer facilities and more money for extracurricular programs. In fact, in today's budget-minded society, it is frequently due to the parents' involvement in school programs and fund-raisers that certain schools can afford to offer better curriculum and equipment. Active parent participation equates to better schools.

The more your child sees you placing an emphasis on schoolwork and showing respect for teachers and the learning process, the more your child is going to value school. The more he values school, the harder he is going to try to do his best at schoolwork and the more he is likely to achieve.

Every parent is going to be applauded by the teacher if that parent emphasizes good work habits, teaches a child to listen intelligently, and holds out high expectations for their child to do his best at whatever he undertakes. Children raised with these parent-instilled behaviors and attitudes are a joy to teach, and your child is going to get more out of school if you do your part in making school a high priority.

## MORAL INSTRUCTION IN THE SCHOOL

A recent survey reported that some 84 percent of parents with children in public school favor instruction in moral behavior provided by the school.[2] My concern is that while these parents may favor involvement from the school, they can rarely define precisely what it is they believe the school should teach *all* children. Every parent appreciates support that reinforces what the parent is teaching at home, but certainly not every parent desires support for values that are *not* being taught at home.

You cannot assume that what is taught at school mirrors what you are desiring to teach your child at home. Fifty years ago that assumption may have been valid, but not today. Some schools are so intent upon teaching tolerance of all opinions and all types of behavior that they consider "tolerance" to be a moral value. Little consideration is given to what is right and wrong, and certainly the Bible is seldom referenced as the criterion for making that determination. Many parents find that private or Christian schools or home-schooling often help them meet their children's needs.

We have enjoyed great success in schools where the P.O.P.S. (Power of Positive Students) program is in effect. We enjoy support from parents, teachers, administrators, community leaders, and students. But because we operate in public schools, we cannot be overtly Christian in the values that we present.

You must recognize that if your child is in public school, there are certain Christian concepts and truths that will not be allowed. Therefore, it is up to you to provide this training at home. Indeed, there is little you can do to ensure that the Bible or that a personal relationship with Christ Jesus can be "taught" at school. Indeed, your efforts would likely meet with hostility. In my experience, I have learned that it is better to try to work *within* the system, rather than attempting to *buck* the system.

Get involved with your child's school by helping as a teacher's aide, serving on various school-related committees, chaperoning school functions, and by running for the school board in your district. As a parent, you should monitor closely the materials your child brings home from school as a part of homework. Volunteer to participate on textbook-review committees. Your school is a great ally in teaching your child, but you also must be an active parent in ensuring that your child's school does not present values which you deem undesirable or destructive.

## SCHOOL PRAYER

Much has been said in recent years about school prayer. During one school prayer debate, a senator was asked to address a men's dinner at a local church. About 450 men attended. The senator began his speech by asking two questions. "First, how many of you would like to see prayer restored to the public schools?" As far as he could tell, nearly every hand in the room was raised with a number of men shouting, "Amen!" Then he asked a second question, "How many of you pray with your children every morning at home before they go to school?" The silence was embarrassing, and only a few raised their hands.[3]

Don't demand anything from your child's school or church that you aren't willing to do yourself, especially when it comes to training in values and morals. Your home and your family are the primary training grounds for your child's character.

## THE LIBRARY

Consider the library as an extension of your child's school, regardless of which type of school your child attends. Both school libraries and public libraries are great resources to you as a parent. Countless books are available to help you develop stronger parenting skills and to give you ideas for activities you can do together as families. Family-oriented magazines often have articles that give good practical tips on improving the quality of your family life. Good family films and fiction are a way of reinforcing to yourself, and to your children, the values you hold to be important. Viewing a film with good morals and values, or suggesting a good book with high moral content, is a natural and easy way to reinforce the values you are teaching and training in more direct ways.

## READING TO YOUR CHILD

One of the most important things a parent can ever do is read to his or her child. Family read-aloud times don't need to stop as a child grows. I know of one father who read to his daughter on a weekly basis when she was in high school. They had a reading time every Monday evening. This young woman loved spending this time with her father and hearing him read exclusively to her the books that he had grown to love as a literature teacher.

As a child grows, of course, a parent might also ask the child to do the reading, which helps the child's reading skills even as it further bonds the parent and child.

What does reading have to do with values? It depends on what you choose to read! Choose stories that promote good values. Choose to read aloud the Bible, in various versions, so that your child can hear God's Word repeatedly.

# Your Relationship with Your Church

Church leaders and church members should be among your strongest allies in training your child in the beliefs, attitudes, values, virtues, and behavior that you consider to be important.

Look for a church home that has a strong emphasis on family life. A growing number of churches have a "family minister" on their ministerial staff. (If you are looking for a church home, this is an obvious clue that the church recognizes the need for families to have church support for their efforts.) Does the church have events or programs for family members of all ages?

If the church has a library with materials available for lending, check out the section on family resources. See what is available that may apply to your particular needs.

### INVOLVE YOUR CHILD IN GIVING

Children come to take pride in what they give to their church. The real-life story is told of a schoolgirl who made a fifty-cent pledge to a special fund drive at her church. The morning after the pledge, the girl's parents outlined for her the chores they expected her to do during the week. Among her chores was cleaning the fishbowl.

"No," the girl moaned. "Anything but the fishbowl! It always smells so bad by the time it needs cleaning." Then she went on to say, "You can ask me to do anything else! You can even keep my allowance this week if I don't have to clean the fishbowl."

Then she remembered her pledge. "No, I take that back," she said. "You can't have my allowance. I need it to pay my pledge. I'll clean the fishbowl!"

Help your child to see a reason for his giving to the church. In nearly all cases, you can find something tangible that is the result of your child's giving, even if your child only gives a few dimes and his giving is only a small fraction of what is required to implement or maintain a large project.

### FAMILY—YOUR CHILD'S "FIRST" CHURCH

Christian family is the laboratory for Christian living. In many ways, your home is your child's "first" church! Family is the crucible in which faith is lived out on a daily, practical basis. It is within the family that we learn how to treat other people. Home is the environment in which the spiritual life of children is formed.

Consider what the church, or the Christian faith in general, gives to an individual: purpose and meaning in life, inner strength, forgiveness, a means of building positive relationships with others, hope for the future. These are also the hallmarks of what a family gives to its members. In many ways, we are wise to think of our families as "mini-churches" or as "cells" within the larger church family to which we belong.

Parents may be tempted to think of the church as the primary place in which one receives spiritual nourishment to grow in faith and Christian values, with the home acting as a supplementary training center. In reality, however, the *home* is the primary place for spiritual nourishment and the development of values. The church supports what has already been learned and practiced within the family. To a great extent, the church becomes the "extended family" of the primary family. This extended family is even more important in single-parent homes.

## Your Relationship with the Business World

At a bare minimum, your family has two strong relationships with the business world: income generation and consumer spending.

Your child should know where you work, for whom you work, with whom you work, what you do in your work, and why you have chosen this means to produce income for your family. Take your child to your place of employment at appropriate times. Speak well of your employer and those with whom you work. Express enthusiasm for the work you *get* to do, as opposed to *have* to do.

Teach your child how to relate to people in business relationships. Involve your child in making purchases. Show your child how to comparison shop, make a budget, and treat shopkeepers with courtesy.

Your business may have specific programs that can help you as a parent. Explore those possibilities. A growing number of employers are offering programs and practices that encourage family involvement with children and schools. A few of those with strong family-related programs are identified below.

- Marriott has a Parenting Resource Center that provides information to parents on child and family issues.

- GTE Corporation has a "College Planning Seminar" that helps employees prepare their children for filling out college admission and financial aid forms.

- Pizza Hut's "Kids Hall of Fame" rewards children eight to fourteen years of age for making a difference in their families and communities.

- John Hancock sponsors educational activities for children of employees during school vacations and holidays. The company also has a special magazine for parents on education, and it sponsors seminars on education for parents.

- Hewlett-Packard has flexible work hours for employees to accommodate a child's school schedule and to allow employees to volunteer in the company's on-site elementary school.

- Hemming's Motor News has "Education Participation Days" to allow all employees, not just parents, two days off with pay to attend classes with children in local schools.

- The U.S. First Cavalry Division at Fort Hood has entered a partnership with the Independent School District of Killeen, Texas, to incorporate parent-teacher conferences as part of military duty for all soldiers with children.

- American College Testing has a "Realize the Dream" program that provides a workshop and resources to help parents become more involved in their teenagers' educational and career planning.

- Toyota has a "Families for Learning" program in Louisville, Kentucky, to help parents improve their own literacy skills and to help prepare preschoolers for school.[4]

A growing number of employers are providing time off for employees to volunteer in schools or participate in tutoring and mentoring programs. Others are helping families with after-school and summer enrichment programs. Some employers have release-time programs so parents can attend parenting seminars or attend parent-teacher conferences.

I have been pleased to see a growing number of companies sponsor on-site child-care programs so parents can be involved with their children during break times and lunch hours.

A nationwide program called "Employer's Promise" is based upon a voluntary pledge that commits businesses and organizations to family-friendly policies and partnerships. A copy of the Employer's Promise and more information about the program is available by calling 1-800-USA-LEARN.

### STATE GOVERNMENT RESOURCES

Government agencies are getting more and more involved in helping families to help themselves. Avail yourself of the help that may be offered by your state government. California, for example, has encouraged its school district staff leaders to develop comprehensive parental involvement programs for their schools. In Utah, the State Office of Education and the PTA cosponsor training programs for parent volunteers, who then teach other parents how to improve the learning environment in their homes and take a more active role in their child's education.

In Wisconsin, the state has trained teams of educators, parents, and business board members in how to develop parental involvement plans. The governor of Idaho signed an executive order in 1992 allowing state employees to take an hour of paid administrative leave each week (or four hours a month) to volunteer in a school.

Find out what is available in your area.

## Your Broader Community

When we speak of a community, we tend to think of a town or neighborhood in which we live. Our definition of community needs to be broader than that. A child's community is made up of all the adults and children with whom a child interacts on a regular basis.

To a great extent, you design and define the community that your child experiences.

### OTHER PARENTS

While you may come to think of your child's peer group as a collective enemy, try instead to think of the parents of your child's friends as your own peer group—a collective ally. Parents who work closely with other parents have far fewer peer-pressure problems with which to deal.

After a state teenager was murdered for a pair of status-symbol athletic shoes, a group of parents came together with their local school board and devised a plan: no expensive jewelry or other expensive items would be allowed at the school. Uniforms were adopted during school hours, and students were prohibited from wearing leather skirts and jackets, and other expensive clothing and jewelry, to after-school social events.

Make friends with those who have kids your children's age. In this way, you'll be helping to choose your child's peer group. One mother had an interesting way of describing the need for a child to keep good company. She said, "You don't work in the garden with white gloves. The gloves will become dirty; the dirt will not become glovey."

### "FAMILIES OF PEERS" PRESSURE

It is critically important that you create a community of support in which other adults and children (especially children older than your child) join together to send a firm, clear message to your child that they support the values you are teaching him or her. This support community should include only those adults and teens who will reinforce that

- violence will not be tolerated
- the use of drugs and alcohol is unacceptable
- the truth must be told
- authority must be respected
- learning is to be valued
- kindness and generosity to others is good

The more you allow other children—both peers and older children—and adults to send opposite messages to your child, the more you are diluting your own message.

### EXPERT VOICES

As part of the community-at-large, there is a vast host of "expert voices"—people through the ages who have uttered words of wisdom that can benefit your child. Bookstores commonly stock collections of famous quotes, which you can use to influence and encourage your child. Sometimes your child will accept what a famous person has said more than he will accept the same truth out of your mouth. Quote speeches, memorize poems and key statements, or hang placards in your home that recite wise words. Post positive quotes where your child will encounter them regularly. You might tuck one into a lunchbox or into your child's notebook. Keep positive statements on your family bulletin board. Here are ten statements made by Thomas Jefferson that are worth posting.

1. Never put off until tomorrow what you can do today.
2. Never trouble another for what you can do yourself.

3. Never spend your money before you earn it.
4. Never buy what you don't want because it is cheap.
5. Pride costs more than hunger, thirst, and cold.
6. We seldom repent of having eaten too little.
7. Nothing is troublesome that we do willingly.
8. How much pain the evils have cost us which never happened!
9. Take things always by the smooth handle.
10. When angry count to ten before you speak; if very angry, count to one hundred.

Don't wait to share truths such as these with your child when he is in the process of procrastinating, making a bad purchase, or is angry. Instill these truths into your child's mind *before* they are needed. Consider positive statements as mental and emotional vitamins. They won't cure an ill, necessarily, but they can do a great deal to stave off behavior maladies.

## A Strong Whole

Not only is there reciprocity between your family and your church, the business world, the school, and the community as a whole, but there is a "symbiosis" in the way these resources can work in your life.

A strong family helps produce a strong church. A strong church produces a strong community. A strong community tends to attract healthy business activity.

In like manner, churches influence schools. Strong businesses in a community help to produce churches that are better funded. Each segment impacts the other.

At the hub is your family.

Draw from your church. But also give back to it.

Draw from your business. But also give back to it. Your loyalty as an employee makes your business a better place to work, and a better place to work is generally a higher quality, more productive place.

Draw from your school. But also give back to it.

Draw from your friends and the broader community in which you live. But give back to them as well.

As you glean help to become a better parent, you are training your children to become better church members, better employees, better citizens, and better neighbors.

# Chapter 6

# *What It Means to Train*

*Let us train our minds to desire what
the situation demands.*
—Seneca
Roman philosopher (4 B.C.E.–A.D. 65)

*Prove yourselves doers of the word, and not
merely hearers who delude themselves.*
—James 1:22, NASB

Education is a two-sided coin. On the one side is *teaching*, which involves imparting information so that people can learn what they do not know. The other side of the coin is *training*, which means teaching people to behave as they do not behave.

Training includes teaching but goes beyond it to include drilling, disciplining, and practicing. Teaching alone is the impartation of knowledge or information. Training is the development of behavior that becomes habitual. Training is required if we are to prepare our children to *act* in an adult, Christlike manner.

The training process is often a painful one for both student and teacher since it requires daily diligence, constant monitoring, the frequent giving of warnings and praise, and, above all, the setting of an example on the part of the "teacher"—who is, for our purposes, the parent.

Teaching can be a largely mental activity. It is marked by lectures and demonstrations, workbooks and lesson sheets, and textbooks and audiovisual presentations.

Training is a largely physical activity. It requires *doing*—action, implementation, experimentation, trial and error, mimicry, rehearsal, discipline, practice, and involvement.

When training involves virtues, the "heart" is trained as well as the mind. Training a child to lead a moral life is not a matter of telling, but convincing. Convincing involves example and the imparting of a conviction that it feels better on the inside to love what is good and hate what is evil.

# Be Dedicated to Training

I believe there are three main components involved in the training of a child in a Christian family. Each of them involves dedication.

*First, dedication of the child to God.* The parent must recognize that everything he or she does is for the purpose of bringing up a child to love and follow God. This dedication provides the impetus to take the training process seriously.

By dedication I don't mean simply participating in a parent-child service—although these ceremonies can have great meaning and be an outward sign of an inward conviction. Rather, dedication is a deep-seated, heartfelt belief on the part of the parents that their child is a gift of God to them and a commitment that their responsibility before God is to train the child in the ways that bring honor and glory to God.

*Second, personal dedication to daily instruction in the home.* Training requires a commitment to daily instruction in the home for the values and behavior that are desired. Training requires perseverance and endurance. It is ongoing; it is seamless, and it doesn't end until a child reaches full maturity. If a parent does not dedicate himself or herself to daily training, any training efforts will appear haphazard, disjointed, and isolated, and ultimately will be ineffective.

*Third, a mutual dedication of both parents and children to develop an ongoing motivation for excellence.* This dedication begins with the parent. If a parent does not desire to pursue personal excellence, it will be quite difficult for the parent either to model or to exhort a child to pursue excellence. Once a parent has dedicated himself or herself to the pursuit of excellence and chosen to motivate himself to this end, it will be easy to also train a child to pursue excellence in every area of life—spiritual, physical, mental, emotional, and social.

Nobody can motivate you *except you!* You must avail yourself of the inspirational input necessary to help maintain your motivation, but ultimately motivation to train must reside within you. To choose excellence in training is a decision of your will. It must be at the very core of your desire to be a good parent. Otherwise, your training effort will be lackadaisical and halfhearted.

Choose to be dedicated to training your child—to dedicate your child to God in your heart, to dedicate yourself to daily instruction in your home, and to dedicate yourself to be motivated toward excellence at all times.

## Training Requires Realism about a Child's Capabilities

In training, it is very important that you be realistic about your child's capabilities (his overall potential in certain areas) and abilities (his present capacity to receive certain information and perform certain skills).

As much as every parent would like to think so, no child is perfect. Every child has strengths, talents, and abilities, but every child also has weaknesses, flaws, and inabilities. Encourage your child's strengths and talents. Help your child develop his abilities and acquire the skills necessary to lead a responsible adult life. Help your child develop compensatory skills for his inherent weaknesses. But never expect more from your child than he or she can physically, mentally, or emotionally handle.

At a children's track meet, the final runner down the straight-away in one of the events was a short, portly child who probably shouldn't have been asked to *walk* a mile, much less run one. His entire body was wobbling toward the finish line, his face a bright red. Suddenly a voice was heard in the stands. It was obviously the boy's mother. "Run faster, Johnny, run faster!"

A look of hopelessness came over Johnny's face. He surely must have been thinking to himself, *Run faster? What am I? An idiot? Can't you see that I'm running as fast as I can?*

I've seen this attitude from parents on numerous occasions, not only at sporting events. Some parents assume that their child *must* be the star performer—that surely something is wrong with the coach, the entire program, or the whole universe if their child isn't a stand-out on center stage. Never mind that the parent was never a star and has not done much to prepare the child for stardom. The parent is hoping, through the child, to achieve some of the glory he or she has never experienced.

This is completely unfair to a child, but beyond being unfair, it is damaging. If a child is sent out repeatedly to fail and is then criticized for failing, that child's self-esteem and confidence will wither. The more the child fails, the louder the parent tends to shout, and the more the child withers. A downward spiral develops.

Instead, encourage your child to do his best. Applaud your child— literally and figuratively—for good effort. If your child is making a specific error or is deficient in a particular skill, work on that area of performance with your child—personally, privately, and always at a time well after the most recent performance. Immediately after a game or in the midst of a performance is not the time for a parent to coach or teach.

It is important not only to be realistic about your child's capabilities and abilities, but also about the rate at which your child can learn new information or acquire new skills. Some concepts and skills are directly linked to your child's physical development. Others are related to your child's ability to manipulate language or handle foundational concepts involving logic and relationships (including mathematical ones). Still other concepts and skills cannot be learned without prerequisite concepts and skills. In addition, some children learn more quickly than others, and some children employ learning styles that may not be the norm. Don't expect your child to be like all other children. Accommodate his or her uniqueness.

## Training Requires a Parent to Set and Enforce Limits

A significant part of training is the setting of limits to behavior. A major part of concept learning involves the teaching of "examples" and "nonexamples"—explaining to a child an example of a concept at work and then pointing out counterfeit examples and opposite examples. In behavior, a child needs to learn what is appropriate behavior and what is inappropriate behavior.

Successful limit-setting involves clearly defining the boundaries between acceptable and unacceptable behavior. There should be no doubt in a child's mind where these boundaries lie. A parent must also establish consequences for crossing over into unacceptable territory, and then stand by his word in enforcing those consequences.

Expect your child to test the limits you set. That's part of the growth process. Many teenage behavior problems stem from the fact that when they tested the "limits" as a child, their parents failed to *consistently* follow through with the threatened consequences. To develop a pattern of right behavior, consistency is the key. When you consistently follow through on the consequences you set for breaking the rules of behavior, your child can trust that you will enforce all other admonitions that you give him.

As much as possible, give your child reasons for rules. There may be some rules, however, that are beyond your child's ability to understand. In those instances, rely on your own authority as a parent to be the *reason* your child must obey you, and teach this concept to your child. But whenever possible, and to the degree your child can understand, give your child a logical, rational basis for behavior.

In turn, invite your child to express his or her opinions. The more you root your rules in logic and reason, the more you can insist that your child express opinions that are based upon logic and reason.

Children benefit from discussing and helping to set family rules. As your child matures, invite him or her to be a part of the rule-setting process. This gives your child practice in decision making and problem solving. It also gives your child a sense of ownership for the order that has been established in the family, as well as being a positive boost to communication.

### POSITIVELY "NO"

While positive talk is important, it's also important that a parent say an emphatic "no" to his child from time to time. It's a word some parents don't say often enough.

There are many different situations in which saying no is quite appropriate. Here are several examples.

*The physical-danger "no."* When you grab a toddler and swoop him out of the path of an oncoming car, you essentially have said no to the child's behavior. At times you need to save a child's life without worrying about injuring his dignity or wrenching his arm.

This "no" also applies to your insistence that your child not drink, use drugs, or engage in illegal or other activities that have potential for physical, emotional, or spiritual harm (such as attending a questionable band concert).

*The forced-choice "no."* At times your child's desires will collide with what she shouldn't or can't have. You can say no to your four-year-old who wants to stay up until ten o'clock just because an older sibling is, and also to your sixteen-year-old who wants to use the car on Saturday night when you've already made plans. Sometimes saying no is easier when positive options are linked to it. For example, you might find it easier to say to your four-year-old, "No, you may not stay up until ten o'clock, but which do you want to take to bed with you—your teddy bear or your doll?" You might say to your sixteen-year-old, "No, you may not use the car Saturday night, but let me know if you want to use it on Friday instead."

*"No" today doesn't mean "no" tomorrow.* This has nothing to do with your consistency in setting rules and boundaries. It has to do with conditions that change. You may say to your daughter, "No, you may not wear lipstick to school, but you can wear it to the birthday party next

week, and starting next summer, you can wear it to church on week-ends."

Your "no" can be conditional. "No, you may not have a puppy now because you haven't shown responsibility for the things already entrusted to your care. If you learn to put your toys away every day, by spring you will have shown me you are grown up enough to have a puppy." This isn't a bribe. It's an agreement entered into and fulfilled by both sides.

*The collective "no."* Parents of teens would benefit from communicating among themselves to adopt a collective "no" to certain behaviors—such as coed sleepovers and unchaperoned gatherings. Don't give in even if another parent does. Stand by your agreements with other parents.

*"No" in advance.* Establish certain ground rules long before a particular issue is likely to arise. You might say to your thirteen-year-old, "Don't expect us to give you a car when you turn sixteen. You should start saving your money right now if you want a car."

*"No," without adult supervision.* This should never be used by an overprotective parent as an excuse to coddle a child. However, situations arise when adult or other qualified supervision is necessary to ensure your child's safety and well-being. "No, you may not swim unless there's a lifeguard," and "No, you may not attend Martie's party unless his parents are home" are good examples.

How do you confirm that Martie's parents will be there without sounding like the meddling parent who doesn't trust her child? Here are two suggestions. First, make it a practice to always get to know your child's friends' parents, including their phone numbers. That way, calling up to say, "The party at your house Saturday night sounds like fun—do you plan to be home?" is the natural outgrowth of an acquaintance rather than a nosey inquiry.

If you feel uncomfortable with this approach, then I suggest getting to know your child's friends personally to the point where you are quite familiar with their lifestyle and background. With this information you can make a reasonable judgment call about whether their parents will be home to supervise the party.

*"No, it's too expensive."* Parents likely heard this a great deal when they were young, yet they seem reluctant to tell their children this today. Is it because of pride? Is it because of a built-in expectation encouraged by the media that parents should provide everything their

child desires? Is it because of parental guilt over spending too little time with their children or being divorced?

Your child needs to learn that he can't have everything he wants in life. The best way to teach him this important lesson is to occasionally say no.

*"No, it's not a good buy."* Even if you can afford something, like a name-brand pair of shoes, saying no can instill in children that "buying wisely" is an easy way to make a budget stretch. Children today, especially teenagers, need to be taught to make wise financial choices.

If you don't say no to your child on occasion now, you are setting an example that will make it difficult for your child to say no to himself or to others later. You are wise to give your child reasons for saying no. In fact, tell your child freely and often why you don't allow certain behaviors.

Give your child reasons for saying no to peers who may try to pressure him into doing things that are wrong. Have "mock" discussions to help your child counteract peer pressure. For example, here are eight things your teen can say to turn down an offer of alcohol:

- "No thanks, do you have Coke or another type of soft drink?"
- "No thanks, I don't like the taste."
- "No thanks, I'm in training and need to watch every calorie."
- "No thanks, I have to drive later."
- "No thanks, drinking just isn't for me."
- "No thanks, I choose not to drink alcoholic beverages."
- "No thanks, the negatives on this are too great."
- "No thanks, I like to stay in control of myself."

For that matter, just saying "No thanks" can suffice!

## THE SKY'S THE LIMIT

In balancing the use of "no" in your child's life, be sure to include plenty of encouragement for your child when it comes to:

- goals
- opportunities
- potential rewards

Help your child feel like an untapped mine of virtually unlimited potential—which, scientists tell us, is true! (Most of us develop only about 10 percent of our capabilities and use a much lower percent of our intellectual power.) Given sufficient effort, time, and training, most children can achieve far more than they can imagine.

This does not mean that you should promise your child unlimited success or automatic rewards. Situations sometimes prevent the attainment of certain goals, regardless of the effort, talent, or skills that your child may employ. In challenging your child to shoot for the moon, don't promise him the moon!

When Sam Findley decided to retire from the garment business, he called in his son Mervyn and gave him this advice: "Son, it's all yours. I've made a success of this business because of two principles—reliability and wisdom. First, take reliability. If you promise goods by the tenth of the month, no matter what happens, you must deliver by the tenth. Even if it costs you overtime, double time, golden time. You deliver what you promise."

Mervyn thought about this for a few moments and then asked, "What about wisdom?"

His father replied, "Wisdom is never making such a stupid promise."

Don't make promises you can't keep. And don't make stupid promises that you shouldn't keep.

## DEFINING CONSEQUENCES

Part of setting limits is defining consequences—either rewards for staying within limits or punishment for failing to stay within limits.

Don't confuse consequences with forgiveness as you train. They are quite different. Too often we assume—and therefore our children come to assume—that to ask for and receive forgiveness erases all consequence. That isn't at all the case. Behavior and misbehavior both have consequences, apart from forgiveness. Forgiveness is saying that a negative experience will not have a negative impact upon the *relationship* in question. Consequences are not related to *relationship*, but solely to the person who has acted.

Many of us are like the little boy who broke the glass of a street lamp. Upset and fearing punishment, he asked his father, "What do I have to do?"

The father replied, "Why, we must report this immediately and ask what you must pay for a new lamp, and then go and settle the account. You will have to work to pay for the lamp's replacement."

The little boy had been looking for an immediate punishment—one that might be momentarily painful but, nevertheless, short-lived. He whimpered, "I . . . I . . . I thought all I had to do was ask God to forgive me."

Forgiveness, yes. Forgiveness must flow freely between you and your child, but elimination of consequences is not the same as forgiveness. One of the greatest lessons you can ever teach your child is that all behavior has consequences.

# Delayed Gratification Is Implied in Training

Training is based on the premise that if you practice now, you improve your chances of succeeding later. An important concept in training is "delayed gratification," meaning a person has to wait for things that are desirable. Sometimes delayed gratification means earning something through proper behavior, or working to acquire an object. Sometimes, mere patience is required.

Give your child opportunities for delayed gratification. Children live very much in the present tense. It's part of your role as a parent to train your child to think further ahead, to learn to plan, and to set goals that cannot be met instantly.

Delayed gratification is an important concept to develop in your child so he can live a balanced life as an adult. Much of our nation's credit problems, indebtedness, divorce rate, and general stress level would probably be alleviated or eliminated if more adults had been trained as children *not* to expect the immediate fulfillment of all their dreams and wishes.

The story is told of a boy who had been looking forward to a fishing trip with Dad for several weeks. His father had promised to take him fishing on Saturday "if the weather permits." It hadn't rained for weeks, so as Saturday approached, the boy was confident that the fishing trip would go as planned. But wouldn't you know it? When Saturday morning dawned, the boy looked out to see that it was raining heavily.

The boy wandered about the house for hours, peering out of this window and that, grumbling as he went. "It seems like the Lord would have known to make it rain yesterday instead of today," he complained to his father, who had settled in to enjoy a good book. The father tried to explain to his son how badly the rain was needed, especially by the farmers in their area. "It just isn't fair," his son complained.

About three o'clock, the rain stopped. There was still some time for fishing, and the father and son quickly loaded their gear and were off to the lake. Whether it was the rain or some other reason, the fish were biting eagerly. Father and son returned with a full string of fine fish.

Some of the fish were cleaned and prepared for supper. When the time came to eat, the mother asked if the boy would like to say grace. He did and concluded his prayer by saying, "And, Lord, if I sounded grumpy earlier today, it was because I couldn't see far enough ahead."

When your child has to work for things, anticipate things, and wait for things, he not only learns more about work, but also about patience. Along with patience, your child gains a clearer understanding that some things in life are *worth* waiting for, and those things that aren't worth waiting for are likely things that aren't worth having at all. In the end, your child will appreciate more and take better care of those things for which he works and waits.

## NO GRATIFICATION

Along with delayed gratification, there are also situations that result in no gratification. A four-year-old named Jimmy was given some quarters to play a video game at an arcade. He put the quarters into a machine, pressed the start button, and waited for the game to begin. The machine malfunctioned, however, and Jimmy lost his quarters.

"I want more quarters," he whined to his sister. His sister replied, "Jimmy, in life we don't always get what we want." Jimmy paused and then shouted, "I hate that rule!"

The sister had learned one of life's toughest lessons, one Jimmy was in the process of learning, whether he knew it or not. Sometimes we *don't* get what we want, even though we work and wait and hope and dream for it. Life simply doesn't always go the way we plan or the way we anticipate. But that's life. That's reality. Your child will not always have things go his way.

The wise parent trains a child to do his best with the best he has in anticipation of the best that's possible.

## PROVIDE REASONS FOR DELAYING GRATIFICATION

When your child is struggling to wait for something which her peers are currently indulging in, it is imperative to give her sound reasons to continue waiting. Teens especially are so eager to embrace some of the freedoms and benefits of adulthood that they often find it difficult to wait.

One such area of anticipation is sex. Teens are told by their peers—and through numerous television programs—that they should be free to engage in sexual behavior.

Teach your child instead that the real freedom comes in saying no to sexual temptation. Arm your child with many reasons for abstinence. Don't discuss this issue only once with your child; discuss it repeatedly. Reinforce through repetition your beliefs and values to help your child develop the fortitude to say no when passion arises.

Part of your discussion could include the fact that the teenager who abstains from sex until marriage is a teenager who is:

- free of the threat of an unwanted pregnancy
- free of the threat of sexually transmitted diseases, (including herpes and HIV [AIDS], both of which are incurable at the present time)

- free from the problems associated with birth-control pills and birth-control devices
- free from the pressure of marrying too soon
- free from abortion
- free from the pain of giving up a baby for adoption
- free of exploitation by others
- free from guilt, doubt, disappointment, worry, and rejection that can come from a sexual affair
- free to be in control of his or her own body
- free to plan for the future
- free to respect self and others
- free to remember high school dating experiences without shame or remorse
- free to form a strong marriage bond with one person for a lifetime

That's true freedom! In discussions related to abstinence, always assure your child that your deep desire is for his best, and that you also look forward to the day when he can enjoy the great pleasures of sex as part of a marriage relationship.

## TRAINING AND CHORES

The doing of chores is an area in which the principles of training can easily be applied.

Children benefit greatly by being required to do chores that benefit the family-at-large. Certain chores around the house can be expected of a child at virtually any age. Even a very young child can be required to empty the tiny trash basket in his room into a larger container elsewhere in the house, to pick up toys that have been taken into communal areas, and to carry a dish from the table to the kitchen sink. These are behaviors that benefit the overall functioning of the family. As your child grows, the chores and degree of responsibility should grow. Chores can include care of the house, yard, automobile, and other family possessions, as well as participation in daily family rituals—meal preparation, washing the dishes, bringing in the mail, or emptying the trash, for example.

A child can and should be required to keep his or her room tidy, but this is not necessarily a chore that builds a sense of *family* responsibility. When a child is required to make his own bed, or keep his room "picked up," he is being trained to take *personal* responsibility. This is certainly important and should be a major part of training. But also make sure your child is given chores that convey this message: "You are a valuable member of this *family,* and your family is valuable to you. What you contribute to the family is important."

What do chores have to do with values?

It is in the doing of chores that a child has a practicum for building and displaying values.

Is your child *faithful* in making sure that the designated dish always has sufficient water for the family dog? Does your child *keep his word*— and display trustworthiness—in completing a chore when he says he will do it? Is your child *honest* when he tells you that he has spent an hour and fifteen minutes in doing a for-pay chore while you were away from home?

While I don't advocate paying a child for chores, I do strongly advocate *praising* a child for completed chores. Thank your child for the contribution she has made to the family. Acknowledge a job done well. Point out to other family members—in the presence of your child—the successful completion of her chore list. Give your child a sense of pride at contributing to her family life. In so doing, your child should find the successful completion of chores to be a rewarding experience.

Finally, chores give a child a sense of routine within the family. Chores *are* routine. In part, that's what makes them chores—daily chores, weekly chores, monthly chores. Because they are a part of a child's routine, they also become a *routine* practicum for the exercise and testing of values. Over time, values of responsibility, authority, steadfastness, discipline and hard work take root in the fertile soil of chores.

The child who learns to do chores well is very likely a child who will be successful at maintaining a part-time job, following through on the volunteer duties expected of club or group membership, and forging a successful career later in life.

### TRAINING AND ALLOWANCES

One of the best ways of training a child may be related to a child's allowance.

The old view of an allowance was that it was a child's "payment" for doing chores around the house. Then a new view took over, that a child should receive an allowance just for being part of the family. The prevailing opinion about allowances—and one which I support—is that they should be given to children as a tool to teach them about financial responsibility and budgeting, and to provide a practical area in which children can learn how to make choices and accept responsibility for those choices.

Decide with your spouse the size of your child's allowance, as well as when and how often you will give it to your child. Reevaluate this every year. I recommend that you do *not* give your child his allowance on a Friday afternoon or Saturday morning. It's too easy for your child to blow it all during the weekend. Saturday evenings are a good time, in my opinion. That way, the giving of a tithe can be the first priority associated with your child's "income."

Start with a small allowance and increase it as your child grows older. Some child development experts recommend adding a dollar a year, beginning at the time of a child's birthday. There's no set amount that's right for every child, however. A study conducted a few years ago by Nickelodeon MTV and Yankelovich Youth Monitor found that six- to eight-year-olds received an average allowance of $3.18 a week, nine- to eleven-year-olds received $4.61, and twelve- to thirteen-year-olds received an average of $9.26.

You probably need to determine your child's allowance, in part, on the basis of how much things cost in your geographical location. A child's allowance should be big enough so the child can purchase some things he wants and learn to make choices in the process. The allowance should not be too large, however, or the child will have no reason to learn to budget or to learn the concept of saving.

Unless an exceptional emergency arises, don't give your child an advance on his allowance. This will only encourage him to live on credit. If you do make an advance, don't lend more than your child can pay back after he receives his next allowance payment. Put the terms of the loan in writing.

Don't withhold your child's allowance because he fails to do chores. Your child should do chores simply because he's part of the family, not because he is getting paid. A better consequence is to withdraw a privilege—such as TV viewing or dessert at a meal.

Be sure to let your child know the "rules" related to allowance giving, and then don't waver in them. Your setting of this example is a part of *training*.

Let your child choose how to spend his or her allowance within the parameters of what you want your child to learn. You can insist, for example, that your child set aside 10 percent of his allowance as a tithe to put into the church or Sunday school offering plate as it passes. You also can insist that your child set aside another 10 percent to put into a savings account. Your child will delight in seeing how this money grows over the months, and he will be especially delighted at the concept of compound interest!

You also can insist that your child not spend more than a certain amount on candy or other food items that you believe to be harmful to your child's general health or dental care. Once general parameters have been defined—with your child fully aware of them—don't put restrictions on what your child buys. Even if you think the purchase is unnecessary or a waste of money, unless the product your child is purchasing is dangerous in some way, allow your child to make the purchase and learn for himself why he has made an inappropriate choice.

Help your child make decisions by being a willing consultant on purchases. Point out the pros and cons of a choice, but only if your child asks. Or you can try saying, "If you want my opinion, I'll give it, but the decision is yours." This gives the child the freedom to ask for your opinion, but also the freedom to make the final choice. You likely will be pleasantly surprised at how often your child seeks out your opinion—as long as it is reasonable and logical, and not a "put down" to your child's decision-making ability.

Help your child determine "value for the dollar" by pointing out the relationship between quality and cost. Help your child learn to budget his money and save for items that cost more than one week's allowance. Discuss with your child what he would like to buy with his money.

How does this translate into training?

First, make sure you are consistent in your giving of an allowance. Stay on schedule. Give your child his or her allowance face-to-face and take time for the transaction.

You may want to count out the money in different ways from time to time—perhaps five dimes and two quarters instead of a dollar bill. Let your child count out the money to make certain the full amount is there. (You are reinforcing math skills and setting a pattern for a child to count and check the change he receives in stores.)

With your child, set aside the amount that is going to be given to your church or put into a savings account. You may want to have a special box or piggy bank for these purposes. For example, give an allowance on a weekly basis and set aside a percentage for savings, but then only make a bank deposit once a month or once a quarter.

When your child advances to the point of having a checkbook, you are wise to teach your child how to keep a simple ledger and balance his checkbook. Periodically audit your child's checkbook or ledger.

This is the real world at work! Your child is rehearsing valuable adult behaviors.

You also may want to teach your child about investing in something other than a checking account. As your child becomes a teenager, explore the options of money-market and mutual funds. Think about matching your child's investment dollar-for-dollar. You can also encourage your teen to start his own IRA. Make saving for retirement a habit for life.

Talk to your child about what he wants to purchase, but not necessarily at the time you give the allowance. The better time for this may be when your child is expressing a desire for an item that is more costly. You may want to copurchase an item with your child, supplementing or matching what she saves. For example, if your child wants a $50 doll, suggest to her that if she sets aside $1.50 a week for twenty weeks, she will have $30 and you will contribute the remaining $20. This makes purchasing the doll possible within a time frame that the child can imagine. Set up a small ledger sheet so your child can see that each week she is getting closer to her goal.

In doing this, you are *training* your child in a practical way to learn delayed gratification. You are teaching a system of paying cash for items, rather than purchasing on credit. You are also instilling in your child a pattern of purchasing items that are truly desired, rather than reinforcing a purchase-on-whim approach to consumerism. Your child is likely to value her purchase more if she has saved for it over time. She will have learned more about setting goals and achieving them on an incremental basis.

The same method, of course, can apply to saving for a bicycle, an automobile, or even a college education.

I once heard of a man who insisted that his children pay for their first year of college. If they paid all of the first year, he agreed to pay half of the second year, three quarters of the third year, and all of the fourth year of their college expenses. He instilled this concept early so that from preteen years his children were setting aside money for college. A large percentage of their earnings from part-time jobs after school and during the summer were set aside for college. The children were taught as they saved that this was a great deal for them—that they would actually be paying for less than half of their college degrees, but would be ahead of most of their peers in that they would be graduating debt free. As an incentive reward, he told them he would buy them a new car as a graduation present from college.

The children took advantage of junior colleges for the first two years of their college training and then went to more prestigious private schools for the completion of their degrees. They all graduated debt-free and with a new car—a great set-up to the start of a career in their chosen professions.

The father benefited in knowing that his children were more focused in their thinking and planning about college. They didn't take this level of education for granted. They didn't waste time at school; they attended class, studied diligently, and earned good grades because they had paid for their tuition and books. All of the children figured out early in the game that if they could earn scholarships they would be better off, so they worked hard to earn good grades in high school. They took advantage of career counseling and aptitude testing in their high schools, and each of them decided early on their college majors, which meant they didn't waste time "experimenting" with classes or degree programs.

This father had trained his children to be fiscally responsible and, in many ways, more responsible for their entire lives. His children had a plan and goal for their lives. They didn't have time, energy, or extra money for drugs, booze, or hours spent roaming the local shopping malls.

In teaching your child to budget and make choices related to an allowance, you are *training* your child because you are actually requiring certain behaviors. Be sure that your child puts his own money into the offering plate. Be sure he is with you when you go to the bank to make a deposit into the savings account. Make sure he is present when you audit his ledger. Money is not a matter of theory; it is a practice of *doing*—of planning, spending, and record keeping.

These money-related behaviors become habits to your child. They also become a mind-set. Your child is likely to have a much better grasp of finances and how to spend money wisely his entire life. Even more importantly, however, he will have learned that money can be controlled and used.

The same holds true for all material resources. He will learn a great life lesson—that money is to be used and people loved, rather than money loved and people used. Children who are given too much money or who never learn the principles related to spending tend to be children who attempt to manipulate others to get what they want and who believe that anything they desire can be purchased with money. The child who is required to budget, save, give, and be accountable for his money is the child who learns that money is a tool and that he must be responsible for its use.

The discipline required in budgeting, saving, and keeping financial records is just that—*discipline*. The person who is disciplined in the use of money is much more likely to be disciplined in the use of time and other resources.

In teaching your child to save for items he desires, you have taught him a valuable lesson about rewards—that rewards are *earned* through hard work and innovative ideas. Such a child is much more likely to give a maximum effort in any job he has. He is also less likely to think that a company owes him something simply because he has been hired.

The child who saves for items is the child who learns much about goal setting and incremental planning. These skills readily translate to a child's ability to set a goal of writing a ten-page term paper and then plan for its accomplishment over a six-week term. These skills also relate to planning for a career in life and setting short-term goals that build toward the accomplishment of larger goals.

You can *teach* your child all of these principles by sitting down one evening and telling your child all that has been presented here about the management of an allowance. The lesson likely won't stick. But if you *train* your child in these principles—to do them week in and week out, year in and year out—you will be creating a habit in your child that *will* stick and will mold your child's ability to discipline his own life to make wise choices.

By now I hope you have noted that when a person is *trained*, the "spill-over benefits" always transcend the immediate area in which training occurs. I have seen this happen countless times as a sports coach and have heard other parents speak of it in relation to practicing the piano or spending an allowance. The discipline and focus required in pursuit of a goal sets a *pattern* for discipline and focus in the child's entire life.

In giving your child an allowance, you certainly are not prohibited from paying your child for specific jobs that are beyond regular family-related chores. For example, a chore list might include raking leaves on Saturday morning before other activities are enjoyed. You might offer to *pay* your child, however, for weeding the flower beds. Differentiate clearly between what is a chore to be done as a family responsibility and what is a paid job.

Be sure to set standards for the job you are paying your child to do. Don't pay for sloppy or half-finished work. Insist that for payment to be received the job has to be done within the time frame *you* specify. If your child doesn't know how to do a particular job, take time to show him *how* you want the job done and train him in the skills required.

Choose jobs that are well within your child's ability to do safely and with a degree of quality. Don't expect your eight-year-old to handle gas-powered yard equipment or your preteen to paint the house.

If your child does an exceptionally good job, give a bonus. Above all, however, praise your child for work done well. Words of praise are as important to your child as the money earned.

In paying for specific jobs, you will be *training* your child for future employment. You are providing a work ethic that readily translates to other areas of life. You are also creating a clear difference in your child's mind between work that is done simply because one is a member of the family or community and work that is done for hire. It's important that your child have experience with both types of work.

Your praise of a child's work, as well as your praise of good choices that your child makes in spending an allowance, are not only motivating to your child, but they build your child's self-esteem and create within your child a concept that every job undertaken is a job that should be done to the best of one's ability. Your praise ultimately is translated into self-motivation and self-praise—the ability of a child to look at his own work and say, "I did that well." This is a great mark of maturity and confidence; it grows from your praise of good effort and good work.

# *Strategies for Practical Application*

*T*he strategies presented in this section are like tools. They are practical methodologies for building the positive values and habits that you desire to see in your life and in the life of your child. In many ways, you as a parent are sanding away the "rough edges" (negative aspects) of your child's character and building into your child the positive values and behaviors that you deem to be important.

Each of the strategies in this section has a dual function of preventing the negative and building the positive.

Good training results in saying no to bad behavior, falsehoods, and poor values, while saying yes to good behavior, truth, and the most noble of values. Good training also helps children learn from their mistakes.

The negative can never be eliminated with one definitive action. Neither can the positive be built by one decision or one act of discipline. A child's character is shaped *away* from the negative and *toward* the positive one thought at a time, one behavior at a time, and one day at a time!

Each of the following five "tools" has a twofold nature:

*They work best when used early and often in your child's life.* Plant positive seeds early! You must start building your family into a team, and developing your child to be a team player from the time she is an infant. The same holds true for the creation of a positive climate in your family through conditioning and reinforcing behavior. Your child is never too young to hear words of encouragement, appreciation, recognition, praise, and love. Soon she will be imitating your actions and attitudes. Be a positive role model worthy of imitation!

*They work hand-in-hand with your good example.* Your use of these strategies with your child will only be effective to the extent that you are also following them in your personal life. You must make a personal commitment to being a team player where you work, worship, do business, and socialize; to developing a positive climate in your own personal life; to engaging in a conditioning and reinforcement process for your own behavior; and to finding and drawing from positive role models as you grow and develop as a person.

All of these strategies combine synergistically so that they are greater than the sum of their components. They are a key to leaving a legacy of love to your children and grandchildren!

As you implement these strategies on a daily basis, I encourage you to do these three things:

First, begin your day with *goals*. Determine personally and as a family what you wish to achieve. Ask God to be with you in the day ahead.

Then, execute your day with *positive actions*. Work hard. Ask for God's help as you find solutions to problems, relate to others, and make decisions and choices. Put your values into action!

Finally, end your day with *assessment*. Take stock of how you have lived your day. What did you think about? How do you feel about your behavior during the day? Did you reach your goals? If not, why not? This process of assessment keeps you and others in your family aware of days in which you have fallen short of your goals. That way, you can take corrective action before bad behavior or weak efforts become a *habit*.

Ask for God's blessing on those things that you did well during the day. Ask for God's forgiveness for those things that you did poorly, or failed to do. Ask His help in setting wise goals for the next day and in imparting to you the ability and courage to pursue those goals.

# Chapter 7

# Tool #1: Team-Building

*The better the team, the better you play.*
—Wayne Gretzky
National Hockey League Player

*So encourage each other to build
each other up.*
—1 Thessalonians 5:11, TLB

Every child who goes out for team sports quickly learns that there are set practice times for the team. Certainly a young athlete can do much of the training necessary for the development of personal skills and physical fitness alone, in the privacy of his own home, gym, or neighborhood—for example, weight lifting and aerobic exercising. As a coach, I always encouraged my students to exercise regularly in the off-season months and to engage in good personal habits of nutrition, rest, and healthful living around the clock, 365 days a year.

But when it comes to *team play,* there must be *team practice.* The drills and routines that make for successful football scrimmages and games are learned *together.* The same is true for certain morale-building experiences. I don't know of any coach who would give his players headsets and tapes and send them into isolation to hear a pep talk before a game. There's much to be said for "togetherness" in building a successful team.

For decades the Japanese have been masters of this in the corporate world. Their young company employees work together *and play together* for weeks and months as part of their internship with the corporation. They are trained to become team players from the day they are hired, and a significant part of this training process is to keep the team members together physically in both business and social settings.

Team-building is based to a great extent on four R's:

- the *routine* of doing things together
- *reciprocity* in the way family members treat one another
- clearly designated *responsibilities* and *roles*

# "Togetherness" Routines

A sense of team spirit in a home is built in part by having set times when the family comes together. Four of the most beneficial times for team-building are these:

1. eating together
2. worshiping together
3. doing chores and errands together
4. playing together

Let's take a look at each of these activities and the way they can work in the training of values and in the building of a team spirit within a family.

## EATING TOGETHER

I strongly encourage families to eat at least one meal together on a daily basis. This gives a family a set time for communicating schedules and agendas, expressing of ideas and opinions, making decisions, and solving problems. Family mealtime is a great boost to a child's sense of belonging. Even the child who may have been punished during the afternoon for misbehavior knows he has a time and place where he can again be united in love with his family.

Family mealtime provides an important time for learning:

- social courtesies and basic manners; for example, waiting for others before eating, using correct table etiquette, and saying please and thank you. In the process, a child is trained in *kindness.*
- a great deal about small-group dynamics; for example, when to speak and when to remain silent in a group setting. In the process, a child is trained in the values of *respect* and *tolerance,* including putting others first and accommodating differences of opinion.
- more about other family members; hearing about their work, friends, and other associations. In the process, a child learns a great deal about how other people interact, solve problems, and make decisions. A child hears how values are put into effect in practical ways on a daily basis.

For example, consider a father who relates to his children over dinner how he dealt with an unhappy customer who came into his place of employment. If the father was angry, upset, or unkind to the customer, that behavior and its attendant values are going to be clearly evident to the child. On the other hand, if the father was kind, accommodating, and helpful—perhaps even in the face of adversity—those values are also going to be clearly evident. No explanation of values or appropriate behavior is going to be necessary. The example will come through loud and clear to the child.

### WORSHIPING TOGETHER

Daily and weekly routines should include times when the family prays or worships together. Some families gather together nightly at a child's bedside for prayer or a Bible story. Other families pray together at the breakfast table about the upcoming day's activities and then have a time of praising the Lord at the dinner table for the good things of the day. Some families have a set time with their children on Saturday afternoons or evenings to go over with them the next day's Sunday school lesson. This way their children are prepared to get even more out of the lesson and to contribute to any discussions that may be part of the Sunday school period. Some families have daily Bible verses that they memorize as a family; they learn a verse together in the morning and repeat it to each other several times throughout the day.

Regular church attendance should be a family event. Nothing instills more effectively in a child the importance of being faithful and steadfast in one's Christian walk than *regular* attendance at church services—week in and week out, month in and month out, year in and year out. The child who attends church regularly with his family is going to be a child who values church attendance and the importance of having a personal faith in God. Such a child, of course, is going to be exposed to weekly spiritual nourishment—sermons, Sunday school lessons, and various church rituals and sacraments that are rooted in values, explicitly or implicitly.

In addition to the direct benefit that your child receives from attending church on a regular basis, the child also benefits in an indirect way because the church family reinforces and supports what the parents are teaching at home. The result is the creation of a more "seamless" environment for the child, one in which family and community are upholding and espousing the same values. The child who learns values only at home has an uphill battle every time he leaves home to face the world-at-large. The child who sees home values and church values reflecting each other is a child who has a more secure foundation for his or her personal values; he knows he has a community of support for what he believes and holds to be important. His behaviors are going to be rewarded—and disciplined—in a consistent fashion from home to the larger group.

Older children and teens should be encouraged to have a personal devotional time each day as part of their daily routine, in which they read the Bible for themselves and spend time talking and listening to the Lord. Family devotional times can be built upon these personal "quiet times" with God. Some families find it easier and more natural, however, to incorporate discussions about the Scriptures and personal devotion into dinner-time, in-the-car, or as-we-do-chores-together conversation. In this way, the Bible and one's relationship with God are applied to daily circumstances and situations, as opposed to being topics of separate conversation.

Part of worship is living out the Christian life wherever one happens to be. Invite your children and teens to take part in your volunteer service to the church and community whenever possible. Take your child along to help you hand out soup and sandwiches to the homeless, deliver blankets to street people, invite others to church in door-to-door neighborhood canvasses, and visit the sick and elderly at hospitals and nursing homes. Incorporate such activities into your family routine, even if it's only on a monthly or quarterly basis.

## DOING CHORES AND ERRANDS TOGETHER

Chores and errands are a part of every family's daily and weekly routine. Invite your children to accompany you on errands. Let them take a part in helping you with home repairs. Whenever possible, do chores with your child. I know of one daughter whose chore it was each Saturday morning to dust the furniture and clean all of the mirrored and glass surfaces in her home, while her mother vacuumed and mopped alongside her.

Another family I know assigned "setting the dinner table" as a chore for their son. Mom and Dad fixed dinner together while the table was set. The predinner chores became a natural extension of the dinner hour and was a lively time for conversation. Over the years, there was some exchange of roles—Mom setting the table so the son and father could cook together. All three were involved in clearing the table and putting away food items, rinsing the dishes, and loading the dishwasher.

The mother in this family pointed out to me that on most nights this gave the family a little more than an hour together—including meal preparation, eating, and clearing—a time they would have found difficult to carve out of their busy schedules any other way.

Doing chores together conveys to your child that all members of a family benefit individually when they work together for the family good. It also conveys the value of *teamwork* and gives lots of opportunities for a child to learn *fairness, cooperation,* and a *stick-to-itiveness* related to mundane activities.

Invite your child to go with you as you run errands and shop. Your child will gain valuable life skills in the process and be a ready observer of your behavior toward others. As you go through your daily routines with your child, you will have ample opportunities to exhibit values of:

- patience—whether in long supermarket lines or with an uncooperative clerk
- kindness—toward fellow shoppers
- honesty—in the purchase and exchange of goods and services
- punctuality—in keeping appointments and handling problems in a timely manner

**PLAYING TOGETHER**

While it may be quite beneficial for parents to get away by themselves from time to time, it is also important that a family have some routine "playtime" together. On a daily basis, this may be a half hour before or after dinner in which Dad plays with the kids—tossing a football around in the front yard or getting down on the floor and playing games with his young children. It may be a story-reading time or an ongoing family chess tournament that is played for ten minutes a night. Such a practice builds an understanding of rest and relaxation being in balance with work.

On a regular basis, a family might have playtimes that revolve around sporting events or other activities, such as Saturday morning at the golf course, tickets to a concert or theater series, or regular attendance at the local high school football games. Periodically the family might enjoy time away at a favorite vacation spot or an annual trip to the beach, amusement park, or into the city for a special performance of some type.

Since many games and activities are competitive—such as board or card games, or volleyball games at large family gatherings—they provide a good opportunity to teach your children the values associated with winning and losing—how to be gracious to opponents, as well as to the fans of the opposing team, whether you have won or lost. Contests of all types are an opportunity to train your child in the behaviors that reflect:

- fairness—rules apply to all who participate without partiality or preferential treatment

- honesty—admitting to faults and not cheating
- respect—for other players (and, in an extended sense, for coaches and officials) reflected both in the way the game is played and in the language that is used
- kindness—toward an injured player or one who is less skilled
- team spirit—playing as a team instead of being a "one-man band."

Not everyone can win first prize in a competition or come out a winner in a contest. But every person *can* be declared congenial and a person who displays good sportsmanship. There are those in our culture today who declare that winning isn't everything; it's the only thing. But as Christians we must hold to a higher standard: winning isn't *anything* unless Christ is honored in the process! The only true victory in life is one in which evil is defeated and the Lord Jesus is exalted.

Not all play involves competition, of course. There are those playtime activities that require cooperation, such as a puppet show, a band concert, or a theatrical production. Encourage your child to be involved in a mixture of competitive and cooperative activities. Adult life offers both types of activities, and it's important to keep them in balance. It is in cooperative play that your child will have an opportunity to learn these values:

- equality. Each position in the group is vital to the success of the whole, and each person has something to contribute.
- equanimity. Being even-tempered whether your child wins or loses.
- communication. Communication is vital in any type of cooperative effort, from playing "making believe" with a friend to undertaking a task together such as building a fort or working on the engine of a car.
- group dynamics. Participants learn how to play the roles of leader and follower, when and how to submit to authority in peer groups, and how to establish communication networks to accomplish a task successfully.

In all these activities, your child will have ample opportunity to display the values of selflessness (or self-sacrifice), generosity, and temperance (avoiding excess). What you teach your child at home about how to play—both cooperatively and competitively—readily translates into your child's behavior at school and in all of life's situations.

These four areas of home routine—family meals, worship, chores, and recreation—are vital to building a "team" atmosphere in the home.

### PERSONAL ROUTINES

It is also important for your child to have personal routines. Within the family structure, personal routines enforce the concept that no family member is an "island" into himself, but an integral part of a whole.

The child who lives in a well-ordered environment, both in time management and routine schedules, as well as a tidy and well-ordered room and home, is a child who develops an appreciation for and an understanding of structure, authority, and constancy.

Such a child has a deep and abiding sense of belonging, which relates directly to the child's self-esteem and confidence. He is also "anchored" as he faces a world that is often in turmoil or in flux. In sum, your child has a sense that he is a member of a solid, nearly unshakable, reliable force: his family. Your child not only knows in his mind he is part of the family team, but he *feels* in his heart he is part of that team. The team identity has partly become his own identity.

Personal routines play an important role, adding a sense of belonging, predictability, and satisfaction to each individual family member. Personal routines should include the following list:

- a set time each day for getting up and going to bed. Children who are on a regular schedule tend to arise more alert and sleep more soundly and peacefully.
- a set time for meals (whether or not the meals are enjoyed together as a family). It is important for a child to have regular meals in order to keep the child's energy level constant throughout the day.
- a set time for devotions, individually or as a family
- a set time for daily chores. A part of the discipline of doing chores is doing the chores according to a schedule, not whenever your child feels like doing them. Some chores may be done on a variable schedule, but usually chores should be assigned with specific time and quality parameters.
- a set time each day for doing homework

# Reciprocity: Choosing to Get Along as a Family

Reciprocity is important if a family ever hopes to be a safe haven for each family member. It requires a commitment to getting along with one another.

Nearly twenty centuries ago, Jesus summed up reciprocity in one statement: "Do unto others as you would have others do unto you." Perhaps the most important rule for human relationships ever uttered, reciprocity (the Golden Rule) requires that *each* family member be a good team player.

We hear a great deal about the importance of being a team player, not only in sports but in business. Rarely, however, is a definition provided for the characteristics of a good team player. There are at least six such qualities in my opinion:

1. both the desire and effort to contribute your best to the team
2. a willingness to sacrifice self for the benefit of the team. Each person must be willing to set aside a certain degree of their own personal likes and dislikes, wants and desires, for the benefit of the entire team.
3. a willingness to let the team leader lead
4. a willingness to compromise. Teams usually move forward more effectively and harmoniously when decisions are made by consensus. Everyone has an opportunity for input, but once a decision has been made, all team members are obligated to support it.
5. a willingness on the part of each person to keep an open mind and look for new alternatives and new ideas that will benefit the team as a whole
6. a desire and effort to solve problems as a team as problems arise

This description of a team player works as well for a family as it does for any group or organization in which a team spirit is crucial for success. Because we are dealing with Christian families as teams, I believe there is another vitally important quality to add: a willingness to share one's life and faith with others on the team.

A renowned heart surgeon once said that the competition in his field had led him to perfect his techniques to a stellar level, but he did not share his techniques with his colleagues. When he later developed cancer and had only months to live, however, his attitude changed dramatically; he wanted to impart all of his knowledge to others. How much more might have been accomplished by this brilliant man if he had been a team player throughout his career!

It's important that you, as a parent, impart to your child what you know about life and, specifically, what you believe about God and have experienced in your relationship with Him. So many parents have never shared with their children how they came to know the Lord and to accept Him as their personal Savior.

In turn, your children should feel quite free to share the spiritual experiences they have and to talk openly about their doubts, fears, and questions regarding God, the Scriptures, and the many practical ramifications of living out a personal faith in an unbelieving world.

# A Clear Delineation of Responsibilities and Roles

Teamwork involves sharing the load.

In team sports, players quickly learn that they fill a "position" that is vital to the success of the team. If they fail to perform their role to the best of their ability, all other members of the team suffer to a certain extent. Some positions have greater responsibility than others and, therefore, have greater authority. But all positions on a team are important.

Successful teams have certain characteristics in common, whether they are teams in sports, business, industry, government, or education. These same characteristics apply to team-building in a family:

### POSITIVE LEADERSHIP

Every successful team has a leader—a person who generally has the greatest authority and, therefore, the greatest responsibility. A developmental psychologist, Thomas Lickona said it well: "Without somebody in charge, you can't run a family, a school, or a country. When people don't respect authority, things don't work very well, and everybody suffers."

Confidence, competence, and compassion are essential qualities in a successful leader. In the home, parents must lead. This may seem obvious, but in many homes across our nation it is the children who are setting schedules and agendas, forcing priorities, and calling key decisions.

### CLEARLY DEFINED, MEASURABLE OBJECTIVES

As we discussed in a previous chapter, most people have only the most general goals for their lives, if any. Successful people, however, have clear objectives toward which they direct and focus their energies.

### AN ACTION PLAN TO ACHIEVE OBJECTIVES

"Plan your work, and then work your plan" is a saying that is common in business-planning seminars. An action plan requires you to focus your attention on specific objectives, establish priorities related to them, coordinate efforts among all parties involved to reach the goal to impart a sense of shared responsibility among the team members, and then work together to reach the goal.

## SPECIFIC ROLE CLARIFICATION

Each member of a team must know precisely what is expected of him or her, to whom they are responsible, and the length of time in which a task must be accomplished.

## OPEN, CLEAR COMMUNICATION

All team members must have ready access to the people and information they need to perform efficiently and effectively.

Give all members of the family as much information as possible about what is happening in any given situation. Like all social organizations, the family thrives on information.

The "strong, silent type" may make a strong movie character, but it is not a leadership style that works well in families. Answer your child's questions to the best of your ability and to the best of his or her ability to understand your answer. Give your child information in advance about what she might expect in new situations. Explain to your child how things work, and why. You don't have to know it all to be a good parent, but you do have to be willing to share what you know.

I never advocate "talking down" to a child, but you should always speak at your child's level of comprehension. Explain things in terms your child can understand. Use language that is familiar to him. Make sure that you have reached an understanding with your child, not merely said your piece.

Of equal importance to being able to speak clearly is the ability to listen carefully. Communication is a two-sided coin—speaking and listening—and a good communicator will know when to do both.

I once heard of a girl who stayed home from school with a virus. Although ill, she was not too ill to study, read, or play quietly. In the morning the girl's mom said, "I want you to do your homework while I'm gone." The child agreed, but discovered after her mother had left for work that the assignment involved an interview with a parent!

Upon arriving home at the end of the day, the mother discovered that her daughter had not completed her homework, and a fairly prolonged discussion ensued. While the mother repeatedly accused her daughter of willfully ignoring her homework, feigning more illness than she had, and disobeying her, the girl kept interjecting, "But I couldn't . . . ." Finally, the girl handed her homework assignment to her mother. You can imagine the chagrin the mother felt when she saw at the top of the page: "Interview Mom or Dad." They spent the next hour doing the interview and agreed that they still had a few communication glitches to work out in their relationship.

Family meetings can sometimes be very helpful in improving overall communication. The idea of family meetings has been presented by numerous people through the years. Some advocate family meetings for coordinating schedules and setting goals. Others advocate family meetings as a forum for resolving family squabbles and differences of opinion.

A family meeting differs from a dinner-time conversation in two important ways: the meeting has an agenda, a reason for meeting; and the meeting has a set protocol of some type for conducting the business-at-hand. Generally speaking, family meetings provide an opportunity for every person in a family to express himself and be included in the information-sharing or decision-making process.

Regardless of the reason that you hold a regular meeting of all the members of your family, you can enhance that meeting by using part of your meeting time to:

- discuss ways in which your family is different from other families, and why
- discuss things you like about your family (be specific)
- discuss your broad family goals (what type of people you are attempting to help one another become)

Regarding communication, you also may want to bring up one or more of these questions as part of a family meeting:

- Do we openly share our feelings with one another?
- Do we talk with, not at, one another?
- Are we courteous and civil to one another?
- Do we speak in ways that communicate trust and love for one another?
- Do we give one another the opportunity to make mistakes?
- Do we help one another to succeed?
- Do we take joy in one another's successes?

## FOCUS ON STRENGTHS AND POTENTIAL

Each family member has strengths and untapped potential. Successful team-building harnesses the strengths of each person and uses those strengths to compensate for built-in weaknesses. Each member is encouraged to recognize and develop his own potential within the context of helping the family as a whole.

*Admit to Imperfection.* Admit to your own weaknesses and failures, and let your child know what you intend to do to overcome them.

You fail; your child will fail. That's life. The important thing to convey to your child is that we learn from our failures and, in most cases, are able to pick ourselves up and move on to greater successes. Teach your child—by example—this critical concept.

Don't try to present a foolproof, failure-resistant, error-free image to your child. He will attempt to live up to your pseudo-perfect example and experience great disappointment later in life—not only in his own failures, but in the realization that you weren't genuine with him.

Do present to your child the image of a parent who is willing to learn from mistakes and move forward after making them. Such an image is one that compels your child to continually strive for excellence and maintain an openness toward learning and growing throughout his life.

*Support in Good Times and Bad.* Find ways to help your children support each other, in both good times and bad. Recognize that every individual goes through various growth spurts of all kinds—physical, intellectual, emotional, relational, and spiritual. Those times are always more stressful for an individual. The same holds true for families as a whole. Support one another in special ways during those times.

You can help prepare your child to support other family members during bad times by emphasizing support for other family members in good times!

Encourage your children to do their chores together, or for one child to agree to cover the chores for another in a pinch, and vice versa. You may even want to assign some all-children chores, such as washing the family car. If one child is good at geometry and the other is good at spelling, encourage them to help each other with their homework.

Let your children do some things together without your direct supervision. Perhaps you can give them sufficient cash and let them get a list of designated groceries while you go next door and pick up the hardware items you need.

## HIGH EXPECTATIONS

Like a team, each family member is regarded as highly essential to the success of the family as a whole. Much is expected, frequently more than some members of the family may think they are capable of being or doing. Goals are challenging to everybody, and in a successful family effort, team members help one another to develop their abilities and skills.

## SHARED RESPONSIBILITY

Teams are formed from individuals with a variety of skills and abilities, melded together to achieve a common goal. Success requires that each family member knows and accepts his responsibility within the family. Most people are quite willing to do this if they sense other family members' faith in them.

Allow your child to participate in meaningful decisions. Richard M. DeVos, for many years the president of one of the nation's leading corporations, and his wife had a practice of allowing their children to participate in deciding where the family's philanthropic dollars would go. Periodically, the family sat down at the dining room table and discussed the requests they had received from various organizations seeking their financial help. After discussing how much money they had to give, DeVos and his family then decided how much, if any, should go to each requester. Each child, without regard to age, had an opportunity to voice an opinion.

### CONTINUOUS EVALUATION

A continuous evaluation of plans and their execution is necessary for continued success. Family members need the reinforcement of periodic successes. They also need to learn why certain efforts have not succeeded. The focus of evaluation should be on the overall plan and its execution, not on the temporary failure of an individual. An individual's failure rarely scuttles the opportunity for family success.

Talk to your child privately about areas that both you and he perceive to be lacking. Talk to your spouse periodically about the overall direction you believe your family is taking. There are no "grades" to be awarded for family success; nevertheless, evaluation should be ongoing, periodic, and intentional.

## Developing a Working Plan for Team-Building

How can routine, reciprocity, responsibilities, and roles translate into a working plan for *your* family?

### DEVELOP A PLAN

With your spouse—or with other adults who have a shared responsibility for training your child (i.e., grandparents)—set specific objectives that you desire for your family, and also develop a plan for achieving those objectives. Here are seven objectives set by one family I know:

1. prepare each child to be a positive and contributing member of the church
2. prepare each child for college or some other form of higher education

3. prepare each child to live independently after graduation from college
4. prepare each child to be a loving spouse and parent
5. help each child discover his or her unique aptitudes and talents
6. prepare each child to be a good citizen in the community
7. help each child learn work habits that will make him a valued employee or employer in whatever field he enters

Under each of these objectives, it's fairly easy to see the types of plans and priorities that were listed by these parents. I've included several examples under each goal.

*Objective*: Prepare each child to be a positive and contributing member of the church.

*Plan*: Attend church, Sunday school, vacation Bible school regularly; pray together *as a family* on a daily basis; encourage each child to read the Bible for himself, and purchase a Bible for each child that he can read and understand; get involved in one outreach or ministry activity sponsored by the church, *as a family.*

In this particular family, the parents also decided that the hour after a family breakfast on Saturday morning would be a good time for Dad to lead a brief Bible study.

*Objective:* Prepare each child for college or some other form of higher education.

*Plan:* Encourage school performance and be present at all parent-teacher conferences and school performances in which the child participates. Talk about the importance of higher education in the normal course of family conversations. Drive through or tour college campuses as a part of family vacations. Read daily with each child and discuss what has been read.

Mom and Dad decided to alternate the "read daily" activity with their children. The parent who had reading responsibilities didn't have to help with dinner preparation or clean-up that day.

*Objective*: Prepare each child to live independently after graduation from college.

*Plan*: Train each child in skills related to laundry, meal preparation, house cleaning, yard upkeep, financial planning and bill paying, and health and nutrition. Mom and Dad divided these responsibilities between them. As much as possible, the family opted to do chores, errands, and meal preparation together.

Once a month, Mom would sit down with each child to go over their "financial accounts" with them.

*Objective*: Prepare each child to be a loving spouse and parent.

*Plan*: Be affectionate to each other (spouses) in the presence of the children, and be affectionate with each child. Spend as much time together as a family as possible. (This young couple realized that within ten years all of their children would be eighteen. Ten years of intentional effort to spend concentrated amounts of time together as a family didn't seem to be an overly burdensome task!) Give children opportunities to help care for younger siblings and cousins.

*Objective:* Help each child discover his or her unique aptitudes and talents.

*Plan*: Allow each child to participate in various clubs and to take extracurricular lessons as the child expresses an interest. (Mom and Dad volunteer their time as mentors, coaches, chaperones, and teachers' aides as much as possible.) Give each child aptitude testing to discover his or her unique talents no later than the second year of high school.

*Objective:* Prepare each child to be a good citizen in the community.

*Plan:* Get involved in at least one volunteer community activity *as a family*. Take children to political rallies, voting booths, local city council, and neighborhood meetings. Discuss the political process. Encourage children to pray for national, state, and local leaders. Tour the state capitol as a family.

*Objective*: Help each child learn work habits that will make him a valued employee or employer in whatever field he chooses.

*Plan*: Assign chores to each child, and require that the chores be completed to your satisfaction.

Open a savings account for each child and require that a portion of her earnings be deposited into it. Help each child get a summer job at age fifteen. Provide opportunities for each child to earn money beyond an allowance by doing "extra" chores around the house.

Writing down these objectives, and ideas on how to implement them, was not a prolonged process for these parents. They went away for one romantic weekend together and spent several hours of that time talking about their family. Doing this on an annual basis allowed them to tailor specific goals and plans to the ages of the children.

### SHARE THE PLAN WITH ALL INVOLVED

Tell your children what you consider to be your family goals and plans. Don't leave them in the dark to figure it out for themselves. Let them know you consider them to be valuable participants in executing the plans. You may want to post your family goals where every member of the family can see them. Let each person know how he fits into the plans and what is required of him.

### REVIEW AND DISCUSS FAMILY OBJECTIVES AND PLANS

How might the objectives be fine-tuned? Periodically discuss how each member is doing in attaining personal and overall goals. Are there areas that need to be emphasized? Does a family member need help? Is more information required?

None of these conversations needs to be conducted in a formal manner. You can discuss family goals in a casual atmosphere using a warm but direct tone of voice and have just as much impact as if you called a "formal meeting." The key is to be *intentional* about doing this. Give thought to where you are going as a family, and why. Discuss your family life. Explore the many ways in which you can help and encourage each other even more, so that each member of your family feels valued, helped, encouraged, and uplifted.

# Taking Responsibility for Personal Problems

Although reciprocity is critically important, so is the taking of personal responsibility for one's own behavior. Make it clear to your child that although there are many areas of shared responsibility within the family, each person is ultimately responsible for her own faith walk, habits, and attitudes.

### OWNERSHIP OF PERSONAL PROBLEMS

The story is told of a small mining town in the Midwest where everyone complained constantly, feeling as though he or she had more problems than the next person, that he had been dealt a stacked deck in life. The complaining continued for years until it reached epidemic proportions.

Fed up with the complaints, the wise mayor of the town finally called a town meeting at the well in the center of town. All the town folk showed up, and each was given a pencil, a piece of paper, and a small bag. The mayor said, "I want everyone to list his problems—debts, responsibilities, ailments, and anything else you consider to be a burden." The townspeople murmured at this, and some were heard to comment that one sheet of paper wouldn't be enough for their list, but all did as they were instructed. Then the mayor told the people to place their lists inside the bag they had been given.

After the people had done this, he said, "You now have a choice. You can toss your bag into the well and take turns retrieving a bag of problems, which, in turn, will become your new personal problems to solve. Or, you can each take your own bag of problems home and deal with them the best you can."

Not one person volunteered to toss his bag into the well and assume the unknown problems of another, and not another public complaint was uttered in the town.

Life is a series of challenges—the evidence of which you can find on the front page of any newspaper you pick up. Some psychologists have speculated that people read newspapers, not for the sake of news, but to remind themselves that other people have problems greater than their own. They draw comfort in knowing that as important and demanding as their problems may be, others face even tougher problems.

Handling our hurts and problems is a major part of life—as one person has said, it's the part found between being born and dying! Author of *The Road Less Traveled,* M. Scott Peck has written about life's problems: "It is in the whole process of meeting and solving problems that life has meaning. Problems are the cutting edge that distinguishes between success and failure. Problems call forth courage and wisdom; indeed, they create our courage and wisdom. It is only because of problems that we grow mentally and spiritually. It is through the pain of confronting and resolving problems that we learn."

Even as you attempt to build a team spirit in your family, you must allow each person to take ownership of his or her personal problems. The family is not the resolver of personal problems; the family is a support system for helping each individual within the family resolve personal problems.

We err when we attempt to "cover" with the cloak of family identity the personal weaknesses and flaws of an individual family member. Families should provide a foundation in the struggle to conquer life's problems and learn from them, not an alibi to avoid confronting tough times and tough problems. The same holds true for personal responsibility and completing one's tasks or roles within a family.

### OWNERSHIP OF PERFORMANCE

One of the practices that kindergartners enjoy mastering is the signing of their names to everything they do. This practice serves multiple purposes. It helps the children with writing skills and helps them to learn to spell their names. It also allows teachers and students to identify everyone's work. Perhaps the most valuable lesson the children learn, however, is that of taking pride and responsibility for their own work.

A growing number of companies are also requiring their employees to "sign their work." This includes line work in factories. Component parts, for example, can be traced back to specific workers as a means of quality control and subsequent correction or reward. Studies have shown that when workers sign their names to their work, they take more pride in what they do and they also produce a better product. It is a practice that is good for both morale and accountability. It is only when a person begins to think, *Who will know?* or *Who will care?* that workers and students alike fail to give their best effort.

Every person in a family needs to be required to "sign" the work he or she does. In other words, there needs to be a means of recognizing who did which chores, who caused negatives, and who produced positives. Children need to know that parents care about the quality of their work and that they reward good effort and achievement. In a very practical way, you can require your children to sign off on "chore lists" that are posted for the entire family.

The reward aspect of a child's efforts within the family should be related directly to the quality of a child's performance. Note that this has nothing to do with *love*—we are to love our children regardless of their performance. We love them because of *who* they are and because they are God's creation bestowed to us for our care and nurture, not because of *what* they do. Rewards, however, should be geared to goals and the accomplishment of assigned responsibilities. At times, the wisest reward we can give is to present a child with the fruit of his own labor.

Many years ago a wealthy rancher decided to retire. He told his foreman of his decision and said, "I will be traveling for the next year, but I have one more project I want you to undertake. While I'm gone, I want you to develop my remaining five hundred acres into a cattle ranch. I have authorized the bank to release fifty thousand dollars for this project. I want it to be the best in the West. When I return, we will celebrate my retirement."

The foreman set out to develop the ranch as he had been authorized, but as he did so, he began to think, *If my boss sells his assets when he retires, I'm going to be without a job. I'd better provide for myself.* So, he began cutting corners, using inferior products and inflating costs so he might swindle money from the rancher.

The year passed and the owner returned. He called a meeting with his foreman. "For twenty years you have served me faithfully," he said. "This past year you have built a cattle ranch on five hundred undeveloped acres. I'm now giving you that ranch. Enjoy it and prosper. Thanks for all you have done."

Every job is a self-portrait of the person who did it.

In matching a reward to a task, a parent must be very careful to reward the effort according to a child's *ability* to do the job. Just as you wouldn't expect a five-year-old child to carry a thirty-pound suitcase aboard an airplane, so you shouldn't expect a child to do an adult's job. Take into consideration the effort involved and the time required, as well as the quality of the finished product.

The story is told of a group of villagers who decided to honor a retiring missionary doctor for his help to them. One of the gifts given to the doctor was a handmade bowl. It was presented to him by an elderly gentleman from a neighboring village some thirty miles away. With tears in his eyes, the doctor thanked the man, noting that he had walked a long way to give him such a special gift. The elderly man replied, "Long walk part of gift."

A child is *learning* to become a responsible adult. The effort—evidence of discipline, hard work, perseverance—is as worthy of acknowledgment as the actual completion of a task. A wise parent acknowledges a willingness to try, an improvement in performance, and diligence and perseverance in rewarding his child for the completion of a chore or task.

Good coaches certainly do this, calling out, "Great job! Good effort! Good workout today!" to individual players. These words of encouragement are not only for those who catch all the passes, make all the plays, or come across the finish line first. They are words of encouragement to all players who give their best effort and who are diligently seeking to improve their performance.

### SELF-EVALUATION OF PERFORMANCE

Children quickly learn that others will judge their work, and that these judgments can make them feel good or bad. Over time, your child needs to learn to evaluate his own work, praise his own efforts, and motivate himself to do better where he has failed. The child who learns to do this will likely become a confident adult with a high degree of success.

# The Waltons: A Family Team

The Walton family, founders of Wal-Mart stores across America, has long employed the team-building strategies identified in this chapter.

Let me share with you a number of quotes from various family members that appear in the best-seller, *Sam Walton: Made in America.*

- "Helen and I did the best we could to promote a sense of togetherness in the family, and we made sure our children had a chance to participate in the same sorts of things we did as kids." (p. 68)
- "I always tried to be home on Friday nights so I would miss very few of their games. . . . We all went to church and Sunday school." (p. 68)
- "Helen and I made it a point to take the whole family out and spend time traveling or camping together. I think that time we spent together has had a lot to do with our close relationship as a family today." (p. 70)
- "We learned to work together, and everybody had their chores, and at night we prayed together. He went out of his way to spend time with us, and he was fun to be with."—Alice Walton (p. 71)
- "We have been happy together, but we've stayed independent to pursue our own interests as well." (p. 76)

Finally, let me share with you Sam Walton's "Rules for Building a Business," which also apply directly to your family and your efforts to build a strong family with a vibrant team spirit. From Sam Walton's original rules, I have replaced "business" or "company" with the word *family*. Any place that mentioned associates or partners has been changed to read *family members*. And "customers" was replaced with the word *children*.

Rule 1:  Commit to your family.

Rule 2:  Share your profits with all your family members, and treat them as such.

Rule 3:  Motivate your family members.

Rule 4:  Communicate everything you possibly can to your family members.

Rule 5:  Appreciate everything your family members do for the family.

Rule 6:  Celebrate your successes.

Rule 7:  Listen to everyone in your family.

Rule 8:  Exceed your children's expectations.

Rule 9:  Control your expenses better than your competition.

Rule 10:  Swim upstream.

# Chapter 8

# *Tool #2: Creating a Climate*

*Rules imposed by external constraint remain
external to a child's spirit. Rules due to
mutual respect and cooperation take
root inside the child's mind.*
—Jean Piaget, Educator and
Developmental Psychologist

*Fix your thoughts on what is true and good
and right. Think about things that are pure
and lovely, and dwell on the fine, good things
in others. Think about all you can praise
God for and be glad about.*
—Philippians 4:8, TLB

*I*n "Apology at Bedtime," Jackie Gleason presented a poignant picture of the family climate we often are guilty of creating for our children:

> *Listen, son, I'm saying this to you as you lie asleep, one little hand crumpled under your cheek, blond curls on your forehead. I've just stolen into your room, alone. A few minutes ago, as I sat reading my paper in the den, a hot, stifling wave of remorse swept over me. I couldn't resist it and, guiltily, I came to your bedside.*
>
> *These are the things I was thinking, son. I had been cross. I scolded you as you were dressing for school because you gave your face just a dab with a towel. I took you to task for not cleaning your shoes. I called out angrily when I found you had thrown some of your things on the floor. And at breakfast too, I found fault. You spilled things. You put your elbows on the table. You spread butter too thick on your bread. As you started off to play and I made for my car, you turned and waved your little hand and called, "Good-bye, Daddy," and I frowned and said in reply, "Straighten your shoulders."*

*And then it began all over again in the late afternoon. As I
came up the hill, I spied you down on your knees playing mar-
bles. There were holes in your stockings and I humiliated you before your boy friends by making you march ahead of me back to
the house. "Stockings are expensive, and if you had to buy them,
you'd be more careful." Imagine that, son, from a father. Such
stupid logic! And, do you remember, later, when I was sitting in
the den, how you came in softly and timidly with a sort of hurt
look in your eyes, and I glanced up over my paper, impatient at
the interruption? You hesitated at the door. "What is it you want?"
I snapped. You said nothing but ran across, in one plunge, and
threw your arms around my neck and kissed me again and
again, and your small arms tightened with an affection that God
had set blooming in your heart and which even neglect could not
wither, and then you were gone, pattering up the stairs.*

*Well, son, it was shortly afterward that my paper slipped from
my hands and a terrible, sickening fear came over me. Suddenly I
saw my horrible selfishness and I felt sick at heart. What was habit
doing to me? The habit of complaining, of finding fault, of repri-
manding. All of these were my reward to you for being only a small
boy. It wasn't that I didn't love you; it was that I expected too much
of you. I was measuring you by the yardstick of my own age, and
son, I'm sorry. I promise never to let my impatience, my nervous-
ness, my worries, ever again muddle or conceal my love for you.*

This monologue presents, in my opinion, a classic example of a parent unwittingly creating a "negative climate" for his child. The father
didn't *intend* to hurt his son—in fact, quite the contrary! He intended
to help him become a fine, upstanding adult. But, along the way, he
*did* hurt his son by failing to create a positive climate in which his child
might take risks and yet feel unconditional love.

The great likelihood is that if you don't make a conscious effort to
create a positive climate in your home, you are going to create a negative one by default.

## The Great Blessing of a Happy Home

A research study of students chosen for *Who's Who Among American
High School Students* revealed some startling results. The students selected for this survey had at least a *B* average in school, were involved

in school or community activities, and had demonstrated leadership. More than three thousand teens were polled.

The survey asked students whether they lived in happy or unhappy homes, and it also asked students about their behavior as teens. Among the findings:

- Teens were nearly five times more likely to smoke if they came from unhappy homes.
- Teens from unhappy homes were twice as likely to drink to the point of being drunk.
- Two percent of teens from happy homes admitted to attempting suicide, while 18 percent from unhappy homes said they had tried to take their own lives.
- Twenty percent of those from happy homes admitted to sexual activity, while 46 percent from unhappy homes had engaged in premarital sex.
- Those from unhappy homes said they were more likely to have sex with a stranger than those from happy homes (44 percent compared to 30 percent).

The survey did not ask about a student's religious beliefs or affiliations, nor did it ask about the spiritual climate of their family. The students were mostly white and had attended public schools. More than half of them came from small towns or rural areas, from families with incomes between thirty thousand and seventy thousand dollars. Any person analyzing the data would likely conclude that these students were among the "cream" of American youth.

Yet 78 percent of those surveyed said they had cheated in school, 19 percent said they drink alcoholic beverages at least monthly, and 17 percent admitted to having stolen something from a store in the previous five years.[1]

An unhappy home can have devastating consequences.

### DEFINING THE HAPPY HOME

The phrase "happy home" struck a cord in me. I recall reading a little booklet written many years ago by A. G. Hobbs, which identified eight traits of a home marked by happiness and harmony. Most of these have been mentioned elsewhere in this book, but I believe they are worth repeating here:

*1. Love abounds.* The happy home is one where a close tie of love binds parents and children together. Love, said the apostle Paul, is the "bond of perfectness" (Col. 3:14, KJV).

*2. Peace prevails.* No home can be happy unless it is free from nagging and fussing. In order for a home to be marked by peace, there must be:

- kindness. Proverbs 19:22 tells us, "What is desirable in a man is his kindness" (NASB).

- the Golden Rule. Jesus taught, "Therefore all things whatsoever ye would that men should do unto you, do ye even so to them: for this is the law and the prophets" (Matt. 7:12, KJV).

- confession of faults. James 5:16 says, "Confess your faults one to another, and pray one for another, that ye may be healed. The effectual fervent prayer of a righteous man availeth much." We must discuss frankly the problems that arise and come to an understanding, rather than give in to the tendency to sulk or pout.

- forgiveness. Ephesians 4:32 commands, "And be ye kind one to another, tenderhearted, forgiving one another, even as God for Christ's sake hath forgiven you."

- courtesy. We should be as courteous to those in our families as we are to those outside the family.

*3. Order and system exist.* There should be a place for everything and everything kept in its place. Chores and responsibilities should be fairly distributed, with each person doing his share.

*4. Discipline is maintained.* Discipline and correction are vital if a child is to learn right from wrong. Discipline instills in a child the ability to ride out the storms of life and to adopt a "give and take" relationship with others. It is the ship that is well-anchored that has the ability to ride the rough waves and not careen into a rocky shoreline.

*5. Fundamental principles of Christianity are taught.* Very specifically, Hobbs advocated that these Christian principles need to be taught in the home:

- an emphasis on spiritual things. Children should be taught that "life is real, and life is earnest; and the grave is not the goal." This does not rob life of its pleasure but adds meaning to it.

- respect. Children must be taught to respect God, Christ, and the church. They must also show respect for all adults—especially parents—and the aged. Lastly, children must respect those in authority and the rights of others, including their wishes and their property.

- responsibility. Children should be taught that accountability implies responsibility, and that we all are accountable to God for what we do with our lives and the resources we are given.
- humility. A parent can encourage a child and commend their work, and at the same time, teach a child humility before God.

6. *Everyone recognizes his right place and stays in it.* The line of authority is maintained. No parent should ever abdicate his or her responsibility and authority to a young child. In Hobbs' ideal home, "everyone recognizes his rightful and God-given place and tries humbly to fulfill the obligations of the same."

7. *There is an impartiality and fairness to all.* No child is favored over another. There is fair distribution and consideration of finances, as well.

8. *Christianity is practiced.* Christian principles are not only taught but lived out. Children learn from the good examples of their parents.

Hobbs concludes, "There can be no real and lasting happiness apart from hope."[2] The happy home is one in which each person has a faith in God and a hope for the future.

Note that these are all *positive* behaviors and attributes. The fact is, a happy home is a positive home. I believe there are four positives that are essential to creating the kind of happy home that Hobbs describes:

1. *positive presence* by parents
2. a prevailing attitude and hope for a *positive future*
3. *positive potential* emphasized continually
4. *positive freedoms* given

Let's take a look at each of these positives as they work together to create a happy climate for your home.

# Positive Presence of Both Parents

The most positive thing you can do to create a positive climate in your home is to be present for your child, physically and emotionally.

Running out the door and shouting "I love you!" to your children as you leave for your work day is not being "present" to your child emotionally.

I must confess that I did not learn that lesson easily. As a young father, I loved my two sons, Billy and Michael, but I was so driven to be a successful high school coach that I left much of the parenting to my wife, Carolyn.

I was ambitious and wanted to provide nice things for my family. Since my salary as a coach and teacher didn't provide much, I got a job working at the post office during the Christmas holidays one year. I worked all night long—11 P.M. to 7 A.M.—taught school all day, coached basketball practice in the afternoon, went home, caught a few hours of sleep, and then went to work again at the post office. If you had asked me why I was doing this, I would have said, "To give good things to my family." Yet I was giving very little of myself to the family.

I developed a bad cold, but since I didn't want to quit working, I went to a physician and got a big dose of penicillin so I could keep going. That night at the post office I started to break out in big hives all over my body. My face, neck, and arms began to swell, and suddenly I was in severe pain; but I finished my shift. At seven that morning, I went home and collapsed. I called the doctor, and he told me to get to the hospital immediately. There they pumped me full of medication, but the condition worsened.

I spent two weeks in the hospital but still was no better. The doctors were very concerned and said they needed to inject a drug into my bloodstream to kill the penicillin mold, the source of the problem. The treatment was dangerous but necessary.

Before the treatment began, I wanted to see my two young sons. Carolyn dressed them up, brought them to the hospital parking lot, and held them up so I could see them and wave to them from my hospital room window. Looking out at those two boys, I suddenly realized that I loved those two children with all my heart. I had let my job so completely dominate my life that I barely knew them. I recognized that my priorities were totally out of line, and I made the decision that if I got out of that hospital I was going to change things.

The treatment was successful, and I was able to go home. I lived my life differently from that point on. My family came first, and then my job.

Being "present" for your children means that you
- spend time with them
- listen to them
- do things with them
- rejoice when they rejoice
- feel sad when they are sad

To a child, your presence is the best present you can give!

If you are a single parent, you will need to make a double effort to be present for your child. If you are divorced, encourage your child to spend as much quality, positive time as possible with the parent who does not live with you. If you are relying on grandparents to help you in the parenting process, encourage your child to spend quality time with those grandparents.

## REGARDLESS OF YOUR CHILD'S MOOD

It is important that you continue to be "present" for your child regardless of your child's behavior, mood, or prevailing attitude. Moods and attitudes are volatile, especially in teens. Don't allow your child to stay locked up in his room for extended periods. Require your child to be a part of the family and to remain accessible to you. (You, actually, are choosing to remain accessible to your child.) Insist that your child talk out some of his problems.

I recently heard of a grandmother who was partially responsible for the care of her son's children. She lived in the home with her son and three grandchildren, and, over time, she took on the responsibility of praying at bedtime with each child. She adopted a policy of allowing a child to go two nights without saying bedtime prayers. She allowed the child the freedom *not* to talk to God in her presence. At such times, she prayed aloud for her grandchild. On the third night, however, she insisted that the child talk to God about what it was that was bothering him or her, and to confess the reason for the estrangement the child was feeling. She said, "I believe it is wrong to let a child build up guilt that can so easily be erased through acceptance of God's forgiveness. It's also dangerous to let a child drift away from a daily walking-and-talking relationship with God."

Allow for your child's moods, but be present physically, emotionally and spiritually, even when he may not want to talk. If the mood persists, insist that your child communicate with you.

Some parents shy away from such confrontations and encounters because they don't want to "rock the boat." Confrontations may, indeed, become a bit explosive, but in the end your relationship with your child is likely to be stronger. Maintain your cool and don't let your child's statements become the source of an ongoing argument. Let your child vent his anger, frustration, or concerns, and assure him of your love for him and that you will take into consideration any accusations he has brought against you.

## CONTINUE TO LEAD

A leader continues to lead regardless of the behavior of those who follow. In other words, the behavior of a leader is not contingent upon the behavior of followers.

A parent continues to love, continues to spend time with his or her children, continues to lead by example, continues to teach and nurture and admonish and encourage, regardless of results. There is no giving up or giving in as a parent!

A modern-day parable has been told of a young woman who went to see a counselor who asked her, "Which of your three children do you love the most?" She answered quickly, "I love all my children the same." The counselor thought the answer had been too quick and too glib, so he probed a bit. "You love all three of your children the same? I think its psychologically impossible for anyone to regard any three human beings exactly the same."

The young woman broke down, cried a little, and then said, "All right, I confess. I do not love all three of my children the same. When one of my three children is sick, I love that child more than I normally do. When one of my three children is in pain or lost, I love that child more than I normally do. When one of my children is confused, I love that child more than I normally do. And when one of my children is bad—not just a little naughty but really bad—I love that child more than I normally do. But except for those exceptions, I do love all three of my children about the same."

I believe God loves us as this young mother loved her children. He doesn't change in His love for us—only in the generosity of His expression of that love.

A parent may need to spend more time with a child or give a child a little more attention during certain periods of the child's life. There's no point, however, at which a parent is privileged to abandon his or her post or allow the child to dictate the values, habits, and attitudes that prevail in a family.

## LISTENING TAKES TIME

Be committed to spending the time it takes to listen with an open heart. Listening takes time, and your time is something your child deeply desires. In fact, your child can never receive enough of your time, attention, and love. This does not mean, of course, that you should "smother" your child with attention and love. True love is manifested when we know how much attention and contact a child needs.

The emphasis in recent years has been on parents giving their children "quality time." While this is very important, it can never be a substitute for availability. Children not only need quality experiences with their parents. They also need as much time with parents as is possible.

A statement about grandparents is one that depicts what many a child would desire to see in a parent:

*A grandmother is a lady who has no children of her own. She likes other people's little girls and boys. A grandfather is a man grandmother. He goes for walks with the boys, and they talk about fishing and stuff like that.*

*Grandmothers don't have to do anything except to be there. They're old, so they shouldn't play hard or run. It is enough if they drive us to the market where the pretend horse is, and have a lot of dimes ready. Or if they take us for walks, they should slow down past things like pretty leaves and caterpillars. They should never say "hurry up."*

*Usually grandmothers are fat, but not too fat to tie your shoes. They wear glasses and funny underwear. They can take their teeth and gums off. Grandmothers don't have to be smart, only answer questions like, "Why isn't God married," and "How come dogs chase cats?"*

*Grandmothers don't talk baby-talk like visitors do, because it is hard to understand. When they read to us they don't skip or mind if it is the same story over again.*

*Everybody should try to have a grandmother, especially if they don't have television, because they are the only grown-ups who have time. [Author unknown.]*

## A CLIMATE FOR LISTENING

Parents often seem surprised when their child misbehaves or says something they consider to be totally inappropriate or in error. The likelihood is that they haven't been listening to the small messages, or alert to the small signals, that the child has been sending all along.

The story is told of a little boy who yelled loudly at a Thanksgiving feast, "Please pass the butter!" All conversation at the table stopped, and the boy's mother looked at him sternly and immediately sent him to his room.

After dinner, one of the relatives present at the family gathering said she had recorded the conversation at dinner to share it with a relative who had been unable to attend. She started to play a little of the tape, and the entire family was surprised to hear a quiet and polite little voice say, "Please pass the butter." There was no response, and a little later on the tape they heard the voice again, this time just a little louder, "Please pass the butter." Again, there was no response on the tape. A third time the voice asked, a little louder still, "Please pass the butter." When no response was given this time, they all heard the child's shout, "PLEASE PASS THE BUTTER!"

It wasn't that the child had failed to ask politely and insistently. It was the others at the table—so caught up in their own conversations—who had not listened.

Listening is an important part of building a climate of trust, value-rich behavior, and positive attitudes within a family. Unless you listen and know what it is that your child is thinking and believing, you as a parent will have a difficult time knowing if you are succeeding in your parenting goals, or determining which corrections need to be made and how to go about them.

## Staying Positive about the Future

One of the greatest inspirational leaders of our nation was born in a small Alabama town in 1880. At the age of only nineteen months, she became both blind and deaf. As a child, she lived in a world marked mainly by frustration.

A young teacher named Anne Sullivan sought a way to help this severely handicapped student, and the student, Helen Adams Keller, responded. Soon she learned to communicate through the sense of touch, but Helen Keller didn't stop there. She stretched her abilities to the utmost, and in the course of her life, she became a celebrity. With the aid of a faithful interpreter, she spoke all over the world. She wrote approximately a dozen books, and she lifted the spirits of millions of people.

Helen Keller always thought she could do more, and so she did. She lived her life in sharp contrast to most blind and/or deaf people of her time, who resigned themselves to a life of misery and self-pity.

What you believe about yourself and your world determines to a great extent the climate you create within your family. If you believe that the future holds great promise, you and your children will work for the fulfillment of that promise and be optimistic about your success. On the other hand, if you believe the future holds nothing but gloom, you will be reluctant or nonchalant about tomorrow's dawn; and you will likely become a family that exhibits laziness, laxness, and pessimism.

## Positive about Your Potential

The greatest barrier in your child's life is likely to exist in his own mind. The barrier will be low and worn with travel if your child believes that he has the potential to be and do more than at present. The barrier will be high and virtually impassable if your child believes that he has reached the full capacity of his life.

Once a lion was kept in a rather frail-looking cage. A visitor stood in awe at the animal's physical stature—its powerful, well-developed muscles, its rich coat and proud mane, and its gleaming eyes. The animal looked the epitome of strength and pride. The cage, in contrast, appeared flimsy and about to fall apart.

He asked the caretaker, "Is that cage really as fragile as it looks?"

The caretaker replied, "It isn't a strong cage at all."

"Then why doesn't the lion break out and escape?" countered the surprised visitor.

The caretaker explained, "When this lion was first caged he was just a cub, not strong enough to break these bars. He learned he wasn't capable of breaking out of the cage, and he soon quit trying."

"But now," the visitor noted, "there's no doubt that those bars couldn't hold him if he wanted to break out."

"True," the caretaker admitted. "But he doesn't think he can escape, so he'll never try."

How true this is for so many young people today! Their minds are locked within four walls: self-doubt, poor self-image, fear of failure, and low self-confidence. They are in a cage of mental barriers. Sadly, few will ever test the invisible barriers that hold them back, or discover that much of what they perceive to be holding them back is a misconception.

From my many years in the public school systems of this nation, I have concluded that students are not hampered so much by lack of financial substance, social background, or environmental restraints as by a creeping paralysis of the mind. They have been overexposed to messages of "You can't do that," "You're not college material," "You're just a loser," "You always mess up," or "You aren't worth the effort." They grow up thinking they can't when, in fact, they can.

## FEAR IS ENEMY #1 TO POTENTIAL

The pursuit of potential requires courage. Fear squelches courage, thus keeping a person from making the effort to achieve or grow.

One of the most courageous young men I have ever encountered is Freddie Steinmark. I watched this young man and his University of Texas football team play against the University of Arkansas in a nationally televised game. Texas had a winning streak of nineteen games going into the game; Arkansas also was undefeated. The president of the United States, Richard Nixon, attended the game—and what a game it was!

In the last two minutes of the game, Texas came from behind and pulled off a victory by one point. Young Freddie Steinmark was the starting defensive safety.

Just a few days after the game, while Texas players and fans were still basking in the victory, Freddie Steinmark had his left leg amputated because of a malignancy. Sports pages and television stations across the nation carried the story of Freddie's tragic loss. Many doubted that Freddie would live to see the Cotton Bowl on New Year's Day—in which Texas would be the host team—but not Freddie. He had a personal goal to be there, and there was no doubt in his mind that he would attend. Twenty days after losing his leg to cancer, he attended the game he had helped his teammates to reach.

Courage? You bet. But attending the game was not the only thing Freddie had in mind. In the face of cancer, he set some new goals in his personal life—to help others become inspired to develop their potential. He was bold in his witness that he depended on God to give him the strength to do what he needed to do. And until the time of his death, Freddie worked diligently to reach as many people as he could with a positive message of faith and hope. As a part of his achievements, he wrote a book, which he dedicated to the Lord.

One remark Freddie made has stuck with me ever since I first heard his story. He said, "I must not be afraid because fear itself is more painful than any pain you fear."

Freddie knew a lot about pain *and* fear. He knew at an early age what many people learn much later in life: fear *is* a type of pain, perhaps the worst type possible.

If fear is allowed to take root in the life of any one individual in your family, it, in effect, has taken root in *all* of your family members. Fear is contagious and pervasive. Don't let it invade the climate of your home.

## YOUR CHILD AND YOUR FAMILY ARE SPECIAL

Believe in yourself. Believe in your child. Believe in the potential for your entire family. Continually repeat to your child that he is important and that having a strong family is something special to be treasured.

In 1912, Harry Leon Wilson wrote one of the greatest books ever on the topic of believing in yourself. In it he told the story of Bunker Bean.

Bunker was a young child when his parents died. He lived in various homes while he was growing up, and many of his childhood experiences were unpleasant. He developed a severe "inferiority complex." He doubted himself, his abilities, and his potential.

Bunker eventually moved into a boarding house where an occultic medium lived. The medium believed in reincarnation and was a very convincing individual. Before long, the medium had Bunker Bean believing that he had lived a previous life—as Napoleon Bonaparte. Bunker asked, "How could this be?"

The medium said that life went in karmic cycles—Napoleon had lived in the upper half of the cycle, characterized by power and courage, and Bunker was living in the lower half of the cycle, characterized by fear and weakness. However, the cycle was changing, and soon Bunker would be ascending into the half where Napoleon had lived.

Bunker felt a stirring within himself that he was soon to be somebody special. He began reading books about Napoleon; and as he faced challenges in his life, he asked himself, "What would Napoleon have done?" He began to model himself after Napoleon's strengths, but since there were no wars to fight, he turned instead to commerce. Soon, Bunker was a success. He turned again to the medium to find out who he had been prior to Napoleon.

This time, the medium told him he had been an Egyptian king for eighty-two years—a tall, handsome man of great strength and character. Bunker again sought to develop himself into the person he had once been. He bought new clothes, stood tall and proud (now that he knew he had royal blood), and developed his strength. He believed in himself, took pride in his achievements, and truly felt he had great potential.

One day Bunker was shocked to learn that the medium was a fake. He had no special powers and had made up everything he had told Bunker Bean about his past greatness. He had tricked Bunker into believing in himself.

Was Bunker devastated? Only momentarily. The fact was, Bunker was now a changed man. He had developed the habits and characteristics of a real winner. He decided that regardless of the lies the medium had told him, he would still think big, live big, and accomplish big things. He had learned that the secret to success was not in who he had been, or even who he was now, but in who he thought he could be!

I certainly don't believe in reincarnation and would never advocate that a parent lie to a child about his potential for greatness. But the story of Bunker Bean does illustrate a key point we need to keep in mind as we create a climate for the success of our children: in Christ Jesus is all the success they can ever hope to have, in great abundance. We need to hold up Jesus as their role model and encourage them to grow into His likeness and become like Him.

## POTENTIAL PRESENTS A CHALLENGE

When you present potential to your child, you are essentially challenging him to leave his comfort zone and launch out into unexplored territory, which can be frightening. Signing up for a contest, joining the school debate team, or trying out for a solo in choir or a part in a church play are all examples of ways your child can stretch his potential. Yet each will likely make him nervous and uncomfortable, at least at first.

Assure your child that he has your support as he takes risks related to growth and development. Help her understand that the purpose of life is not to live in comfort, pleasure, and ease, but to serve God and others—to love and to give to the best of our ability from the storehouse of resources we have been given in the form of talents, abilities, skills, experiences, relationships, education, family, and faith. We know true *joy* when we are fulfilling our purpose in life.

## ALWAYS A "CAN DO" ATTITUDE

Praise is the perfect accompaniment to potential. As you hold out a challenge related to your child's future, also provide praise for who your child presently is and what your child has already accomplished in life. This creates a "can do" attitude as your child embarks on a new endeavor.

At the "Can! Academy" in Dallas, high-school dropouts are actively taught personal responsibility, examples of which are openly rewarded with praise. One student said of the program, "It's totally different than a regular high school where there's really no one to pat you on the back. I'm going to walk away from here with a lot of values I didn't have before." At the academy, 98 percent of the students earn a high school equivalency degree, compared to 35 percent for other area programs designed for dropouts.

My son Michael and I presently are involved in the development of "Youcan University for Kids," a character building daycare center where Christian values are taught. A can-do attitude among administrators and teachers will be a must. Preschoolers need the challenge of potential. So do the elderly. Potential is never fully achieved. You must continue to have goals and embrace challenges *all the days of your life*. Teach that principle to your child.

# A Positive Climate Is Marked by Freedom

In a positive climate, each person feels free to be fully himself or herself—to express one's creativity, to voice opinions and ideas, to move about within the broader boundaries that have been established.

Freedom includes the concepts of flexibility, responsiveness, and risk.

## FLEXIBILITY

A positive climate is not one in which rules and boundaries are so rigid that there can never be exceptions. A family, for example, may have a fixed bedtime for children of 9 P.M., but on the night of the Olympic finals in an event about which one child may have a keen interest, the bedtime might be extended an hour. The key is to let the child know that this is an exception to the rule, not a laxness in enforcing the rule.

## RESPONSIVENESS

In a positive climate, procedures, rules, boundaries, regulations, and policies help people move toward positive ends. When not imposed as harsh judgments or entrapments, they become standards of excellence that can help a child achieve more and receive more rewards. In evaluating your own family goals, plans, rules, and standards, make certain that you aren't setting certain practices into concrete only for the sake of appearing firm or in charge. The goals, plans, rules, boundaries, and standards within your family should *benefit* every family member in ways each person can recognize and appreciate if they truly are objective about them.

## RISK

Cocoons are special environments in which very fragile creatures can develop in safety until they are ready to break out into a larger world to fulfill their purposes. Although temporary shelters, cocoons are safe havens in which a child can take risks without any fear of being criticized. I strongly encourage parents to make their homes such cocoons.

One teacher placed a large sign at the front of her class stating, "It's OK to make a mistake." What freedom that gave students to take risks, ask questions, engage in the trial-and-error process so essential to learning! In the end, the students in that environment actually achieved as much or more than students in classrooms that were run in a much more autocratic manner—the students given the freedom to fail actually made fewer mistakes than their peers!

The same principle holds true for a family.

# Positive All Day!

On a very practical level, a parent can create a warm and friendly atmosphere in the home by doing just a few things consistently every day.

At the start of the day, schedule your morning routine so that you have a few minutes to talk to your child in a relaxed and positive way. Let him know that you love him and will be thinking about him during the day. Have a moment of prayer together and give him a motivational quote, word, or verse of Scripture to carry with him through the day.

Keep a bulletin board in your kitchen or family room for posting positive ideas, awards, articles, quotes, and success stories related to your child. Update it at least once a week.

Have a quiet time with your child after work or school. Unwind together. Discuss your day. What happened at school? What did your child learn? What happened at work? Share positive encounters you may have had during the day with others in your family.

Here are some other questions you might ask your child:

- "What did you see that was beautiful today?"
- "What was the best thing about your day?"
- "Which part of your day would you like to repeat because it was so good?"

Listen to your child's answers and ask follow-up questions. This should not be a time for your child to "report" to you as much as a time for a good two-way conversation. Be prepared to tell your child the beautiful, good, positive, "best" things about your own day!

Let your child help you (even in a small way) to get dinner on the table or do chores that need to be done before bedtime. Even young children are capable of putting salt and pepper shakers on the table or putting a napkin beside each plate. Young children are also capable of picking up clothes that are lying on the floor and carrying them to a hamper.

Spend a few minutes in the evening having fun with your child. This might include a story read together after homework is finished or a few minutes spent playing an outdoor game before the sun sets.

End your day by giving your child an opportunity to express any fears or feelings he may have about his day. Pray with your child for forgiveness of sins and safety through the night hours. Assure your child of your love, accompanied by a hug and kiss goodnight.

All of these activities can be woven into the normal pattern of your day without interruption or excessive time. In fact, you can easily do all of the above in a matter of minutes. What counts most is your attitude, your tone of voice, and your relaxed manner. In this way, you are expressing to your child, "You are a valuable part of my life. I like being with you."

# Positive Results Can Be Expected

Positive climates help produce positive people. A positive home is not simply a nice place to live. It is a productive, effective training field.

In her familiar poem, "Children Learn What They Live," Dorothy Law Nolte expressed this well:

> *If a child lives with criticism,*
> *he learns to condemn.*
> *If a child lives with hostility,*
> *he learns to fight.*
> *If a child lives with fear,*
> *he learns to be apprehensive.*
> *If a child lives with pity,*
> *he learns to feel sorry for himself.*
> *If a child lives with ridicule,*
> *he learns to be shy.*
> *If a child lives with jealousy,*
> *he learns what envy is.*
> *If a child lives with shame,*
> *he learns to feel guilty.*
> *If a child lives with encouragement,*
> *he learns to be confident.*
> *If a child lives with tolerance,*
> *he learns to be patient.*
> *If a child lives with praise,*
> *he learns to be appreciative.*
> *If a child lives with acceptance,*
> *he learns to love.*
> *If a child lives with approval,*
> *he learns to like himself.*

*If a child lives with recognition,*
*he learns it is good to have a goal.*
*If a child lives with sharing,*
*he learns about generosity.*
*If a child lives with honesty and fairness,*
*he learns what truth and justice are.*
*If a child lives with security,*
*he learns to have faith in himself and*
*in those about him.*
*If a child lives with friendliness,*
*he learns that the world is a nice place*
*in which to live.*
*If you live with serenity,*
*your child will live with peace of mind.*

May it be so in your family!

# Chapter 9

# *Tool #3:  Conditioning*

*By constant self-discipline and self-control you
can develop greatness of character.*
—Grenville Kleiser
American author (1863–1953)

*If ye know these things,
happy are ye if ye do them.*
—John 13:17, KJV

Al Capone once said, "Everyone has his price." Capone was implying that anyone faced with enough temptation would sacrifice right for wrong, the lawful for the lawless. Granted, some people do sell themselves out for monetary or material possessions. More common, however, is the person who simply moves away from his or her values inch by inch, small decision by small decision. Most of us don't *expect* to renege on the values we hold dear. We don't *want* to go against what we know to be right. We simply respond to circumstances and situations before we have time to think fully about the potential consequences or the impact on our value structures.

Sliding away from values is easy to do in a society that places less and less importance on right and wrong.

In his book, *Living without a Magic Eightball,* Sidney Sowers tells of a study conducted by a psychology professor in which 652 people were asked, "What is the least amount of money you would take to push a button to kill a person inside a black box, providing no one would ever know what you did?" Some 25 to 45 percent of the people said they would kill for money, for as little as $20,000 to $50,000! Al Capone would no doubt have said, "See, I told you so."

When you consider today's crime rates, the scandals rocking virtually every profession (from politicians to attorneys to sports heroes to religious figures), and the myriad of other anti-social behaviors plaguing our culture today, it is obvious that people are willing to sell out their values, with a disastrous result to the overall fabric of our society.

There's an old fable about a farmer who went to a cotton gin to sell his wagonload of cotton. While the gin owner was adjusting the balance, the farmer stepped onto the scales to add his weight to that of the cotton. The gin owner noticed what the farmer had done, although the farmer didn't think anyone had spotted his move. As the gin owner totaled the weight he said, "Well, John, I always thought you valued yourself pretty highly, but today you sold yourself for $2.27."

In times of temptation, people of integrity stick to their convictions and values. They refuse to be sold or bartered at any price. They believe as Thomas Jefferson did, "In matters of style, swim with the current; in matters of principle, stand like a rock." Values are not negotiable.

How can we keep from giving in to the spur-of-the-moment temptation to compromise what we believe or take short-cuts with our values?

Part of the answer lies in conditioning.

## Good Conditioning

Regarding physical fitness, we know what contributes to good conditioning:

- drink eight 8-ounce glasses of water a day
- exercise thirty minutes, four times a week
- eat fresh fruits and vegetables, and avoid fatty foods
- take vitamins, minerals—especially antioxidants—on a daily basis
- get sufficient sleep

As a football coach, I knew the exercises that would help my young athletes develop the physical strength, agility, stamina, and coordination necessary for success.

In the mental and emotional realm, we also must be concerned with certain actions that result in good conditioning:

- give to others
- smile often
- give positive affirmations to others
- set positive goals
- enjoy each day's success
- keep a mind-set of "always learning"

Likewise, in the spiritual realm, we know there are certain principles that help condition us for strong faith:

- pray frequently
- read the Bible daily

- stay in close fellowship with other Christians
- practice the Golden Rule at every opportunity
- ask the Holy Spirit to renew our mind daily

Knowing what makes for good conditioning, of course, is no substitute for actually *doing* these things in our lives. Furthermore, doing these things once or twice in a month is not sufficient. True conditioning requires repeated behaviors that become habits.

A working definition of conditioning is this: "doing the right things repeatedly until doing the right things becomes an automatic response."

Conditioning is habit-building. As Plato once said, "Habit is no little thing!"

# The Power of Role Playing

You can help condition your child in good habits by running "practice games." Every coach knows the benefit of intrasquad scrimmages and practice games with other teams before the competitive season begins. In parenting terms, such practice games are often couched in activities called "scenarios."

A scenario is a make-believe situation that you construct for a particular training purpose. In a scenario, each person is given a role to play. The situation is "set up" with the various roles and the dilemma which the characters find themselves in. The question is asked, "What happens? What do these characters say and do in this setting?" Each person who participates must respond "in character."

Children usually regard this as a fun activity. In fact, much of a child's unstructured play involves scenarios of his own creation. Parents can employ this same technique to teach valuable lessons and to give children "practice" in various situations, some of which a parent hopes his child never encounters!

### TALKING ABOUT VALUES IN SCENARIOS

It is very important that you talk about values with your child and actively relate them to the behaviors you are training your child to develop as habits. Children do not automatically conclude that certain behaviors are linked with certain values. A young child isn't going to know, for instance, that your calling an error in your favor to the attention of a store clerk is an example of honesty and integrity. It's up to you to make this connection for your young child. You can simply say, "Sometimes it's hard—even more expensive—to do the honest thing, but it's always right to be honest with others."

Be sure to talk about values as a part of your scenario training sessions. Otherwise, you are simply playing a game with no point and no training benefit.

## SEX, DRUGS, AND ALCOHOL

Scenarios can be quite helpful in training your child to cope with those who might attempt to entice him or her to engage in premarital sex, take drugs, or use tobacco products or alcohol. Children and teens often give in to pressure from peers because they are caught off guard and don't have ready comebacks. Scenarios help your child become prepared.

Talk to your children openly, candidly, and repeatedly about sex, drugs, and alcohol. Give information and opinions to your child at the level on which your child can receive and use the information. The life you save may be the life of your child! Include a frank discussion of inhalants, pornography, and what it means to "abuse" a substance (which nearly always results in the person being abused *by* the substance). Don't expect or wait for a teacher or pastor to talk to your child about these important matters. Your child first should hear about sex, drugs, and alcohol at home.

Some parents are in denial about how prevalent drugs and alcohol are in their children's world. Consider these statistics:

- Seventy-five to eighty percent of young adults have tried an illicit drug. More than half have experimented with an illegal drug other than marijuana.[1]
- More than half of American high school seniors say they get drunk at least once a month. Two of five get drunk at least once a weekend.[2]
- In a study done by the University of Michigan, one-quarter of high school seniors, almost one-fifth of tenth graders, and almost one-tenth of eighth graders reported using some form of marijuana in the past year.
- The use of inhalants, LSD, and stimulants is on the rise among teenagers.

Many parents are also in denial about the sexual behavior of teenagers. They don't want to think *their* child is engaging in sex or considering sexual behavior. However, even if your child is not actively engaging in sexual behavior, he or she is likely fantasizing about it.

One of the major concerns parents have about sex education is that their children are taught the biology of sexual behavior without any relationship to values. The fact is, *parents* should be teaching their children the values related to sexual behavior—as well as the biology of sexual behavior—long before these matters are brought up at school! The parent who teaches his child about sex and values related to sexual behavior will feel more comfortable that his child can put into perspective the sex education lessons taught at school.

Sex, drugs, and alcohol are topics around which numerous values can be discussed, among them:

- *respect* for one's own body, as well as for members of the opposite sex
- *personal courage* to say no to peers and pushers
- *self-control* and the desirability of avoiding potentially dangerous, seductive, or tempting circumstances
- *trust* and the need to be trustworthy and supportive of one's friends so that a peer group is developed in which each member of the group has the strength and courage to say no to immoral behavior and to the use of illegal substances

The use of drugs and alcohol, as well as illicit sexual behavior, often becomes "secrets" that teens want to keep from their parents. Teach your child early in life these important principles:

- Things done in secret eventually come to light (1 Cor. 4:5). As Christians, we are to live in such a way that our behavior is a "light to the world"—a ready example to all who observe us. Jesus taught, "Let your light so shine before men, that they may see your good works, and glorify your Father which is in heaven" (Matt. 5:16).
- Secrets breed guilt. Bad behavior according to God's viewpoint—which is a way of defining sin to your child—always causes us to feel guilt (Ps. 32:5). Guilt is a heavy burden to bear. It weighs us down on the inside and causes us to lose heart and hope.
- All sin has consequences, but all sinners can be forgiven (1 John 1:9). Always assure your child that she can be forgiven in Christ. And while you may discipline her for bad behavior (with the intent of correcting the behavior for her ultimate good), you will always love her regardless of what she does and forgive her any time she asks for your forgiveness.

If you teach your child these things, you are making yourself available for him to come to you and talk to you about what he has done or what concerns he feels.

When your child asks questions about sex, drugs, or alcohol, answer him immediately and fully—according to the intent of your child's question and his ability to understand your answer. If your child asks you, "How was I born?" he may be asking whether he was born at a hospital or at home, rather than seeking a full explanation of sexual behavior.

In order to talk to your child intelligently about sex, drugs, and alcohol, you may need to educate yourself more fully on these subject matters. A great deal of material is available through your public library, the parent resource center at your child's school, or through organizations which support parenting. Some of the materials are ones that you can use *with* your child in giving explanations and presenting facts clearly and concisely.

Above all, present information to your child along with your own opinion about *why* he should behave in certain ways when it comes to sex, drugs, and alcohol. Give your child reasons to abstain—these are likely to be the reasons your child gives to his peers or to those pressuring him to act immorally or illegally.

Although there are many good reasons to abstain from sex, drugs, and alcohol, the best reason is found in God's Holy Word; such activities are simply wrong in God's eyes. God's commandments are for the benefit of humankind, to keep us from doing things that will hurt or destroy us in the long run. Sin is pleasurable for a "season," the Bible says. But the end result of what appears to be fun, pleasurable, or beneficial is spiritual—if not physical—death. All behavior that is wrong in God's eyes is behavior that ultimately has the power to destroy us.

Furthermore, God has designated a *way* for us to use and be a part of His creation, and in that way is great freedom. Some things are a matter of timing. Sexual behavior, for example, is normal, beneficial, and pleasurable in the context of marriage. In that context, sexuality is marked by fidelity and faithfulness. Drugs in the form of medication are also beneficial. They enhance life rather than destroy it.

Teaching your child about context invariably involves issues related to values—when and how and where one behaves is always linked to how a person sees himself in relationship to other people and to God.

### SAFETY

Scenarios are also quite helpful in preparing your child to encounter unsafe situations and dangerous people. Again, set up "what if?" circumstances and give your child an opportunity to rehearse responses and actions.

Discuss with your child the danger of getting in a car with strangers. Role play with your teen scenarios which involve riding in automobiles driven by a person who has been drinking or who is high on drugs.

Teach your child to stay away from guns and those who use them. Talk to your child about gangs, why kids are attracted to them, and the negatives associated with being in a gang. Give your child the tools he needs to keep himself and his property safe. A self-defense course, or other kinds of personal safety courses, may be quite useful to your child.

As parents, we desire for our children to communicate well and be open toward other people with a kind, generous, caring, giving spirit. At the same time, we must teach our children caution and restraint to help them avoid evil or dangerous situations. Balancing the two concepts can be difficult for a child to learn, and sometimes difficult for a parent to teach. The value in question may be considered *discernment*. As you give your child clear definitions of good behavior and good character traits—and attempt to model those behaviors and traits—you also must give your child clear definitions and examples of bad behaviors and bad character traits. If you attempt to shield your child from all exposure to the bad in our world, you will be creating in him a naivete that can work to his disadvantage and harm. Innocence is knowing evil exists but not *experiencing* it. Ignorance, however, is not knowing that evil exists or not knowing how to recognize it.

The Bible gives us two clear directives we can teach our children:

1. "Abhor that which is evil; cleave to that which is good" (Rom. 12:9).
2. "Prove all things; hold fast that which is good. Abstain from all appearance of evil" (1 Thess. 5:21–22).

How does this translate into training?

Do you remember what you were taught to do if your clothing caught on fire? "Stop, drop, and roll" is the message that most preschoolers are taught. This principle is also good anytime your child suspects that something may be evil.

*STOP* immediately. Teach your child not to engage in any aspect of a suspicious activity until he has checked it out with an adult—ideally you, the parent—to see what the full ramifications might be related to the activity. Teach him to question the character of the person who is engaging in the behavior in question.

*DROP*. Move away from or "drop out" of the group that is engaging in bad behavior. Teach your child to distance himself from the situation or person in question until he has determined whether the activity is a good one.

*ROLL*. Actively "roll" toward something good. Teach your child to redirect his focus toward a wholesome activity. Break the spell of the moment. This may mean changing the conversation, walking away, or suggesting a new activity. Your child doesn't need to confront the person who is engaged in wrong behavior. He simply needs to move on, call for help, align himself with another group, or divert attention to something else.

All the while, talk to your child about *why* he should behave the way you are teaching him to behave. Again, keep your emphasis on positive values and the positive consequences of doing the right thing.

## The Power of Suggestion

To suggest means to introduce a thought into the mind from an external source. We are always receiving suggestions from outside sources—other individuals, reading materials, the media—and we are constantly either accepting or rejecting these suggestions.

Part of our challenge as parents is to filter out what is harmful or unhealthy for our children, and teach them to do the same. However, given the enormous number of suggestions that we receive daily, it is quite difficult to consciously control all the thoughts that enter one's own mind, let alone another person's. To maximize the possibility that most of the suggestions your family receives are positive, it's important that you create positive climates and surround your family with positive people.

Many suggestions come to us in verbal form. We *hear* people say things to us, or we overhear things that people say to others. Other suggestions come to us in visual form—we read billboards and books, see graffiti, or catch a few random minutes of a television program.

Be aware that, as a parent, you are the source of many suggestions to your child, and, to a great extent, you are responsible for filtering out poor, inappropriate, or harmful suggestions so that they never reach your child.

## The Power of Self-Suggestion

Self-suggestion is a process of introducing thoughts into one's own mind, usually through one of two methods: imaging and self-talk.

### IMAGING

Imaging is the act of forming mental pictures. By picturing ideas or settings in the mind's eye, a person can introduce positive feelings and thoughts into the subconscious.

Professional athletes often use imaging to improve their athletic abilities. They view in their mind's eye the correct techniques for hitting a golf ball, serving a tennis ball, or making a free throw. They see themselves succeeding.

Imaging can be used positively by everyone. The subconscious cannot discern the difference between thoughts related to real-life situations and thoughts of imagined behavior. It is the subconscious that largely determines attitudes and directs subsequent actions. When you see yourself succeeding in certain areas of your life, you are actually setting into motion a form of rehearsal in your subconscious. Your subconscious will not find it abnormal or difficult to use that rehearsal in helping you at the actual time you are called upon to take action.

## SELF-TALK

We talk to ourselves constantly, even if we aren't aware of it. The vast majority of this self-talk is mental, not verbal. We continually analyze situations, people, and events in our minds and make judgments about our own performance, relationships, actions, attitudes, and potential. These judgments or thoughts reinforce existing attitudes. They impact the opinion that you have of yourself. If you think to yourself, in the aftermath of a mistake you have made, *That was a stupid thing to do*, you are reinforcing to yourself the concept that you do stupid things and, therefore, must be a pretty stupid person. If you think to yourself, *I can do better than that,* you are reinforcing to yourself the concept that you are a person in a constant state of improvement in the pursuit of excellence.

*The Importance of Positive Self-Talk.* Why is positive self-talk important? First and foremost, what you put into your mind is what you get out of it! The person who hears your self-talk the most is *you.* If you are speaking positive messages to yourself, you are going to have a more positive outlook on life. Your self-image will be reinforced in a positive way. Negative self-talk, in contrast, produces a negative self-image.

The subconscious mind takes in whatever it hears. It doesn't have a built-in, objective filter that separates truth from lie. It imprints *whatever* is fed to it. The statements we hear about ourselves—from others and from our own lips—become the foundation on which we form our attitudes and, subsequently, our behaviors.

Over the years, most people mentally "swallow" thousands of negative messages about themselves and others. The result is a deep-seated cynicism and sarcasm that contends, "I'm bad, you're bad, and we're in a bad way together."

Consider some of these examples of negative self-talk:

• I just never have enough time.
• I'm terrible at remembering names.
• I simply can't lose weight.
• It will never work.
• I always seem to make this stupid mistake.
• I hate doing this (or taking this class, or going to this meeting).
• I can't decide.
• I'll never get it done (in time).
• I'm tired—I just don't have any energy.
• I can't help it! It's beyond my control.
• I feel lousy today.
• I never have enough money.
• I just don't have any willpower.
• It's going to be another one of those grindstone days.
• With my luck, I don't have a chance.
• I never win at anything.
• You can't trust anybody.
• There's no way that will work for me.

How would you like to be around a person who talks in this way *all* the time? You'd probably do your utmost to avoid such a person!

Research has long shown that negative, unhappy, miserable people attract the same kind of people. Misery truly does love company. Even so, most of us don't *like* being around negative people for very long. They are annoying or troublesome to us, often in ways we can't pinpoint. We much prefer to be around positive, happy, forward-thinking people.

Most of us engage in negative self-talk without even realizing it. It has become such a part of us, we no longer think about what we are saying to ourselves or what the effects will be. As a result, we begin speaking negatively and attracting others who are equally mired in the mud of negative thinking and speaking.

*A Simple Test for Self-Talk.* How can you know if your self-talk is positive or negative? Listen to yourself the next time you make a mistake. The positive person will say to himself, *I know better than that. Next time I'll do better.* The negative person is likely to say to himself, *I'm so stupid. I never do anything right.*

Or, listen to yourself the next time you get angry. The positive person will say to himself, *I need to control my emotions.* The negative person will say, *They deserve whatever they get. I'm going to let it all out.*

Finally, listen to your friends. We just agreed that negative people attract negative people; if the majority of your crowd speaks and acts in a pessimistic manner, that may be an indication of your own attitudes and speech.

The key to acquiring positive self-talk is this: practice, practice, practice. Nobody automatically thinks about himself in a positive way all the time. It takes practice.

*Acquiring the Habit of Positive Self-Talk.* To help you acquire this habit of positive self-talk:

- Make a list of your strengths and positive qualities—ones you either have or are working to acquire. For example, you might identity yourself as honest, courageous, and patient.
- Take these positive attributes and put them into a noncompetitive statement in the present tense, using personal pronouns.

Say, "I am an honest person," not, "I'm honest most of the time."

Say, "I am a courageous person," not, "I'm a courageous person in most situations."

Say, "I am a patient person," not, "I'm a patient person with most people."

Reaffirm to yourself daily the attributes that you possess, or desire to possess. From a scriptural standpoint, you are identifying the person that the Lord is calling you to be. You are identifying yourself with the character traits of Jesus—not that you necessarily have these traits already, but that you desire them, are seeking to develop them, and believe in faith that, with God's help, you *are* going to manifest them.

You may ask, "But am I lying to myself when I talk like this?"

Well, are you generally honest, and striving to be more honest all of the time? There may have been occasions in the past when you weren't patient, courageous, or honest, as in our example. Ask God to forgive you for your shortcomings. Then, make your statement in the present tense. State who you are and what you want to be like. In so doing, you are placing your emphasis on the positive side of who you already are in Christ Jesus, and you are reinforcing your own belief in who God is helping you to become.

Dale Carnegie once addressed this issue by saying, "Is giving yourself a pep talk every day silly, superficial, or childish? No, to the contrary. It is the very essence of sound psychology."

It takes three to six months of practice to change a deeply ingrained habit, including changing the habit of negative self-talk to one of positive self-talk.

## NEGATIVE SPEECH PATTERNS

Until the age of twelve, children tend to speak in terms of what is. Adults, by comparison, speak in terms of what isn't. Ask a child about his recent trip to Disneyland and he is likely to say, "It was awesome!" Ask the child's parent, and he's likely to say, "We survived." While we don't necessarily set out to be negative, it's easy to allow pessimism and cynicism to creep into our conversations by oversight. Dr. J. Mitchell Remy has concluded that "most people speak 80-90 percent of the time in exclusion."[3] We narrow our focus to eliminate possibilities, people, and opportunities, rather than explore the "what if's" and "why not's" that come our way.

Remind yourself of the qualities associated with positive and negative talk:

| Positive | Negative |
|---|---|
| Optimistic | Pessimistic |
| Inclusive | Exclusive |
| Builds up | Puts down |
| What is | What isn't |

Consider two approaches taken by major credit card companies in our nation. American Express has had as a slogan: "Don't leave home without it." American Express has about 13 percent of the credit card market share.

VISA by BOFA, with more than 50 percent of the market share, has as its slogan: "VISA—it's everywhere you want to be." This approach is a positive one, whereas American Express focuses on a negative.

A negative speech pattern can be quite subtle. Consider the three examples of negative talk below:

1. Why don't we go to . . . . ?
2. Why don't we get together on Monday?
3. Why don't we consider another option?

While the questions themselves may point toward positive change or a positive activity, the questions are posed in negative terms.

As an alternative, here are three examples of positive talk:

1. Let's go to . . . . OK with you?
2. I suggest we get together on Monday.
3. How about considering another option?

Researchers tell us that only about 7 percent—or one hundred minutes—of our daily communication is verbal.[4] In those one hundred minutes, more than 90 percent of our statements are negative in nature. In other words, the vast majority of our communication is rooted in criticism, complaint, and argument!

The same doesn't have to hold true for your child. Listen to what your child says about himself. Does he call himself "stupid," "a jerk," "dumb," or "ugly"? Does she refer to herself as a "dunderhead" or complain that nobody likes her or that she can never seem to do anything right? Don't let your child get away with such negative talk. Insist that they speak in positive terms about themselves and about others.

Ask others to help you develop positive speech patterns and habits even as you help your child to do the same. Their "correction" at first may be irritating to you. In fact, if you ask your children and spouse to help you by pointing out your negative talk, you may become downright frustrated and angry since they are likely to enjoy this game of catching you speaking negatively! Control your temper. Keep a positive frame of mind and thank others for their help. Remember that you are trying to change a pattern in your life that you likely have had for many years, perhaps several decades.

You are likely to find that as you change your speech patterns, people become more cooperative. They become more supportive of you personally. They desire to spend more time with you and are more open with you.

A wonderful way to help each other think and speak positively is a family "pep talk." I recently heard of a family who—during their Sunday dinner—goes around the table saying one nice thing about every other member in the family. The compliment must be genuine and spoken in a kind tone of voice, never sarcastically. The comment can be about something the person has said or done, or about a character trait the person has. A tremendous new atmosphere of appreciation, warmth, and loyalty has come into this family since they started doing this several months ago.

I would take this one step further. As each person finishes his remarks about others in the family, he should be invited to say something positive about himself! Again, this could be a statement about something he did or said during the week, or something he believes to be true about himself.

Remember, don't feed yourself a diet of junk thoughts, including negative self-talk. The brain gives back only what you put into it.

# The Power of Habit

Each of us forms habits, and our habits form our futures. Some researchers have estimated that as much as 90 percent of what we do in a day we do out of habit.

A habit is a disposition or tendency to act in a certain way. Most of us have numerous highly developed habits related to eating, dressing, driving a car, studying, organizing our work, or talking on the phone. We developed those habits in the past, and if we do nothing to change our habits, they predict with a high degree of accuracy how we will live out our day tomorrow.

It takes about twenty-one days to form a new habit, good or bad, yet it takes about three to six months to break one! In many ways, bad habits are like a disease. In the early stages of development, they are easier to cure but hard to recognize; and in later stages, they are easy to recognize but hard to cure.

People are not born with habits; but, rather, they acquire habits as they grow and mature.

Two things seem to be required to break a bad habit. First, recognize what you are doing. Ask others to call to your attention when you display a habit you want to break. As you recognize what you are doing, *stop doing it!*

Second, you must replace your bad habit with a desired behavior. The process is not unlike gardening. Pulling out a weed isn't enough. Another weed can grow in its place if the ground is left bare. You must establish a good plant in the place of the weed if your garden is to prosper and be beautiful.

Habits relate not only to the things we do, but to the way we think, believe, and feel. We develop habitual responses to circumstances. We become "fixed" in our way of thinking about things. When we have a positive faith and an optimistic, hope-filled, love-motivated outlook on life and eternity, great! When we become habitual in negative thinking and have a pessimistic, downtrodden, distrustful approach to God and other people, we can be in eternal trouble.

Much in our society attempts to compel us to be freewheeling people who are spontaneous and not bound by habits. I have two responses to that point of view.

In the first place, it isn't realistic. People who consider themselves quite "spontaneous" are often simply lazy. An amazing number of the things they *think* they do spontaneously actually follow a fairly predictable pattern or routine. In other words, they are predictably spontaneous, which may also be defined as unfocused. We are all creatures of habit whether we think we are or not.

Second, a person who places too high a value on spontaneity and living "outside the boundaries" of society is a person who is frequently alone—without close family ties or friendships. Most people don't desire to be isolated. They may want moments alone or sufficient personal space; but when a person is truly alone and without love, concern, and compassion, that person tends to become bitter, angry, and frustrated— in a word, miserable.

Not only are we creatures who need the security of habit, but we were *commanded* by God to be this way. Take another look at the many feasts, commandments, and rituals established in the first five books of the Bible. God was quite precise in telling His people how to build strong habits into their daily lives.

## Suggestion and Habits Work Together

Suggestions from the external world are directly related to our self-talk. External suggestions reinforce what we think about ourselves, and, in turn, our self-talk creates a filter by which we take in the outside world. Suggestions and self-talk build attitudes. Attitudes prompt, shape, and are manifested in behavior. Repeated behaviors and repeated attitudes become habits.

Cicero once said, "Virtue is a habit of the mind." Plato saw it this way: "Virtue is a kind of health, beauty, and good habit of the soul." Either way, the point is made: virtues are habitual behaviors. They can be learned and acquired through conditioning.

# Chapter 10

# *Tool #4: Providing Reinforcement*

*Punish if you must, but let the
sugarplum go with the rod.*
—Martin Luther

*He is a rewarder of those
who diligently seek Him.*
—Hebrews 11:6, NKJV

When the words *conditioning* and *reinforcement* are used, we sometimes think of Pavlov's dogs, or perhaps of brainwashing and mind-control techniques. Actually, conditioning is the most basic form of learning. Educators and psychologists have studied it for more than a hundred years now and have come to realize that it is quite a natural process—a built-in way in which humans and animals function. Reinforcement is a vital part of the conditioning process.

## Two Types of Reinforcement

Most people do not fully understand the concept of reinforcement. When a child receives a *response* from a parent for behavior, whether good or bad, that response reinforces the behavior.

One of the basic tenets of conditioning is likely to sound like common sense to you: behaviors that are followed by rewards tend to occur again, and those that are followed by punishment tend not to occur again.

Contrary to what some people think, however, punishment is not nearly as effective as reward in shaping behavior in a child. Encouragement is by far the stronger "reinforcer." Praise what your child does that is *good*. In doing this consistently and frequently, you probably will find that you are having to punish your child for bad behavior far less often.

## REINFORCE WITH LOVE

All reinforcement should be accompanied by love. We must never withhold love when we discipline our children, or chastise them for errors committed, in an attempt to teach them to pursue what is good and right behavior. Scolding should be reserved for inappropriate attitudes, not innocent mistakes. At all times we are to love our children and show them love.

## REINFORCE IMMEDIATELY

Good reinforcement should happen at the time a deed is done. This requires, of course, that a parent not only spend quality time with a child, but also a quantity of time. A parent must be present when a child suffers a loss or scores a victory.

A recent study reported in *Education Week* indicated that of the sixteen average hours that a four-year-old child is awake in a day, fathers in the United States are available to their four-year-olds only .7 hours.[1] This translates to less than forty-five minutes a day! Spending time with your children is a matter of setting priorities.

## MATCH REINFORCEMENT TO THE DEED

In providing reinforcement, a parent must be careful to match the reinforcement to the deed. A positive reinforcement that is too lavish or extravagant can ring hollow. A negative reinforcement that is too harsh can injure a child's self-esteem and willingness to pursue his best.

In fact, children who are punished frequently tend to develop an overall behavior pattern that is less active and spontaneous. Such children are far less likely to ask questions, display creativity, and take risks that are essential to learning and acquiring basic life skills.

Furthermore, children who are punished excessively tend to be more hostile and aggressive than those whose behavior is shaped primarily by reward. Therefore, keep the emphasis on *positive* reinforcement, in amounts that are appropriate for the achievement of your child.

# Positive Reinforcement

Use positive reinforcement to reward positive behavior and increase the probability of such positive behavior recurring. It is the most effective means of showing support and approval for another's behavior, while encouraging that person to repeat the desired behavior.

Every parent I know desires that their children be happy and successful in whatever they attempt in life. They want their children to have positive attributes, to be accepted, approved, and recognized by others, and to have high self-esteem and plenty of self-confidence. Parents want *positive* things for their children.

The way to encourage these positive attributes is through positive reinforcement, *wherever* and *whenever* the positive attribute is displayed.

I always encourage teachers and parents to be "good-finders." Seek out your child's successes, achievements, improvements, good attitudes, and behaviors that reflect the values and virtues you desire your child to have. The more you look for good, the more you will find to praise, reward, and appreciate.

Good is not limited to your child's performance. Not every child is going to be an *A* student. Good can reflect effort, attitude, and improvement. If your child has gone from *C* work to *B* work, that's an achievement worth high praise. If your child displays honest, trustworthy behavior, that is worth your encouragement and praise. If your child shows great teamwork, even from the bench, that's worth praise. Look for the "winning aspects" of any victory or loss. These aspects go far beyond a point total or a first-place finish.

Several years ago my son, Michael, was playing an exciting game of Tiddly Winks with his four-year-old daughter, Michelle. The competition had been intense, but Michael eventually prevailed and announced himself the winner after successfully maneuvering all his "winks" into the bowl. He left the room, unaware that Michelle continued to play the game.

About five minutes later, Michelle found her father and proudly announced, "Daddy, guess what? I'm a winner too!"

"You are?" he questioned.

"Yeah," she said, "I got all my winks in the bowl!"

Michael realized that, like most of us, he had been conditioned to think of winning primarily in terms of only one winner. Michelle saw winning as accomplishing a goal, completing a task, getting the job done satisfactorily. From that perspective, most people can be winners on a daily basis!

This does not mean that every child who completes a race should be given a blue ribbon indicating first prize. Our society is a competitive one, and part of learning how to participate in our culture is learning how to win and lose graciously. Everybody has both winning and losing moments in life.

What it does mean is that every child can be supported or reinforced for the display of right behaviors and good values in the face of a victory or loss.

Lou Holtz, the great head football coach at Notre Dame, has said, "Winning is a goal." But Holtz defines *win* in a way most people don't: "*W*hat's *I*mportant *N*ow." Every person can glean a "what's important now" message from nearly every experience in life. If we do what is important, and take away from a loss that which is valuable for the future, we are winners.

# The Goal Is Not Control

Never use reinforcement techniques to manipulate or control your child. Your child is not a puppet. In reinforcing behavior, take great care to preserve your child's feelings of independence, individuality, creativity, and satisfaction, as well as the joy of discovering one's own potential and aptitudes.

Positive reinforcement should direct your child toward the positive, but it should not be used to engineer your child's future or manipulate your child into total compliance. Keep in mind that God has a plan and purpose for your child's life that may not be the plan and purpose you would choose. If you encourage your child to seek out God's plan, he will find fulfillment in life. If you encourage your child to fulfill your personal wishes and desires—which may be your own unfulfilled dreams—you are setting your child up for disappointment, frustration, and eventual resentment.

In reinforcement, we are reinforcing the good traits, abilities, talents, attributes, and godly virtues and values that are part of your child's uniqueness. Positive reinforcement should never be used to force a child into a preconceived set of career or social-status expectations. Nor should positive reinforcement be used to encourage negative behavior, i.e., encouraging your child to pursue homosexual feelings.

**SIX METHODS OF POSITIVE REINFORCEMENT**

The six most positive methods of reinforcement are:
- praise
- appreciation
- rewards
- recognition
- encouragement
- success

As you read through a more detailed explanation of each of these methods, think about ways you can use them with *your* child.

# Praise as a Reinforcer

Praise needs to be linked to the behavior that is to be reinforced. Don't praise an incorrect choice. Some people have concluded that praise, in and of itself, is valid regardless of a child's performance. Wrong! Praise only what is praiseworthy.

Never praise your child falsely for ideals or goals that aren't rooted in reality. Don't say, for example, that your child is a great athlete if he can't hit the ball. Don't tell your child he's on his way to the top of his class when he scores a *C-* on a test paper. You can offer praise and encouragement to your child and still be realistic and grounded in truth. What you want to do is to reinforce the *good*, not deny the error. In reinforcing the good, you are emphasizing achievement and pointing toward fulfillment. If you emphasize the error, you are emphasizing mistakes and pointing toward failure.

"Am I bragging by voicing praise for my child?" a parent might ask. No, not if he has done good work. Bragging implies a better-than-thou attitude, while praise simply acknowledges a job well done.

Following are some special thoughts about praise:

- Deal with specifics. Don't limit your praise to broad, generalized statements about your child's character. Put your praise for your child's values into the context of behavior. Praise your child for being trustworthy "in feeding the cat every night this week without being asked." Praise your child for being diligent "in practicing a piano piece until it was learned well." Praise your child for being honest "in pointing out to the store clerk that he gave back too much change."

- Be timely in giving your praise. Note your child's effort or accomplishments as quickly as possible. The more recent and more concrete your example of noteworthy behavior, the greater the encouragement to your child. From time to time, of course, you might recall an incident in your child's past in which your child exemplified good behavior or good values, but it is *today's* behavior that should be noted on a regular basis.

- Give praise related to things that are important to your child, as well as those things that are important to you. Get to know your child's likes and dislikes well enough to know that Jonny's patience with Christopher is especially noteworthy because Jonny thinks Christopher is too boisterous. Discover what your child considers to be valuable so that you can praise with enthusiasm: Claire's acquisition of a new art technique, or Deanne's ability to dance an intricate tap-dance step, knowing full well that Claire desires to be an artist and Deanne is attempting to overcome large-muscle coordination problems by taking tap dance classes.

## Appreciation as a Reinforcer

One of the simplest ways of showing appreciation is simply to say to a person, "I appreciate you," or "I appreciate what you are doing. . . . what you have done. . . . having you as a friend," and so forth. Those few simple words can make an otherwise ordinary day a great one!

Written notes are appreciated because they can be preserved. William James, the father of American psychology, once stated that 90 percent of what we do each day stems from a need to feel appreciated. We all need to feel appreciated by those people who are important to us.

I once gave a keynote address to a group of school district parents and patrons. Earlier that day I had addressed a meeting of school administrators for the district.

After the meeting with parents, a woman came up to me, reached for my hand, and told me she had something important to share with me. Tears began to stream down her face as she said, "Dr. Mitchell, I came here tonight to share with you something that happened after your address this afternoon to our school administrators. I work in the district office. My boss came by my office after the session and told me he appreciated me and thanked me for what I did for him. I said to him, 'Do you realize this is the first time in the twenty-six years I have been working here that anyone has ever said that to me?'"

The woman continued, "I just wanted to share that information with you and let you know how touched I was by his words. Just because I am paid to do my job, he thought that was sufficient. We all need to be reinforced and told we are appreciated."

You may think it's enough to meet your child's basic needs and tell him occasionally that you love him. But your child also needs to experience your appreciation, praise, and recognition on a daily basis. He needs to hear it—and feel it.

# Rewards as Reinforcer

Rewards are not limited to trophies, ribbons, gold stars, or certificates. They can be anything of value or significance to the person receiving them. Thus, rewards can include privileges, special honors, and public acknowledgment.

Rewards can be given for participation in an event or for completion of a task. They need not be limited to winners; they can be given for any type of positive action or behavior. A note of warning, however: Overuse of rewards can cause their value or significance to be diminished. No person should expect a reward for every positive action or behavior.

Think carefully about the rewards you give to your children for good behavior. There are several rules governing a reward.

1.  Your child should never come to expect a reward for good behavior or for doing the right thing, unless you have promised one for a specific accomplishment. If you have promised a reward to your child, deliver.

2.  You set the rules and requirements for a reward that is to be earned. Don't change the rules midway through the child's effort to earn the reward. At the same time, don't compromise your own standards and give the reward before the child has met your requirements.

3.  Give rewards that are safe and appropriate for your child. Don't reward your three-year-old with a collector's edition doll that sits on a top shelf in her room or your six-year-old with a Swiss army knife like the one you gave to his older brother. Rather, give both children rewards that are age-appropriate.

4.  Don't reward your child for doing his routine family chores. Reward your child for *extra* effort—that significant accomplishment or the attainment of a goal. Reward your child for work done well.

A son who had just celebrated his sixteenth birthday went to his father and said, "Dad, I'm sixteen and have my license. Can I drive the family car?"

His father replied, "Son, driving the car is a big responsibility. First, you must prove you are responsible. One way you can show me that is to bring up your grades. They are below what you are capable of achieving. Second, I would like to see you reading your Bible every day. And finally, as a reflection of this family, I want you to keep your hair cut short."

The son began fulfilling his father's requirements by reading his Bible daily. When his report card came out, he went to his dad with a big smile. "Look, Dad, all A's and B's. Now can I drive the family car?"

"Very good," the father said. "Now, when are you going to get that hair cut?"

The son, thinking he might outsmart his dad, replied, "Well, I don't see why I should get my hair cut to drive the car. I've been reading my Bible like you asked, and I raised my grades. Jesus had long hair; I don't see why I can't have long hair."

The father looked at his son and said, "That's right, Son. And Jesus walked everywhere He went."

Don't let your children talk you into different requirements, bigger rewards, or undeserved rewards. Stick to your original agreement. Your own trustworthiness and integrity are on the line.

## Recognition as a Reinforcer

There are many forms of recognition. The nature of recognition, however, is that it is most effective when it is *public*. In recognition, others are informed of your child's accomplishment or good behavior. (Private recognition tends to be perceived as praise or encouragement.)

Recognize the good work that your child does and the good values your child is exhibiting. Recognition can extend to the very basic fact that your child exists and is a part of your family!

Some ways in which you can recognize your child are listed below. All of them require care and attention, but virtually no money.

- Introduce your child to adults you meet. Adults frequently encounter old friends or business acquaintances in public places and engage in conversation with them, totally ignoring the children at their side. Recognize your child by saying, "Have you met my daughter?" or "You may not recognize him by his height, but this is my son."

- Host a dinner in your child's honor. Fix a special meal of your child's favorite foods, or designate a meal in your child's honor at his favorite restaurant. Give a toast to your child at the beginning of the meal and include a prayer of thanksgiving for your child as part of the meal's blessing.

- Post your child's good work or school report in a place where other family members can see it. Don't limit yourself to grade cards and good grades on assignments. Lean a photo of your child in front of a pile of raked leaves, or cut out letters from a magazine to spell: "No cavities!"

- Carry recent photographs of your children in your wallet—ones they approve of—and have photographs of your children in your office or private study at home. This conveys to your children the message that they are important to you at all times and in all situations.
- Help your child assemble a scrapbook or photo album. You might label it, "It's Nice to Be Me" or "My Wonderful Life!" Occasionally sit down and look through the book with your child or add entries to it. Recall happy memories, good times, and good work accomplished by your child.

# Encouragement as a Reinforcer

Encouragement is the process of helping someone believe in himself, his abilities, and his potential. There are significant differences between praise and encouragement:

- Praise is used as a reward for an accomplishment. Encouragement is an expression of confidence in one's ability.
- Praise is generally based on an external evaluation of past performance. Encouragement focuses on internal potential and can relate to future performance.
- An expression of praise would be, "I think you did a great job in the play." An expression of encouragement would be, "You have a lot of talent!"

Encouragement focuses on strengths, not weaknesses. It builds up a positive self-image in the person who receives an encouraging word. Encouragement conveys, "I think you're valuable."

### EFFECTIVE ENCOURAGEMENT

In order for encouragement to be most effective, try the following:

- Give your child tasks, chores, and responsibilities that she is capable of doing, and doing well. Success at a task is its own reward. When success is coupled with parental encouragement *before* the task is undertaken and praise *after* the task is completed successfully, the child is far more willing to engage in the task or chore in the future, as well as undertake new challenges.
- Encourage your child along his way toward completion of a task or chore, especially if you see he is becoming frustrated with a problem or obstacle. Say, "I can tell you're working hard at this. Good effort," or "Keep working. I have faith that you can do this."

- Put your encouragement in writing from time to time. Write your child a special love letter or thank you note to express your appreciation for his good efforts. Doing so gives your child something tangible that says, "I'm proud of you. Keep it up!"
- Encourage your child to encourage others. Help your child find creative ways to motivate his friends and siblings to do well. Handmade cards are a great way for children of all ages to offer encouragement.

## A CLIMATE OF ENCOURAGEMENT

Here are several other ideas that build a sense of ongoing encouragement in a child:

- Provide your child with positive posters or statements for his room or desk. Let him help choose the posters or desk placards he finds most inspiring. A wall that is decorated with positive messages is less likely to be covered with negative images, movie posters, or pictures of rock stars who lead largely negative lives.
- Help your young child to write mini-booklets about how she and her friends have performed good deeds for others. Keep the stories in a special magazine holder on your family bookshelf.
- Clip out positive and interesting newspaper and magazine articles to share with your children and teens. Place an emphasis on creative or unusual ways in which people are helping other people or exhibiting positive behaviors.
- Send your child off to school or camp with a smile and a positive word: "You look great," "You're going to do great," "This is going to be a great experience." These statements all create a positive mind-set for your child to take with him as he leaves your presence and embarks on his own life adventures.
- Finally, verbally encourage yourself with words like, "This shouldn't be too difficult," or "If I stick with it, I'll be finished in no time." If your child hears and sees you acknowledging your own good efforts, he will be more likely to do the same in his own life. To give your encouragement the greatest amount of validity, *always speak the truth*. Don't lie to your child by acknowledging an effort that has not been made. Rather, find some virtue or accomplishment that your child has made great strides toward, acknowledge that effort, and encourage further efforts. A child can never receive too much encouragement as long as it is rooted in truth and values that are of importance to you and your child.

# Success Is Its Own Reinforcer

When a child enjoys a successful experience, he intrinsically feels rewarded and positively reinforced. As a parent, you can set up incidences in which your child *will* experience success. Every child has the potential to succeed at something. Make it happen for your child!

Make a connection whenever possible between your child's behavior and the stories or lyrics your child hears, and encourage your child to embody those behaviors that are positive. In other words, let your child "try on" positive values by "acting out" good books or songs. The success he experiences in relationship to these adventures will be a strong means of reinforcement.

For example, a parent once challenged her bored son and his friend to read the book *Swiss Family Robinson* during the second week of a summer vacation. The boys were dismayed at first, especially when they saw how thick the book was. But Mom gave an incentive: a day at the water park near their home when they finished the book. After a couple of hours of reading, the boys needed no further encouragement; they were hooked on the story. They spent a good portion of the rest of the summer building their own backyard tree house.

Along the way, both Mom and Dad had many opportunities to encourage the two boys to dream big and work hard. They praised their ingenuity, creativity, and perseverance in finishing the tree house, their willingness to work together on a project, and the fact that they had both finished reading the book that had triggered the idea to begin with. Mom and Dad also had opportunities to discuss with the boys the need for maintaining hope in difficult circumstances and making good use of what they had (rather than pining away for what they didn't have).

The tree house and the completed book on the shelf were testaments to a "success" which was highly rewarding to both boys, who went on to create a business together later in life. Now they have full confidence that they can build a strong and successful company, in part because as boys they had turned a dream into a reality.

# Overcoming a Negative Disappointment

A failure or disappointment can "feel" like negative reinforcement to your child. Teach your child that failures and disappointments are a normal part of life; specifically, they go with the territory of risk-taking.

Keep in mind that disappointment can bear as much of a sense of loss to a child as any tangible loss or defeat. The world always promises more than it can deliver—especially from a child's point of view. Recognize that there are times when your child is going to be disappointed at the way things turn out, in the way things *don't* materialize, and even in his own reactions and responses to life. In those moments, seek to reinforce who your child is, what he possesses, and what he has accomplished. Teach your child that not everything she perceives as a loss really is one.

A Norwegian fisherman and his two sons were fishing one day when their boat was engulfed by heavy fog. To make matters worse, darkness fell before they could reach home, and a storm was threatening. They were unable to see the shoreline and had no idea which way to row their boat.

Meanwhile, back home, the fisherman's wife faced troubles of her own. A kitchen fire blazed out of control, and by the time the fire fighters arrived, the home was completely destroyed. As the wife sobbed in front of the ruins of her home, her husband and sons arrived. "Everything is lost!" she cried as her husband tried to console her. "We've lost everything."

"Not everything," he said. "Earlier, our sons and I were lost at sea, and for hours we feared we would perish. Then we saw a light through the fog, and we headed our boat in its direction. The light grew larger and brighter as it safely guided us to the shore. My dear, the same fire that destroyed our home also saved our lives."

There may be times when you think your child's failure, mistake, or bad behavior is a "loss" of major proportions. On the other hand, it may very well be that this negative is actually the beginning of something quite positive. Keep looking for the good in every circumstance—the turning point may be just around the corner. Memorize Romans 8:28, and encourage your children to do the same. Make it a hallmark verse for reinforcement.

> *We know that all things work together for good to them that love God, to them who are the called according to his purpose.* (KJV)

# Chapter 11

# Tool #5: The Parent as Role Model

*Children have more need of*
*models than of critics.*
—Jonhert (1754–1824)

*Treat others as you want*
*them to treat you.*
—Luke 6:31, TLB

While on a flight to Atlanta a number of years ago, I was sitting across the aisle from a mother and her two young daughters. We had a hard landing in Atlanta; the plane hit the concrete runway with a jolt. The mother began cursing the pilot, muttering loudly that he needed to go back to flight school.

As we began filing off the plane, the pilot was standing near the exit wishing the departing passengers a good day. As this woman reached him, she flew into another tirade, telling him what a poor pilot he was. I was shocked to hear her two little girls chime in, also loudly berating this middle-aged professional for incompetence.

I smiled at the pilot and told him I had enjoyed the flight, and then left the plane behind this woman and her daughters who were still muttering about what a terrible experience they had been through.

*What a great example of negative modeling,* I thought. I can almost predict the outlook those two girls have developed over the years. If the mother had laughed and made a little joke about the bumpy landing, the girls no doubt would have done the same. Instead, she showed them quite a different response, and, like little sponges, they soaked it up.

# Three Types of Modeling

"Models" come in three varieties:

1. Human models
2. Philosophical models
3. Operational models

As we take a look at the three types, consider how you are providing, or might provide, good models to your child.

# Human Models Are People

Human models are, quite simply, all the people your child encounters! Those people encountered most frequently are the strongest models.

When we think of role models, we often think of those who are rich, powerful, or famous. However, a child's first—and always foremost—role model is his or her own parent. Your child will "copy" what you do and say, perhaps even in ways that are humorous or embarrassing to you. Children readily imitate a parent's walk, speech patterns, and gestures. They will also adopt your values and character traits, whether you like it or not. In fact, you can't help but be a model for your child.

A child will learn what it means to be a mother from his mother. A child will learn what it means to be a father from his father.

Your child will likely grow up:

- dressing the way you dress
- using the same facial expressions you use
- displaying the same gestures and general conduct that you display
- listening in the way you listen
- talking like you talk (including your vocabulary and your accent)
- posturing himself in the way you posture yourself.

The poem below, by an anonymous writer, expresses the nature of modeling:

> I'd rather see a sermon than hear one any day, and
> I'd rather one walk with me than merely show the way.
> For the eyes are better pupils, more willing than the ears,
> Fine council is confusing, but example is always clear.
> And the best of all the preachers are those that live their creed,
> For to see the good in action is what everybody needs.
> For I can soon learn how to do it, if you'll let me see it done.
> I can watch your hands in action, but your tongue too fast
> may run.

*For the lectures you may deliver may be very wise and true,*
*But I'd rather get my lesson by observing what you do.*
*For I may misunderstand you and the high advice you give,*
*But there's no misunderstanding how you act and how you live.*

The kind of person you are is the kind of person your child will be. Given that, perhaps you should determine what kind of person you want your child to be as an adult and then strive to be that kind of adult yourself!

As your child attends Sunday school and church, various leaders within your church will become role models for your child. The same holds for adult friends you may have and the parents of your child's friends.

When your child enters school, teachers, coaches, and other adults also will become human models, but they are unlikely to become a more important model than you, the parent.

## THE TYPES OF VALUES YOU MODEL

There is an old story about two neighbors, a baker, and a farmer. The baker began to be suspicious of the farmer, suspecting that he wasn't getting his money's worth when he paid for a full pound of butter. He weighed the farmer's butter on several occasions and finally had him arrested for fraud.

The judge asked the farmer at the trial, "I presume you have scales?"

"Yes, of course, Your Honor," the farmer replied.

"And weights?" the judge asked.

"No," replied the farmer. "I don't have a set of weights."

"Then how do you hope to weigh accurately the butter you sell to your neighbor?" the judge asked.

"That's easy," the farmer said. "When the baker began to buy from me, I decided to buy my bread from him. I've been using his one-pound loaves to balance my scales. If the weight of the butter is wrong, he has only himself to blame."

When we see behaviors in our children, we are wise to ask ourselves, "Is what I see a reflection of me?"

Lawrence Kohlberg, the famous Harvard psychologist who studied moral development in children, was fond of saying that values are "caught, not taught." By that, he meant that children are more likely to absorb their parents' values by being around them constantly than through the intellectual processes of logic and reasoning. In truth, actions do speak louder than words.

To a great extent, you will model for your child *all* the values and virtues that you possess. Very specifically, however, your child will copy your example in these ways:

*Division of labor.* Your child will learn this concept best if you delegate certain family-related chores or responsibilities to him and allow him to complete them on his own, with suitable rewards or consequences associated with completion of the tasks. If you "do it all" for your child—including picking up his clothes, cleaning his room, preparing his meals, taking care of his laundry—you will be training him to be a totally dependent adult, one who has no concept of assuming responsibility for his share of labor in accomplishing group goals.

*The Golden Rule.* "Do unto others as you would have them do unto you" can be taught to children at quite an early age. Say "please" and "thank you" to your child, even as you require her to say "please" and "thank you" to you. Don't interrupt your child when she is speaking, even as you insist that she not interrupt you.

*Citizenship.* Discuss with your child your activities which benefit the community. When elections are held, vote. Take your child with you to the polling place, even into the polling booth. Attend town hall and city council meetings that are related to issues you believe to be important.

*Self-control.* If your child sees you lose your temper, he will copy your behavior. If your child sees you maintain your cool in a tough situation, your child will do the same.

*Industry.* An industrious parent who takes work seriously and tries to do his personal best at tasks, who values work and has steady employment, is a parent whose child will likely develop this same work ethic. This certainly does not give a parent license to become a workaholic, which allows work to become a detriment to the family. It does mean that a lazy parent is likely to produce a lazy child.

Perhaps the foremost maxim related to human models is one from Josh Billings (1815–85): "To bring up a child in the way he should go, travel that way yourself once in a while."

## THE SPECTER OF HYPOCRISY

Because children watch what you *do* so closely, they are likely to be the first people to see discrepancies between what you do and what you say, or what you tell them to do. When a person's "talk" doesn't match his "walk," we describe him as a hypocrite.

The story is told of a man who sat down to eat supper with his family. During the grace, he thanked God for the food, the hands that prepared it, and for God being the source of all life. Then during the meal, he complained about the staleness of the bread, the bitterness of the coffee, and the sharpness of the cheese. His young daughter asked him, "Dad, do you think God heard the grace tonight?"

He answered confidently, "Of course!"

She asked, "And do you think God heard what you said about the coffee, cheese, and bread?"

Not as confidently, he answered, "Well, yes, I believe so."

"Which do you think God believed?" she pressed.

The man realized that his mealtime prayer had become a rote habit rather than an attentive, honest communication with God. He had left the door wide open to let hypocrisy march in.

This man did something wise, however, and it is what all parents must do when they realize that their "talk" and their "walk" don't match. He apologized to his daughter, saying, "You're right. My prayer and my comments didn't line up. Thank you for calling this to my attention. I'm going to try to do better on that score."

Never be afraid to apologize to your child for the mistakes you know you have made or the errors in which your child catches you. To err is human. To insist that you never err is foolish. To ask forgiveness for your errors that impact your child brings healing, growth, and a spirit of righteousness into your home.

Some children, of course, might use "catching Mom and Dad in errors" as a kind of power-play game. Don't let that happen. If you suspect that your child is baiting you, goading you, or chiding you for your shortcomings and mistakes, insist that he apologize to *you* for his disrespectful, overly critical behavior. To be constantly critical of another person is as great a sin as any mistake you may make. Luke 6:37 (KJV) tells us, "Judge not, and ye shall not be judged; condemn not, and ye shall not be condemned; forgive, and ye shall be forgiven." This is a good verse to memorize as a family and a good one to recall anytime any member of the family is overly critical of others.

When you ask your child's forgiveness for hypocrisy, you are paving the way for something good to come from your behavior, even your negative example.

Clarence Jordan saw hypocrisy at work at an early age. His father was a prosperous banker and merchant in a small Georgia town. They lived within one hundred yards of the Talbot County jail.

One hot summer night during a revival meeting, Jordan noted how carried away the warden of the jail's chain gang became while singing,

"Love Lifted Me." He was inspired at how deeply the prevailing spiritual atmosphere had impacted this man.

Later that same night, however, Jordan was awakened by agonizing groans coming from the direction of the chain gang camp. He knew what was happening; he had heard these sounds before. Someone had been placed into the "stretcher" and was being tortured. He also knew only one person could be responsible for inflicting such torture—the same man who had been singing "Love Lifted Me" with great emotion and conviction only hours before.

That realization tore at Jordan's heart. He identified with the man who was in agony and became angry with the church as he understood it. Jordan didn't reject his faith or launch a protest, however. He stuffed his anger deep inside until such time as he could make a difference, which he certainly did in writing the Cotton Patch versions of the New Testament and in founding Koinonia Farm.

Not all such examples of hypocrisy have such a good ending. Many times the hypocrisy that a child witnesses turns into guilt, fear, or deep anger and bitterness.

Don't dismiss your child's concerns over what he perceives as hypocrisy. Answer his questions. Talk over issues with him. Own up to, and apologize for, your own hypocrisy. Only then can a truly good outcome occur.

## INTEGRITY

The opposite of hypocrisy, of course, is integrity—a good match between what a person says and what a person does.

Bubba Smith is someone who knows the cost of integrity. Bubba didn't drink himself, but he sold a great deal of beer by making cute television commercials. Then came a turning point:

> "I went to Michigan State for the homecoming parade. . . . I was the grand marshall, and I was riding in the back seat of this car. The people were yelling, but they weren't saying, 'Go, State, go!' One side of the street was yelling, 'Tastes great!' and the other side was yelling, 'Less filling!'
>
> "Then we got to the stadium. The older folks are yelling, 'Kill, Bubba, kill!' But the students are yelling, 'Tastes great! Less filling!' Everyone in the stands is drunk. It was like I was contributing to alcohol, and I don't drink. It made me realize I was doing something I didn't want to do."

Finally, Bubba's integrity took over. He contacted the brewery which he represented and told them to find someone else for their commercials. As far as I know, Bubba Smith is the first athlete who ever gave up a lucrative, easy, legal, amusing job because he decided he was involved with something that was morally wrong.

"I loved doing the commercials," Bubba has said. "But I didn't like the effect it was having on a lot of little people. I'm talking about people in school. Kids would come up to me on the street and recite lines from my commercials, verbatim. They knew the lines better than I did. It was scary. Kids start to listen to things you say; you want to tell 'em something that is the truth."[1]

### IDEALS

Most parents want their children to live in the "real world." What they sometimes fail to realize, however, is that focusing on ideals can make the real world a better place.

In his newspaper column, Cal Thomas once wrote, "When Harriet Nelson died . . . some stories noted how unrealistic 'The Adventures of Ozzie and Harriet' was. But that show was not about realism. It was about idealism. If we lose the ideal, what good are we striving for? Showing a functioning and loving family on TV encouraged the rest of us to consider right from wrong, good from bad. That is what is missing in our culture."

Talk to your children about the *ideals* you believe in and that you would like to achieve in your life. Own up to the fact that you aren't there yet, but you're striving toward your goals. Challenge your child to claim his own ideals, and then teach him how to work toward them.

## The Philosophical Models You Teach

Philosophical models are systems of belief and ideas. Children come to appreciate these models over time by accepting a set of theories about how the world works, how success is defined, and what must be done to survive.

The philosophical model you espouse will flow not only from conversations you have with your child about what is right and wrong, but from what you say to your child about the world as a whole, your own hopes and dreams, and how you regard other people and institutions.

Young children will follow examples, but it is also important that you explain to your child why you do certain things and why you deem certain habits to be important. This type of conversation usually flows quite naturally out of your attempts to answer the many "why" questions your child poses to you.

Immediately after presenting to the Jews the Ten Commandments, as well as the great commandment to love God with heart, soul, and strength, Moses exhorted the people to teach these principles to their children—on an ongoing basis (Deut. 6:6–9). This implies many conversations over a period of years, in the midst of a variety of activities.

The Israelites' calendar was filled with spiritual rituals and celebrations. Knowing that the meaning of events could get lost over time, Moses said, "And when thy son asketh thee in time to come, saying, What mean the testimonies, and the statutes, and the judgments, which the LORD our God hath commanded you? Then thou shalt say unto thy son, We were Pharaoh's bondmen in Egypt; and the LORD brought us out of Egypt with a mighty hand: And the LORD shewed signs and wonders, great and sore, upon Egypt, upon Pharaoh, and upon all his household, before our eyes: And he brought us out from thence, that he might bring us in, to give us the land which he sware unto our fathers" (Deut. 6:20–23).

The children of Israel were to tell their children what had happened in the past that gave rise to certain habits and traditions, and how God had authorized certain laws and statutes for the *good* of His people.

Many traditions and habits seem boring to children. They don't understand why things are done certain ways. When they know the meaning that undergirds habits and rituals, they are much more likely to want to participate and make those habits their own.

Fairly early in life, your child will begin to compare your philosophical model of the world with models presented by others. The teen years, especially, are a time when children are exposed to a wide variety of "world views." If your child grows up in an atmosphere where the home and the church are homogeneous in their belief structure and philosophical model, your child is going to acquire a fairly strong "life perspective" early on. This may be modified later, but rarely is it completely overthrown.

## Operational Models Involve Experience

Operational models represent "a bank of experience." Your child will learn most of the life skills he needs through trial, error, and repeated practice. You show your child how to brush his teeth, and hundreds upon hundreds of times a year, a child brushes his teeth. You show your child how to balance a checkbook, how to sing a hymn, how to tie shoelaces, how to cast a ballot, how to converse, how to . . . ad infinitum. Then repetition reinforces the lesson to form a habit.

Here are only some of the areas in which parents are the foremost providers of operational models:

- personal hygiene
- child care
- communication (visual, verbal)
- money management
- problem-solving skills
- decision-making skills
- good nutrition
- use of machines and tools
- prayer
- travel
- manners
- reading
- food preparation
- home care and repair
- health
- management of nature, care of environment
- volunteer or community service
- learning and study

If there is an area of life in which your child needs experience or an operational model and you cannot provide it, find someone who can.

Keep in mind that operational models—life experiences—do not exist in a vacuum. Every operational model has an attitudinal dimension to it. You can teach your child the rudiments of good nutrition, for example, by saying to your child, "Eat a balanced diet and avoid foods that are bad for you." You can proceed to show your child what that means by involving your child in shopping, menu planning, and meal preparation. As you continue to serve nutritionally sound, balanced meals in your home, your child is going to receive the message that balanced eating is something you value. As you talk about the importance of good health, your child is going to adopt an attitude toward eating that is positive. What you say about good nutrition is going to be matched by what you do, and the message is going to be more effective.

The key is twofold:

1. *Meaning.* Link experiences to beliefs and values. Let your child know *why* you are teaching him certain skills and enforcing cer-

tain rules. Give him sound reasons. In so doing, you will be expanding his understanding, strengthening his self-esteem, and giving meaning to the ways in which your family lives life.

2. *Consistency.* Be consistent in the experiences you give your child. Taking your child to church on Christmas and Easter is not enough to build a strong Christian foundation. Take your child to church every week. To develop a love for reading, taking your child to the library once a year or sitting down to read together once a month isn't enough. Take her to the library every week or two, and encourage her to read every day by reading with her.

Meaning and consistency. A child who is exposed to operational models that fulfill these two vital criteria is going to be quite self-confident in his own personhood, with a positive foundation of values on which to build his life.

# You Are Your Child's "Model Guardian"

As a parent, you are the foremost "guardian" over the kinds of models your child is exposed to, keeping in mind that no one will influence your child as much as you will. Decide what kind of person you choose to be, and then be that person—genuinely and with the utmost integrity—before your child.

Monitor the messages that come into your home from outside sources. What type of worldview is presented to your child by the programs you allow him to watch on television or the movies you allow him to see? What kind of example is set by people who come into your home for dinner parties? What types of literature do you have in your home—not only for your child's reading enjoyment, but for your own?

# Send a Clear Message

To build a strong family, you must seek to be the best possible role model for your child and provide other positive models throughout your child's life. You must instill in your child a philosophical model that is founded upon Christian values and virtues. You also must try to provide appropriate experiences that will prepare your child for life by reinforcing the values and virtues that you desire.

Regardless of the type of modeling involved, always reveal your thoughts, ideas, motives, values, faith, and dreams to your child. Don't make your child guess about how to do something or what it is that you expect. A model is only as good as your child's understanding of it.

My granddaughter, Michelle, recited this poem in a program when she was in fourth grade. It says volumes about modeling.

## WALK A LITTLE PLAINER, DADDY

*Walk a little plainer, daddy,*
*Said a little one so frail.*
*I'm following in your footsteps*
*And I don't want to fail.*
*Sometimes your steps are very plain,*
*Sometimes they are hard to see.*
*So walk a little plainer, daddy,*
*For you are leading me.*
*I know that once you walked*
*this way years ago*
*And what you did along the way*
*I'd really like to know.*
*For sometimes when I am tempted*
*I don't know what to do.*
*So walk a little plainer, daddy*
*For I must follow you.*
*Someday when I'm grown up*
*You are like I want to be.*
*Then I will have a little one*
*Who will want to follow me,*
*And I would want to lead him right*
*And help him to be true.*
*So walk a little plainer, daddy,*
*For we must follow you.*
—Author Unknown

# Chapter 12

# $\mathscr{R}$unning the $\mathscr{D}$rills

*What we hope ever to do with ease, we*
*must learn first to do with diligence.*
—Samuel Johnson
English author (1709–84)

*Work hard and cheerfully at all you do.*
—Colossians 3:23, TLB

$\mathscr{O}$ne of my favorite stories about a child's concept of time is this: A little boy was riding with his father from New Mexico to Colorado on a fishing trip. The trip covered 250 miles, a good five hours of driving not counting rest and restaurant stops. After about fifty miles, the excited son asked his father if they were almost there. The father answered that they had quite a ways to go.

Fifty miles later: "Now are we almost there?"

"No, not yet."

Another fifty miles later: "We must be just about there, right, Daddy?"

"No, not yet. We have about another hundred miles to go."

Fifty miles later: "Daddy, am I still going to be four years old when we get there?"

Stay aware that your small child doesn't measure time the way you do. He doesn't remember from day to day what you have said or what you have provided. Every day is fresh and new: "What are you going to say to me *today?* What are you going to do for me *today?*"

## The Importance of the "Dailies"

As a former high school coach, I have drawn great encouragement through the years from others who are or were coaches. John Wooden, the former coach of the UCLA Bruins, openly admits that the values he holds today are rooted in his faith. He has said, "Dad read the Bible daily; he wanted us to read it, and we did. That is probably why I keep a copy on my desk today. It's not a decoration, but it is well marked and read."

A written creed of seven statements given to him by his father also has given guidance to Wooden's life. Notice as you read through them how "daily" and practical this advice is:

1. Be true to yourself. Being true to yourself requires that you first have values and then that you stay true to them regardless of situations and circumstances that may arise. Be more concerned about your character than your reputation. Character is what you are. Your reputation is only what others think of you. Ability may get you to the top, but it takes character to help you once you are there.

2. Make each day your masterpiece. Learn as if you were to live forever; live as if you were to die tomorrow.

3. Help others. You cannot live a perfect day without doing something for someone who will never be able to repay you.

4. Drink deeply from good books, especially the Bible.

5. Make friendship a fine art.

6. Build a shield against a rainy day.

7. Pray for guidance; count and give thanks for your blessings every day. Things turn out best for those who make the best of the way things turn out.[1]

## The Best Practice Is Daily Practice

We all know the phrase, "Practice makes perfect." Practice is what children do daily, whether they know it or not. They are practicing life skills and rehearsing mental concepts, even subconsciously, which will form the foundation for their future.

Every coach knows that an athlete's game is only as good as his practice. Arnold Palmer once made a great chip shot, only to have a commentator note, "Lucky shot!" Palmer grinned and replied, "I notice I get a lot luckier when I practice."

The best practice is *daily* practice. Each day of our lives is an opportunity to practice the values and behaviors we hold true, according to our Christian beliefs.

A runner knows that to maintain physical conditioning he must run nearly every day. A professional writer realizes she must write regularly to keep her mind focused and alert. It is a law of nature that all matter is constantly moving toward a state of disorder or entropy. Without upkeep, houses eventually fall down, bridges collapse, and machines break.

When it comes to parenting, the day a parent stops "running the drills" is the day that the development of a child's godly character begins to decline.

# Three Daily Disciplines

In 1993, the U.S. Secretary of Education, Richard Riley, made three recommendations to parents. They reflect a three-pronged daily discipline you can establish with your child that encompasses many of the tools we have discussed in the previous five chapters:

1. Read aloud with your children.
2. Limit television viewing to no more than two hours a night.
3. Make sure homework is completed.

As you read through the information related to each of these daily disciplines, think about how you might incorporate these practices into your family's schedule.

### READ WITH YOUR CHILD

If every parent of a child aged one through nine would spend only one hour a day reading or working on schoolwork with his or her child, five days a week, American parents would be devoting 8.7 billion hours a year in support of their child's learning. The benefits to the next generation would be incalculable!

We hear so much about the importance of reading with children, and yet only half of parents with children under age nine read to their children every day. Only 13 percent read with their children ages nine to fourteen on a daily basis.[2]

Reading with a child is something every parent *can* do. It costs no money and little effort. But it yields tremendous rewards for the child and for the parent-child relationship.

Children who read with their parents (either reading to their parents or listening to their parents read to them) are children who:

• have a much richer vocabulary and a much easier time learning grammar, both of which translate into school and career success
• are more likely to communicate with their parents about issues, questions, and problems that are not related to the materials they are reading
• have a much broader base of common knowledge on which to build their own aptitudes and talents

- are more creative
- are better problem solvers and more logical thinkers (in part, because they have more knowledge of how others have solved problems or reasoned their way through mysteries)
- feel closer to their parents emotionally and physically
- have less desire to watch television or engage in passive activities, and are more likely to choose activities that require participation and mental exercise
- are more likely to finish college—which can translate into a higher standard of living. The difference in lifetime earning between a student who does not graduate from high school and one who does is more than $200,000; the difference for a student who receives a bachelor's degree or higher and a student who doesn't graduate from college is almost $1 million over a lifetime. (Both figures come from a 1994 U.S. Census Bureau report.)

## Controlling the Media in Your Home

Most parents desire to limit their children's television viewing. A study done in 1993 revealed that 73 percent of parents both desired to and thought they should limit their child's TV viewing.[3] Even so, 43 percent of seventh graders recently reported watching three or more hours of television a day.

The amount of time children spend in front of a television set greatly impacts their academic achievement. Children who watch more than ten hours of TV a week (or an average of two hours a day, Monday through Friday), exhibit a sharp drop-off in their academic grades and test scores.[4]

TV viewing also has a high correlation to a child's emotional well-being. Children who watch a great deal of television are less sensitive to the pain and suffering of others, have more fear of the world around them, and have an increased likelihood of engaging in aggressive or harmful behavior.[5]

We often hear people make claims that "there's no proof that television violence causes people to be violent." That's true, but the statement is largely a function of the way scientific research is conducted. Most scientific studies do not reveal cause-and-effect relationships. Rather, they show correlations—in other words, they reveal the degree of likelihood that if "A" is present, "B" will also be present.

The correlation is quite high between acts of violence and the viewing of television violence, especially among teens and children whose parents do not discuss or mediate the impact of the programs their children watch. The sad fact is, by the time an average child graduates from high school in our nation, he or she has seen eighteen thousand murders in twenty-two thousand hours of television viewing. You cannot pour thousands upon thousands of violent images into a child's mind over a decade and a half without producing some very negative effects. This is common sense.

Children who watch a great deal of television also tend to:

- develop stronger stereotypes for race, age, and sex—with less tolerance for individual differences
- be less patient and have shorter attention spans
- have more nightmares after watching a sustained level of television violence
- be less able to cope with moments of boredom, which can lead to increased frustration and manifestations of frenetic energy
- have a greater desire to explore their sexuality as they watch sexually-oriented segments of soap operas and prime-time shows

By the time a child reaches driving age in our nation, he or she has seen more than one hundred thousand beer commercials: "Beer tastes good, and those who drink it have fun!" Driving fast cars is also portrayed as fun through commercials. What chance does a "don't drink and drive" message really have? Our children are being conditioned by these two industries, among others, to engage in behavior that leads to an incredible number of serious injuries and deaths.

## VIDEOS AREN'T ALWAYS THE ANSWER

Some parents opt for videos rather than television in their homes. This may be a wise choice for younger children, but be aware that "older" videos are sometimes *more* insidious than TV programs.

One study done several years ago pointed out that Christian teens are watching R-rated movies at the same rate as non-Christian teens. The only difference is that Christians rent them from video stores and watch them on the family's "second" TV set, rather than go to the theater and risk public scrutiny.

## NON-CHRISTIAN MESSAGES

Keep in mind, too, that a great deal of children's television programming is based on non-Christian values and behaviors. Some programs even include symbols and activities associated with the occult. Most parents turn on cartoons for their children without ever looking at the content of the programs. They would be amazed at the number of programs that present various aspects of witchcraft and sorcery, including the use of shamans and divination by both good and bad guys. These messages become commonplace to a young child, who has little ability to differentiate what is real and what is fantasy—what is true and what is false.

Do you really want your child engaging in the practices of the occult as part of their play? If not, you need to make certain that the television programs and movies they see don't instill a tolerance or desire for these behaviors!

## MEDIATING THE MESSAGE

To increase the chances for the negative messages of television *not* to have a negative impact, they must be mediated by positive messages and conversations. That's where parents play a critical role.

As you watch television with your child, discuss what you have seen after the program is over. Weave the program into your dinner-time or next-day conversations. Ask your child questions that can lead to a critical evaluation of the behaviors and situations that were portrayed. Such questions might be:

- How did this story make you feel?
- What was right about the action that a particular character took? What was wrong?
- What are the possible consequences for the behavior that was portrayed?
- What about this story was real? What was fantasy?
- What would you do if you were in a particular character's shoes?

Use your television viewing as an opportunity for discussions about important issues in life. Encourage the free-flowing expression of opinions and ideas. Allow your child to say why he liked or disliked a program, without too much parental comment. At times, of course, the story may be one of pure silliness and fun. That's great! Not everything you watch should be serious or heavy in content.

Ultimately, you are responsible for what your child takes into his life—both physically and mentally. That's a part of your parenting responsibility. And because it is your responsibility, you also have authority as a parent to say no to anything that you believe has the potential to harm your child's body, psyche, spirit, emotional health, or ability to relate positively and in a loving manner to other people.

You don't need an excuse to turn off the television set. Simply turn it off.

I strongly recommend that parents limit their children's TV viewing to no more than one hour a day, and that they select the programs a child is allowed to watch. Place your emphasis on wholesome programs, educational documentaries, sporting events, and classic performances of plays and concerts. If a special program is coming up—such as the Olympic Games, a political convention, a positive two-hour movie, or a championship game—budget that longer program into the total hours of viewing for the week. This likely means a night or two without television *before* the desired program. Save children's videos or family-friendly movies for weekend viewing as a reward for the entire family to enjoy.

At other times, encourage your children to:

- go outdoors to play—or stay indoors and play games that they make up from their own imaginations
- read a book
- play board or card games with their friends (especially games that require reasoning or logic, such as chess)
- write a letter to a friend who has moved away
- work puzzles
- draw, paint, or work on craft projects
- do extra-credit homework projects
- work in a garden they have planted
- practice a musical instrument
- write a story or create a play, puppet show, or talent review

Each of these activities helps a child develop skills that are useful later in life.

### AUDIO MESSAGES

The television is not the only potentially dangerous medium in your home. Your child's stereo or radio can be as polluting to your child's mind, emotions, and spirit.

Parents tend to dismiss the sexual and violent messages that are conveyed in today's popular teen music. In the six years covered by grades seven through twelve, the average student spends 10,500 hours listening to music. That's only 500 fewer hours than the total time spent in twelve years of formal training in a public school! Many of the songs have themes that deal with rape, incest, suicide, murder, or other types of deviant behavior. The National Education Association has estimated that five thousand suicides a year are linked to depression that has been fueled by fatalistic music and lyrics.[6]

## COMPUTERS

Also limit the amount of time that your child spends at a computer or playing computer games. Working at a computer for long hours can have an isolating effect on a child. It also can impact a child's vision—too many hours of staring at one fixed focal length and too many hours of sitting close to a CRT screen can have negative effects. Limit your child's computer time. Emphasize instead a balance of activities that include physical exercise, reading (off screen), and interaction with others. Thus far, studies have shown only two benefits to computer games: quicker eye-hand coordination and an enhanced ability to perceive elements in a focused field. These are not broad learning skills, but narrow ones.

Most computer games have an element of violence to them. Others have a strong occultic message. Some, however, are quite creative in teaching a child special relationships and encouraging a child to respond quickly and decisively to environmental changes. Choose your computer games wisely.

Images and messages are permitted via phone line to your home computer that would *not* be allowed on television, including graphic sexual material. Monitor what your child is viewing on the Internet.

## UNPLUGGING YOUR LIVES

As a family, there are a great many things you can do to "unplug" your children from television sets, stereos, and computers. Encourage your child to

- get involved in school- or church-related clubs and sporting activities (ones that are properly coached or supervised)
- get involved in scouting or other youth-development programs
- be part of a volunteer effort (perhaps through your church) to help those who are underprivileged or in need of special help. Teens make great tutors for young children, and one positive experience frequently leads to many others.
- go with you as you perform volunteer work or engage in wholesome hobbies. Invite your daughter to go golfing, or your son to help you distribute baskets of food to those who are in need.

The more your child is actively involved in life—as opposed to sitting passively in front of a television set or idly playing repetitive computer games—the more your child is going to have experiences that give him *practice* at skills that are valuable to adult life and which give him an opportunity to *put values to work*. It is in interacting with other children and adults, in a variety of life situations, that your child has the opportunity to learn and practice a wide range of skills and values.

A child who is involved with others tends to be a better communicator, feel a wider range of emotions, and be more experienced in dealing with situations outside the norm. On the contrary, the child who is isolated from others is a child who attempts to learn about values without a real-life practicum to reinforce and reinstill their importance.

## The Daily Discipline of Doing Homework

Why is it important that your child do his homework—not merely complete it, but do it to the best of his ability? Children who complete their homework enjoy greater school success. They make better grades and perform better on standardized achievement tests.

Those who make poor grades are more likely to be discipline problems in school and further down the line. They suffer in self-esteem. One study showed that students with poor grades are three times more likely to threaten someone with a gun or knife and four times more likely to threaten a teacher.[7]

Doing homework gives a child a sense of accomplishment—taking on and completing a specific body of work. This translates into greater success in school and beyond.

Monitor your child's homework. It isn't enough to say to a child, "Go to your room and do your homework," and then, "Is your homework done?"

Instead, ask your child to show you his homework when he has completed it. Review it with him. You likely can spot errors in logic or procedure that your child is making and be able to help him resolve those errors before he returns to school.

Praise your child for work well done. Never imply to your child, "You're stupid for not knowing this or for being incapable of doing this." Instead, encourage him that you believe in his ability to learn, accomplish, and succeed. Work with your child to overcome gaps that may have occurred in his understanding of a concept or procedure.

It is quite difficult for a child to work quietly on homework if you are watching television or a sibling is at play in another room. Make homework time a quiet time throughout the house. Encourage every person in your family to use the early evening hours for homework, reading, or quiet work. Later evening hours can be for rest and relaxation, conversations, family fun or devotion time, and getting ready for a good night's rest. Too much stimulation—mental, physical, or emotional—too close to bedtime can be disastrous to a child's schedule and need for sleep.

Provide a suitable place for your child to do homework assignments. Every child should have a desk or small table to call his own, a place where he can keep his books, papers, and other homework-related supplies secure, clean, and tidy.

Make homework a priority on school nights. Insist that it be finished before a child is allowed to watch television or engage in other leisure pursuits.

Engage in an ongoing dialogue with your child's teacher. If you question a homework assignment, take that up with a teacher privately. If you think your child needs clarification of certain concepts or procedures, send a little note to your child's teacher. The TIPS program (Teachers Involving Parents in School Work) has designed math and science homework activities in a way that encourages parents to comment to the teacher on the student's success with each assignment. You may want to ask your child's principal about this program.

# Fitting It All into a Day

How do parents fit it all in?

### UNENDING PRACTICE, UNWAVERING PERSEVERANCE

Every parent learns quickly that telling a child something once is not enough. A child needs to be told certain things repeatedly, long after a parent has grown weary of the telling!

The great preacher Charles Haddon Spurgeon once said this about perseverance in training children:

> *In dibbling beans the old practice was to put three in each hole: one for the worm, one for the crow, and one to live and produce the crop. In teaching children, we must give line upon line, precept upon precept, repeating the truth which we would inculcate, till it becomes impossible for the child to forget it.*
>
> *We may well give the lesson once, expecting the child's frail memory to lose it; twice, reckoning that the devil, like an ill bird, will steal it; thrice, hoping that it will take root downward, and bring forth upward to the glory of God.*

The Scriptures refer to the way we learn lessons in life as line upon line, precept upon precept, here a little and there a little (Isa. 28:10). Daily discipline provides the opportunity for this kind of learning and practice.

## NO END IN SIGHT

Practice should not only be daily, but also "unending." We never reach a stop-point in our need to practice and implement the values, beliefs, abilities, talents, and natural gifts that we have.

As we teach our children to "run the drills"—to practice daily the habits that produce godly character—we must also prepare them to run these drills every day for the rest of their lives. The goal in practicing character-related habits is not "to arrive," but "to continue."

The Scriptures promise a great deal to those who persevere or endure. In the Book of Revelation, John writes seven messages which he says the Lord told him to give to the seven churches under his leadership. Each church received a warning from the Lord—one or more admonitions to change something in the way they served God. Note how the message to each church closes. The Lord holds out a wonderful promise to those who will hear what the Spirit is saying to them and then act to "overcome"—which includes enduring, persevering, correcting their ways, and continuing to pursue a right way of living while withstanding evil.

- To the Church of Ephesus: "To him that overcometh will I give to eat of the tree of life, which is in the midst of the paradise of God" (Rev. 2:7, KJV).
- To the Church in Smyrna: "He that overcometh shall not be hurt of the second death" (v. 11).
- To the Church in Pergamos: "To him that overcometh will I give to eat of the hidden manna, and will give him a white stone, and in the stone a new name written, which no man knoweth saving he that receiveth it" (v. 17).
- To the Church in Thyatira: "He that overcometh, and keepeth my works unto the end, to him will I give power over the nations" (v. 26).
- To the Church in Sardis: "He that overcometh, the same shall be clothed in white raiment; and I will not blot out his name out of the book of life, but I will confess his name before my Father, and before his angels" (3:5).
- To the Church in Philadelphia: "Him that overcometh will I make a pillar in the temple of my God, and he shall go no more out: and

I will write upon him the name of my God, and the name of the city of my God, which is new Jerusalem, which cometh down out of heaven from my God: and I will write upon him my new name" (v. 12).

- To the Church of the Laodiceans: "To him that overcometh will I grant to sit with me in my throne, even as I also overcame, and am set down with my Father in his throne" (v. 21).

Regardless of how you interpret these various promises, the bottom line is that those who overcome will be blessed.

There's much in life to overcome. Every person is born with a set of strengths and weaknesses. It is in overcoming our weaknesses and building upon our strengths that we put ourselves into a position to succeed, win, and be rewarded.

As Christians, we overcome our weaknesses through the help of Jesus Christ—as Paul wrote, "I can do all things through Christ which strengtheneth me" (Phil. 4:13). We overcome our weaknesses as we rely upon Christ *daily*. There is no point in our lives in which we can say with pride, "I have overcome," without the help of Christ.

Many parents, Christian and non-Christian alike, prepare their children to win victories or reach goals throughout life. Indeed, guiding children toward successful careers and relationships is a challenging and rewarding task. But there's a bigger perspective to be gained—that of eternity.

Help your child keep the big picture in mind. Every success, and every failure or short-fall, should be regarded in the greater context of eternity. We are so geared in our culture to live in the "now," to capture every bit of gusto we can, that we tend to lose sight of what really matters—leading a life that pleases God and directs others to Him.

Our society tells us, "Been there, done that, and move on." The Bible repeatedly tells us, "Stay steady in your faith, continue to do what you know is pleasing to God, and never leave what you know to be good."

# Chapter 13

# *Facing the Unexpected*

*No one knows what strength of parts*
*he has till he has tried them.*
—John Locke
English philosopher (1632–1704)

*I am the vine, ye are the branches: He*
*that abideth in me, and I in him, the*
*same bringeth forth much fruit: for*
*without me ye can do nothing.*
—John 15:5, KJV

I have always believed in being well prepared. As a student I studied diligently. In fact, as a graduate student I went to my professors on a number of occasions and asked them to give me test questions of the type that I might encounter on the final qualifying exams so that I might practice answering such questions under strict time limitations.

I knew the importance of being well prepared when I was in the military. Being prepared has been one of my foremost goals in every job that I have ever had.

In coaching, one of my main goals was to prepare young athletes for any kind of unexpected incident that might take place in a ball game. I spent countless hours in football practice, teaching young athletes how not to get trap-blocked or hit on their blind side, the types of blows that generally result in the worst injuries. We constantly asked and answered "what if" questions and set up possible scenarios to work through. Much of what I coached my players to anticipate never happened, but I wanted them to be ready should the unexpected occur.

As I have spoken to countless groups of educators and parents through the years, I have placed great emphasis on being prepared, expecting the unexpected, and teaching our children to be prepared for life's challenges and opportunities. However, I also know you can't predict or plan for some of life's events; you can only prepare yourself to react in a positive way. This realization hit home in May of 1996.

Two days after my wife Carolyn and I hosted a party for about fifty persons in our home, we flew to San Antonio, Texas. I spoke to an audience gathered for the USAA Mentor and Junior Achievement Appreciation Breakfast. While in San Antonio, Carolyn began to feel ill. Upon returning home, we made an appointment with her doctor. He said she had a spastic colon and prescribed medication.

Carolyn began to feel worse, however. Our granddaughter Michelle noticed Carolyn was looking "yellowish," and we knew something was wrong. During our next visit to the doctor, he ran a series of tests. The look on his face when he entered his office told us the results were something that we did not want to hear. Carolyn had a tumor on the head of her pancreas.

The next day we were in a hospital in Charleston, South Carolina, for another series of tests—a gastrointestinal test, a sonogram, and a CAT scan. All the tests confirmed the cancer and, in fact, showed the cancer had spread to the liver.

The next few days were a blur to us. Nothing seemed to make sense—Carolyn had been one of the healthiest women I had ever known. She was seldom ill. We had followed good health and nutritional habits for years. She was one of the kindest and most generous women on this earth—a gracious Christian woman and, in my book, a true saint. Nothing had prepared us to anticipate such a battle in our lives.

Carolyn and I had been married for forty-three years, and, without any doubt, she had been the hub of the Mitchell family. Now it was time for the Mitchells to rally around their leader and face this most serious challenge.

I learned a great deal about cancer in a short period of time. I also learned that as much as medical science can do, there is also a great deal that medical science *cannot* do. A woman who has worked in the oncology department at Duke University for about ten years told me that, over the years, she had become convinced that the people who are able to come out well against this disease are those who keep a positive attitude and remain emotionally strong. We agreed that we would not let fear dominate our lives but, rather, trust the Lord, cherish every moment we had together, and cope with this tragedy in a positive way. During the next four months, which were Carolyn's last, I learned the true meaning of courage by watching her deal with this adversity. Unfortunately, a friend of ours had a father who was also battling cancer. He asked me to help him make a battle plan so he and his father could wage their own war on cancer. Carolyn and I reflected back on the many events and emotions that had shaped our past few months, and we concluded there were five things that had helped us face and cope with the unexpected. We shared this list with our friend.

# 1. Graciously Accept the Great Outpouring of Love, Prayers, and Concern from Others

It is not always easy to admit that you need help. When the blows of life hit, you need to be able to accept, draw strength from, and appreciate what is given to you.

We were inundated with calls, flowers, cards, letters, and the good wishes of countless friends, business associates, and fellow church members. I recall one day in which I heard from the chairman of one of the world's major corporations and also from our local automobile mechanic, both of whom expressed the same genuine, heartfelt concern for Carolyn and told me of their great admiration for her—almost in identical words. Friends and colleagues flew in to visit Carolyn and to encourage her; others sent tangible gifts of nutrients and inspirational materials to help her. Still others stopped by to pray.

One day several weeks after Carolyn's surgery, a friend, Randy Cox, came to our home with a special gift. It was a gold bracelet with animal figures on it that depicted the story of Noah and the ark. As he placed the bracelet on her wrist, he told her how much he loved her and that he was praying for her. What made this moment especially touching was that Randy's wife was also suffering from inoperable cancer. Even in his time of personal sorrow, he reached out to comfort a friend. It was a tender moment in our lives, one that far transcended the value of the bracelet in meaning and worth.

Through many other expressions of love and care, Carolyn and I quickly found ourselves in a position of being overwhelmed. It was this overflowing love, however, that sustained us in the darkest moments of our lives.

In preparing your child for the unexpected, encourage your child to accept the help and guidance of others. While independence is to be valued and praised, it is equally important that your child be able to ask for, accept, and appreciate help given by others.

Teach your child that when he is in need and others offer assistance, he should accept it graciously. No one can "go it alone" in life. Life is to be lived in relationship with others, and part of life's journey involves helping others to carry their burdens and, in turn, receiving their help in times of trouble.

Invite people to your home and into your family life who can contribute good things to your children. Encourage your children to participate in conversations with these guests and to learn all they can from them.

Take your children to events, seminars, and special lectures where they can hear notable people speak about their faith and about positive values and virtues.

As you train your children to openly receive what others have to offer, be sure to train them to express appreciation and thanks. Children of all ages can thank hosts and hostesses verbally and write thank-you notes to those who give them material gifts, as well as the gift of time together and advice shared.

Encourage your child to look for and receive all that God has. God desires to bestow great blessings on your child. Train your child to look for those blessings and appreciate them when they come.

God never promises to give us an escape route for life's problems. He does promise to walk beside us through our problems and encourage us with His presence and unconditional love. Train your child to look to God for comfort and help in times of trouble, rather than blame God or turn away from Him in times of crisis.

## 2. In Facing an Unexpected Battle, Keep Your Goals and Adjust Them as You Must

Our goals changed, of course. On some days right after her surgery, our goal was simply to have Carolyn eat a few bites of food or swallow a few chips of ice. But each week we charted some realistic goals that we would strive to achieve.

After a particular hospital visit, when the news we had received was not optimistic, Carolyn and I spent most of the ride home discussing this book and the plans we had made for the establishment of Youcan University for children and senior citizens. As sick as Carolyn was in that moment, she was still looking toward the future and to a day when she might be well enough to take on responsibilities related to this new venture.

If your child finds himself in a crisis—however big or small—remind him to set goals for himself. Goals point toward the future and are a part of having hope. They are an outward expression of an inward faith.

There are times when we each need to readjust our goals in life, not necessarily setting them higher but resetting them to accommodate the circumstance in which we find ourselves. Still, we should have goals.

# 3. Don't Neglect Activities That "Fill Your Cup" Each Day

Every day we each face negative comments and experiences that drain us of energy, creativity, and enthusiasm for life. It's important, therefore, that we devote time each day to filling our lives with the good things that give us energy, faith, and hope.

Carolyn and I established a pattern of morning prayer and reading devotional material together, as well as conversation that helped us establish a good attitude and a positive spirit. Listening to inspirational music also helped us to redirect our thoughts, stay focused, and keep our perspective on life.

Especially when you are hit with a crisis, it's critical that you continue to "fill your cup" daily. Doing so will encourage you in the present and give you hope for the future.

Teach your children that the onset of a crisis is not the time to start developing a faith relationship with God or building relationships with others. Those relationships need to be established early and sustained through time. While your children are young, begin to fill their cups daily with positive thoughts, actions, words, and examples so that they will acquire good habits, attitudes, values, and virtues.

# 4. Live "in the Day" and Savor Each Moment

We are commanded by Jesus to live one day at a time, yet few of us actually live our lives with a *full* appreciation and joy for what each day holds.

When a Christian is faced with a personal catastrophe of some kind, every experience in a day takes on heightened meaning. Sunsets are more beautiful. The loving expressions of children are more dear. Words of kindness are exaggerated. Life seems richer and more meaningful—not because of external circumstances, but because we take time to enjoy and appreciate the small snatches in life. A rich and fulfilling life is not one that is made up of events, hours, or even minutes, but rather moments.

Encourage your child not to look past the present in anticipating the future. Children are often eager for the future, so much so that they fail to enjoy the moment. I once heard a little girl ask her aunt repeatedly how many more minutes she was allowed to stay up. Her aunt had granted her an extra hour before bedtime, and this little girl spent a good portion of that hour counting its minutes, rather than enjoying the story-telling time with her aunt.

Train your child to enjoy what is at hand. While he may anticipate the future with hope and be eager for new experiences that will come his way, there is much to be gained in the *now* of his life. Encourage your child to find the good in the present hour and to enjoy it to the max.

# 5. In a Crisis, Learn a Deeper Meaning of "Commitment"

During the months in which Carolyn had cancer, we became more determined than ever to work through life as a team. We made vows forty-three years earlier that we would love, honor, and cherish each other through good times and bad, sickness and health, for richer or poorer. We lived within that commitment in our marriage and also in her illness.

We also gained a deep appreciation for those who maintained their commitment to our friendship during this trying time. There really is no substitute for committed family members and friends. They are the ones who endure by your side and stand with you through thick and thin.

Train your child to make commitments to friends and family—to stand by siblings and friends when they are in trouble, to speak well of siblings and friends even if others are criticizing them. Train your child to be loyal to the clubs or groups that he joins. Don't let your child be an "easy quitter"—a person who starts things on a whim and then gives up the minute the going gets tough or he thinks he has found a better or more enjoyable opportunity. Insist that your child persevere in some tasks she doesn't particularly enjoy but which you know are good for her to complete.

Train your child never to promise more than he can deliver and, above all, never to make promises when he has no intention of keeping them.

From time to time there may be legitimate reasons why a child cannot keep a commitment—such as illness, a family emergency, a conflict in schedule, or plans that your child didn't know. In those instances, the child should let the person know he isn't going to be able to keep the commitment and why—and with as much advance notice as possible.

Teach your child that vows are serious business. They reflect one's ability to commit and be trustworthy. Keep your vows. They are at the core of your integrity.

# A Fivefold Approach that Benefits Everyone

During the summer of 1996, as Carolyn fought her last battles against cancer that ravaged her body, we watched part of the Olympic Games on television. I was aware as I watched how each of the five practices just mentioned had played a part in preparing the athletes to face the supreme challenge of their careers:

*Receive Help and Support.* They had received openly the help of friends, financial backers, fans, and coaches.

*Setting and Reevaluating Goals.* Even athletes who held world records were setting and reevaluating goals to run a little faster, vault a little higher, and earn one more medal.

*Fill the Cup Daily.* Athlete after athlete expressed in interviews the importance of keeping within their own daily habits and sticking with the basics of training that had brought them to the Olympic Games. They didn't abandon their training programs once they arrived at the Games; rather, they stuck by the regimen that had brought them that far.

*Live in the Moment.* The truly great athletes take competition one step at a time, never getting ahead of themselves or living in the aura of past performances.

*Commitment.* Olympic athletes commit for months and years ahead of the event to training for that hour in which they will compete at the Olympic Games. They persevere and endure in their commitment to excellence.

You may not be able to prepare for the *precise* catastrophe, trouble, or suffering that may come your way in life. But you can "steep" yourself in the attitudes, values, virtues, and morals that will last into eternity. And in the end, that's the very best preparation you can make for the present as well! Our time here on earth is fleeting, even if it's a hundred years. Only what is done and learned that is of an eternal nature is going to count.

To this end, train your child to have a "heavenly perspective." Talk about heaven with your child. Emphasize the importance of living a life that is heaven-bound. Anticipate with joy the eternity you will spend with those you love in Christ Jesus.

# Chapter 14

## *Legacy of Love*

*Recommend to your children virtue; that
alone can make happiness, not gold.*
—Beethoven (1770–1827)

*Do not merely look out for your own personal
interests, but also for the interests of others.*
—Philippians 2:4, NASB

Have you ever watched a young child notice for the first time how a mysterious silhouette mimics his every move? No matter how quickly he turns or how fast he runs, the shadow is always there. Depending on the position of the sun, the shadow may be tall or short, or it may even seem to disappear. Eventually, the child learns to accept that his shadow is there to stay, and it is soon ignored.

We each cast shadows into the lives of others. Some shadows are highly visible, their manifestations readily evident. Other shadows are nearly invisible, not to be noticed for many years.

Henry Ward Beecher, the great nineteenth-century preacher, once said, "The humblest individual exerts some influence, either for good or evil, upon others." Our actions are imitated, both consciously and unconsciously. The question is not whether we will influence others, but whether the influence will be positive or negative. Will our shadows inspire or will they instill fear?

A famous, well-respected individual once issued this statement after he had been accepted for a teaching position at Princeton University: "I am coming to Princeton to do research, not to teach. There is too much education altogether, especially in American schools. The only rational way of educating is to be an example—if one can't help it, a warning example." It wasn't that this person was against classroom lectures or other formal ways of teaching. Rather, he was in favor of teaching by example and deed, not only word. He realized that significant and long-lasting learning was the result of students watching, observing, and imitating. His name was Albert Einstein, and certainly his shadow was a tall and positive one.

# Looking to the Long View of Life

Student drivers often make the mistake of using the center line of the road to guide them in keeping the car moving in a straight line. This may work fine for a long stretch of road, but on curves and hills, such drivers tend to overcompensate and have difficulty. The best advice is to look one hundred yards down the road and see the lane more fully. It's the long view that is most beneficial. So, too, with parenting and growing up. Parenting is filled with many joys and challenges and frequently many sorrows and heartaches as well. But God offers a hopeful future if we say with Joshua, "As for me and my household, we will serve the LORD" (Josh. 24:15). Look down the road to eternal benefits of your daily efforts to raise children who love and honor God. Envision yourself standing someday before the throne of God, with your children by your side!

Children, especially teenagers who are coping with hormones and the challenges of moving from childhood to adulthood, can feel as if they are on an emotional roller coaster. Minor details and small gestures seem to take on monumental proportions. But things will not always be like they are today. Help your child maintain a perspective of "tomorrow" and the "future."

We have heard a great deal in recent years about the despair and futility that the current "generation X" feels about the future. According to some analysts, most of the young people in this generation don't have much hope that their lives will be as good as their parents' lives, and few hope for things to be better. These young people are basing their dreams on what *is*, not on what can be.

Hold out to your child the possibilities of what *might* be through hard work, creativity, and good relationships with others. There is no certainty of doom in the future, only a fear of doom. That fear can be wiped away by faith and hope.

Consider the tale of two families.

Max Jukes lived in New York. He did not believe in Christ or in Christian training. He refused to take his children to church, even when they asked to go. He has had 1,026 descendants; 300 were sent to prison for an average term of thirteen years; 190 were public prostitutes; 680 were admitted alcoholics. His family, as of 1986, has cost the state of New

York in excess of $420,000. His descendants have made no known positive contribution to society.

Jonathan Edwards lived in the same state at the same time as Jukes. He loved the Lord and saw that his children were in church every Sunday. He served the Lord to the best of his ability. He has had 929 descendants. Of these, 430 were ministers, 86 became university professors, 13 became university presidents, 75 were authors of good books, 5 were elected to the United States House of Representatives, and 2 were elected to the United States Senate. One was vice-president of the United States. His family never cost the state one cent but has contributed immeasurably in both taxes and service.

What will be the legacy of your family a hundred years from now?

# The Ripple Effect

A spiritually strong family contributes to a spiritually strong church, and a spiritually strong church helps create a spiritually strong community. A spiritually strong community contributes to a spiritually strong nation. A spiritually strong nation contributes to making the world spiritually stronger.

In recent decades, the concept of a "global village" has become popular. We all have a growing awareness of remote areas of the world becoming more accessible, our lives becoming more connected with those who live in different nations and are of different cultures, races, and language groups. The stock markets are tied together. Trade knows few national boundaries. War in one area of the world impacts us all.

The ripple effect is ongoing.

This principle is true first and foremost in the family. A baby's dependence on others is clearly evident. A baby must be fed, bathed, clothed, sheltered, and nurtured by another person—or several others—each day. The baby's life depends on the support of others.

As a child grows older, he becomes less dependent on others for these basic needs, but no less dependent on others for emotional, mental, and spiritual nourishment. Many people lose sight of that truth.

No matter how old you become or what level of financial and societal status you achieve, you still need others to love you and to whom you can show your love. Your faith is made stronger by being around others who believe as you do. Your mind remains sharper by being around others who are continuing to learn and to create.

Sir Isaac Newton once humbly said, "If I have seen farther, it is by standing upon the shoulders of giants." We need to remember that fact.

We owe a great debt to those in countless professions who have given us the life we enjoy today—the soldiers who have fought for the freedom we cherish; the teachers who prepared us for the careers we know; the inventors who gave us technologies we take for granted; the researchers who discovered the medicines that contribute to our health; the preachers, Sunday school teachers, and evangelists who faithfully shared the gospel with us.

We make a serious error any time we think that we have achieved something entirely on our own strength, creativity, or ingenuity. We also err greatly any time we think that we have a *right* to live unto ourselves and not leave a legacy for others.

# Ripples Start with Pebbles

Don't become overwhelmed by the idea that your family will have a far-reaching and eternal impact on others. The job that God places before you is to be and to do your best as the parent to your children. Leave the full extent of the consequences up to God. He calls us to be faithful and to do our best. He is the one who gives the increase and engineers whatever success we have.

You may have heard the story about the little boy who was asked by his father to work out a jigsaw puzzle that was a map of the world. The father had hoped the puzzle would be difficult enough to keep his son occupied for quite awhile, but to his amazement, the boy came back to him a short time later to announce that he had finished the puzzle.

"How did you know how to put this puzzle together so quickly?" the father asked. "You haven't studied world geography."

The little boy answered, "Oh, I didn't work on the map side. On the other side was a picture of a man. So I put the man together and the world came out all right."

Therein lies our challenge today. Your goal lies with your family; leave the world to God. Always remember that changes are made most effectively:

- one person at a time
- one thought at a time
- one day at a time

Persevere. Don't give up.

# The Legacy of Love

After Carolyn was diagnosed with cancer, we not only discovered new insights into what it means to prepare for the unexpected, but also what it means to leave a legacy in this life. After wrestling with this issue over many months, we decided the best legacy is the legacy of love.

One day Carolyn and I were walking with our grandson, Matthew, to play five holes of golf. The area in which we were walking had poison ivy growing in it, so I said to Matthew, who was wearing short pants, "Matthew, watch your step. There's poison ivy." I didn't hear any response so I repeated my warning to him. "Matthew, there's poison ivy in this area, so watch where you walk."

Matthew replied, "Don't worry, Pappy, I'm just walking in your steps."

Sure enough, I turned around and there he was, carefully placing his feet where mine had made an imprint.

Your children and grandchildren will walk confidently in your footsteps if you have walked with love in your relationship to them. They will *want* to be with you, be like you, and follow your example—step by step by step. No matter how they may rebel from time to time, they will return to the loving example you set, and desire to have a faith like your faith and values like your values.

The greatest virtue, as is so clearly stated throughout the New Testament, is love. Love embodies all the attributes of God. It is the foremost character trait we associate with the fruit of the Holy Spirit.

Walk in love, as Christ walked in love. You will leave the greatest legacy possible to your children, one which has the greatest potential for being passed on from generation to generation.

# The Legacy of Humility

Humility is often equated with a person being a wimp. It is also equated with shame. Humility, however, is neither of the above. Humility is giving place to another person out of respect and appreciation for that person's right to hold his own opinions, make his own decisions and choices, and act freely out of his own personality. To have humility before God and others encompasses all of these traits.

# Leave a Legacy of Obedience to God

When we meditate on God's Word we discover several principles that are directly related to parenting.

## A DAILY WALK OF OBEDIENCE

One of the foremost principles in God's Word is this: we must follow God's Word *daily*. This is sometimes called "walking in the Spirit" or "walking out our faith." (See Gal. 5:22–25.)

In a daily walk, we are commanded by God's Word to

- confess our sins daily. Come to your heavenly Father whenever you realize you have erred in His sight, and receive His forgiveness.
- yield to God daily. Go to your heavenly Father and ask for His help on a daily basis to resist temptation and make choices for good, not evil. Remind yourself daily of His commandments, His authority over your life, and His loving provision.

We must invite the Holy Spirit to direct our lives and lead us to right actions and right attitudes. How might you do this in your family on a practical level?

Pray with your spouse and your children on a daily basis. Invite each person in your family to participate in the prayer time.

Include in your prayers a time of confession. Admit to God that you have sinned and ask His forgiveness. Include a time of praise and thanking God for His presence, provisions, and guidance. Acknowledge in your prayers that God is sovereign over your life and the lives of each of your children, and that Jesus is your Savior and Lord forever. Invite the Holy Spirit to lead you and reveal to you His plan for each member of your family.

Mornings are a good time for voicing petitions for specific help during the day. Evenings are a good time for recalling God's answers, protection, and guidance during the day that has past.

You don't need to wait for a habitual prayer time, of course, before you voice your concerns or praise to God. Shoot "arrow-prayers" of concern to God throughout the day, as things enter your mind. Turn praise into "arrow-prayers" as well. Make praise a normal part of your conversation with your children—on the way to school, as you drive to the supermarket, or as you take your child to Little League practice.

If a need arises, pray immediately for God's help, protection, or guidance.

If your child commits a sin that he openly acknowledges, pray with your child immediately to receive forgiveness. Don't let guilt build up in your child.

In praying spontaneously and often with your children, you are training them to believe that:

- God is present with us always, eager to lead us into His perfect will for our lives
- God is a loving God who is concerned about all the details of our lives
- God is a forgiving God who desires that we be in a close relationship with Him at all times

## OBEDIENCE IN TEACHING GOD'S COMMANDMENTS

God's commandments might also be called God's rules, God's laws, or God's statutes. As a whole, they are God's blueprint for how human beings are to live successful, happy lives in relationship with Him and with each other.

It is important that we always teach God's commandments from the perspective that God desires us to obey His rules for *our* benefit. God doesn't give us His commandments to punish us or put us in straight-jackets. Rather, He gives us rules so we might prosper, grow, and be blessed in every area of our lives.

Teaching God's commandments is to be given a high priority in your parenting. As one man said, "I'm to do the teaching; God does all the exams." Give your children the commandments, and trust God to seal them in their hearts. Trust God to give your children the desire to follow them. You are not your children's judge; you are their mentor.

Don't rely on the pastor or Sunday school teacher to be responsible for your children's spiritual education. What they do for a few minutes once a week should reinforce or bolster what you are doing in the home seven days a week.

Teaching God's commandments means teaching the *whole* of God's Word, from cover to cover. All of the Bible works together to present a clear picture of who God is, what He has done for us, and how he expects us to live. This means knowing how to *apply* the principles in the Bible to daily living.

## OBEDIENCE IN LIVING OUT OUR FAITH IN THE "REAL WORLD"

God's Word isn't mere theory. It is quite practical. It relates to everyday living. Throughout the Bible, we have countless examples of real people struggling with real problems and facing real consequences for actions both good and bad. God's Word is meant to be lived out, not simply learned as head knowledge.

You must always insist that your child live in the real world. Fantasy is fun and entertaining in brief spurts; fantasy play is a way that children learn by trying on various roles and types of characteristics. Fiction is fun to read. But in the end, your child must be able to distinguish fantasy from reality and live out a life that is productive and meaningful.

The Bible confronts us repeatedly with truth. We must do the same with our children and never accept lies from them.

The Bible also confronts us repeatedly with a knowledge and responsibility concerning evil. Encourage your children to develop their consciences by remaining sensitive to the Holy Spirit. Furthermore, never justify evil or sinful behavior as acceptable.

## A Legacy of Good Memories

Edith Schaeffer uses a phrase I like. She speaks of creating a "museum of memories" for children. She advocates that parents should plan very consciously the traditions and memories that they hope to instill in their children.

Family rituals, which may be likened to family habits, don't just evolve or happen. They are an intentional part of parenting. Develop family rituals and customs. Some may be shared with others, while others will remain unique to your family. In so doing, you will be creating special moments and memorable events for your child.

## Building a Legacy Isn't Always Easy

Doing what is *best* for your child isn't easy. Doing what's "best" means doing far more than merely providing food, shelter, and clothing. It means providing spiritual training and an atmosphere conducive to physical, mental, and emotional growth. All of this cannot be accomplished haphazardly. It takes a tremendous amount of effort, energy, and focus, as well as time and money.

Choose today to be and provide the best for your children, and then plan how you will accomplish the task. You won't regret it.

## Start Where You Are Today

It's never too early or too late to start building a legacy for your family.

1. *Start where you are.* Don't give up, thinking that you are too late to build a strong family. Ask for God's forgiveness for mistakes you have made in the past, and, if necessary, apologize to your children for errors you now recognize. Begin anew. Decide that you want to build a strong family, and start doing the things that strong families do.

2. *Ask for God's help.* Pray for your spouse daily, as well as for your children. Also pray for yourself, for your family as a whole, and for all the things that you are facing *as a family*.

3. *Avail yourself of all the resources available to you.* Get help if you need it to mediate problems or get through a crisis. Draw upon the many resources available in your community, at your child's school, or at your church. Ask for help from other family members, close friends, and members of your church family who seem to have strong families.

4. *Recognize that you are not alone in your concern for a strong family.* Find those who share your interest and concern. Encourage them, share activities and events with them, and share practical advice.

The important thing is to start! Parenting is practical and active. You can hope and wish for positive values in your child; you can desire to be a good parent and raise children with great values. But values and good behavioral habits don't happen without PARENTAL *action*.

## Your Family Legacy Is Your Family Treasure

There is a story about a family who had quite a valuable treasure: an antique vase that was kept on the living room mantel.

One day when the woman of the house came home, she was greeted by her daughter, who said, "Mama, you know that vase which you told us has been passed down from generation to generation?"

"Yes," her mother said. "What about it?"

Her daughter replied, "Well, Mama, this generation just dropped it."

The values you have been given by God, grandparents, parents, pastors, teachers, and other adults are a treasure in your life. Don't drop them as you pass them on to your children!

Be assured that as you make your best and most enduring attempt to build a strong family, God will be with you. He will bring honor to Himself through your example. He will take your legacy of values and faith, and build it into an unshakable foundation that does not fail.

# Epilogue

My wife Carolyn is now in heaven. She "graduated" from this earthly life to her heavenly home on September 15, 1996. Shortly before she died, she said to me, "A moment of happiness is worth a lifetime, and I have had lots of happiness."

God's gift to us is life. Our gift to God is what we do with it. Carolyn gave love—abundant and selfless love—to all who knew her.

The tribute given by Pastor Wayne Brown at Carolyn's funeral is a wonderful reflection to me of her life and the strong family she created.

## A Tribute to Carolyn Mitchell

*Beautiful, supportive, caring, gracious, and kind,*
*Thoughts of God and others were always on her mind.*
*A daughter, sister, wife, mother, and friend;*
*To her, relationships were precious and without end!*
*A mother-in-law and a grandmother, too.*
*She put others first in all she would say and do.*
*Unselfish, positive, cheerful, a million-dollar smile,*
*She learned from Jesus to go the extra mile.*
*Patient and always loving with a spirit that was truly glad,*
*In all things she sought to find the good and not the bad.*
*Throughout her life, in all she did or said,*
*She was gentle and consistent, serving where she was led.*
*Bill and Carolyn, the epitome of a happy home, an example for*
*    all to see.*
*They made forty-three years of marriage full of bliss, fun,*
*    and glee.*
*A beauty on the outside, as well as deep within,*
*Carolyn Mitchell's beauty came from her faith which had no end.*
*In valleys deep, or mountains tall, she showed us how to live,*
*For in her life, in sickness or strife, she taught us how to give.*
*For she gave to God her burdens, her cross He helped her bear.*
*And never once did she complain, for she knew His*
*    constant care.*

*Her faith did not waver and she proved, with God's help, she was
strong,*
*For even when life's cup was bitter, she trusted Him all along.*
*And when in death's sweet sleep, she closed her eyes in peace,*
*With her inimitable smile, a hand clasped in love, her soul found
sweet release.*
*Yes, it was on the Lord's Day, the first day of the week,*
*And, as always, she was humble, calm, sweet, and meek.*
*Surrounded by those she loved, she smiled her loving "good-bye,"*
*For the battle now was finished, and she breathed the victor's
sigh.*
*What a noble dream, Building Strong Families now!*
*Thank you, Bill and Carolyn, for showing us how.*
*This wonderful dream you were inspired to begin will continue
to be led by God above,*
*And, yes, we can most certainly know Carolyn is joyful, for she
left us all a "legacy of love!"*

A memorial scholarship fund has been established in Carolyn Mitchell's honor to assist needy children in obtaining quality day-care. If you would like more information about Youcan University for Kids, write to:

Dr. William Mitchell
Pops Foundation International
4325 Dick Pond Road
Myrtle Beach, SC 29575

# Notes

## Introduction

1. U.S. Census Bureau (1994).

2. "Strong Families, Strong Schools," U.S. Department of Education (c. 1995).

3. "Myths, Men, and Beer," a study published by the AAA Foundation for Traffic Safety..

4. Joanne Ross Feldmeth, "Life with an Alcoholic," Focus on the Family (February 1996), 11.

5. "Schools without Drugs, U.S. Dept. of Education (Washington, D.C., 1987).

6. Cited in Interim Report of the National Commission on Children (April 1990).

7. "Character Education and Clinical Intervention: A Paradigm Shift for U.S. Schools, Phi Delta Kappan (May 1987), 667-73.

8. National Center for Health Statistics.

9. "Age-Specific Arrest Rates and Race-Specific Arrest Rates for Selected Offenses (1965-88)," Federal Bureau of Investigations (Washington, D.C., 1990).

## Chapter 1

1. "How Can the Family Survive?" copyright Radio Bible Class (Nashville: Thomas Nelson, Publishers, 1988).

2. *Parables, Etc.* (January 1990), 8.

3. Executive Summary of the U.S. Secretary of Education Report 1996 (published in 1997).

4. In *Parables, Etc.* (June 1987), 7:4:8.

5. H. Norman Wright, *Communication and Conflict Resolution in Marriage* (Elgin, Ill.: David C. Cook, 1977), 6.

## Chapter 2

1. National Commission on Children (1991).

## Chapter 3

1. Gary Smalley, *The Key to Your Child's Heart* (Waco, Texas: Word Books, 1984).

2. *The Best Loved Poems of the American People* (Garden City, N.Y.: Garden City Publishing Company, 1936), 102.

3. Cited in "Building Self-Esteem," American Association of School Administrators (1991).

## Chapter 4

1. Child Development Project Survey (San Ramon, Calif.), quoted in Eric Schaps, Daniel Solomon, and Marilyn Watson, "A Program That Combines Character Development and Academic Achievement," *Educational Leadership* (Dec. 1985-Jan. 1986), 32-34.

2. Benjamin Bloom, *Developing Talent in Young People* (NewYork: Ballantine Books, 1985).

3. *Parables, Etc.* (April 1990), 7.

4. As reported in *Preaching,* reprinted in *Parables, Etc.* (April 1987).

5. S. Truett Cathy, *It's Easier to Succeed Than Fail* (Nashville: Oliver Nelson, 1989).

## Chapter 5

1. "Strong Families, Strong Schools," U.S. Department of Education.

2. "First Things First: What Americans Expect from the Public Schools," the Public Agenda Foundation (New York, N.Y.)

3. Richard C. Halverson, *Executive Guide to Ethical Decision-Making* (Executive Leadership Foundation, Inc.), quoted in *Theology News and Notes* (October 1988).

4. *Community Update* 32 (U.S. Department of Education, Jan./Feb. 1996).

## Chapter 8

1. Gallup Poll.

2. A. G. Hobbs, *Harmony in the Home* (Hobbs Publications, n.d.)

## Chapter 9

1. University of Michigan's Social Research Institute.

2. "'Code Blue': A Health Emergency for American Teenagers," *The Times Union*, 9 June 1990, 1.

3. Quoted in article in *USAir* magazine (1996).

4. Wright, *Communication and Conflict Resolution in Marriage.*

## Chapter 10

1. IEA Preprimary Project, *Education Week* (January 1995).

## Chapter 11

1. Scott Ostler, "That Little Voice Just Kept Chanting, 'Stop, Bubba, Stop."

## Chapter 12

1. John Wooden, *They Call Me Coach* (Word Books, 1972).

2. "Strong Families, Strong Schools," U.S. Department of Education Executive Summary.

3. Steve Huntley and Harold R. Kennedy, "What Entertainers Are Doing to Your Kids," *U.S. News & World Report* (28 October 1995).

4. U.S. Department of Education (1989).

5. Huntley and Kennedy, "Entertainers . . . ," citing Murray and Connborg, 1992.

6. Ibid., citing NEA.

7. *The American Teacher 1994,* survey conducted by Louis Harris and Associates, Inc., for Metropolitan Life Insurance Co. (1993).

# More resources for
## Building Strong Families

**Friends, Foes & Fools**

Fathers Can Teach
Their Kids To Know
The Difference
**James Merritt**
0-8054-6354-2

**You Can Raise A Well-Mannered Child**

Meeting & Greeting,
Going Out In Public,
Table Manners &
much more.
**June Hines Moore**
0-8054-6076-4

**The Complete Book Of Christian Parenting & Child Care**

A Medical & Moral
Guide To Raising Happy,
Healthy Children
**Dr. William & Martha Sears**
0-8054-6198-1

**Raising Achievers**

A Parent's Plan For
Motivating
Children To Excel
**Nita Weis, Ph. D.**
0-8054-6160-4

**Grandparenting: It's Not What It Used To Be**

Expert Answers To The
Questions Grandparents
Ask Most
**Irene Endicott**
0-8054-6200-7

**Letters To Baby**
Letters To The Next Generation
From Many Of Today's
Prominent Personalities
**Chaz Corzine**
0-8054-6299-6

**It's You & Me, Mom**

25 Cool Devotions
For Moms & Kids
**Greg Johnson**
0-8054-5394-6

**Small Beginnings**

First Steps To Prepare
Your Child For
Lifelong Learning
**Barbara Curtis**
0-8054-6287-2

**Coming in Fall 1997**

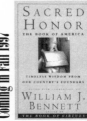

The new book from the
best-selling author of
*The Book Of Virtues*
**William Bennett**
0-8054-0149-0

AVAILABLE AT FINE CHRISTIAN BOOKSTORES EVERYWHERE